Praise for
THE DARK HEART OF ITALY

"Tobias Jones had me seduced before I finished his preface. He writes about the dark side of Italian life with a very light touch, examining the warts with impartial and carefully researched dismay, leavened on occasion by a truly Italian love of hyperbole, and balanced by a contagious enthusiasm for all the pleasures that bind the expatriate to Italy."
—Mary Taylor Simeti, author of *On Persephone's Island*

"[An] almost indispensable book . . . It should be packed in the travelling bags of all visitors to the *Bel Paese*."
—*The Independent on Sunday*

"[Jones's] is a combination of the best of scholarly research and first-hand encounters, complemented by his obvious love for the literature of the country . . . *The Dark Heart of Italy* is essential reading for anyone who seeks to see beyond the Leaning Tower of Pisa and Pavarotti arias."
—*Scotland on Sunday*

"Jones is . . . an ideal guide to anyone who wishes to probe deeply into contemporary Italian life and society. An acute, open-minded, cultured observer, his enduring attachment to Italy combined with his deep anger at the wrongs perpetrated on Italians give him a critical perspective denied both the casual visitor and the native resident."
—*The Herald* (Glasgow)

DAVID JONES

TOBIAS JONES

THE DARK HEART OF ITALY

Tobias Jones studied at Jesus College, Oxford. He was on the staff of the *London Review of Books* and of *The Independent on Sunday* before moving, in 1999, to Parma, Italy.

THE DARK HEART OF ITALY

The

DARK HEART

of

ITALY

TOBIAS JONES

NORTH POINT PRESS
A division of Farrar, Straus and Giroux
New York

For Walter Donohue

North Point Press
A division of Farrar, Straus and Giroux
19 Union Square West, New York 10003

Copyright © 2003 by Tobias Jones
All rights reserved
Printed in the United States of America
Originally published in 2003 by Faber and Faber Ltd, London
Published in 2004 in the United States by North Point Press
First North Point Press paperback edition, 2005

The Library of Congress has cataloged the hardcover edition as follows:
Jones, Tobias.
    The dark heart of Italy / Tobias Jones.
        p.   cm.
    Includes index.
    ISBN 0-86547-700-0 (pbk. : alk. paper)
    1. Italy—Description and travel. 2. Italy—Social conditions—1994–
3. Italy—Social life and customs—1945–   4. Italy—Politics and
government—1994–   5. Political corruption—Italy—History.
6. Berlusconi, Silvio, 1936–   7. Jones, Tobias—Homes and haunts—Italy.
I. Title.

DG430.2.J66 2004
945.093—dc22

                                                                    2003024207

Paperback ISBN-13: 978-0-86547-724-7
Paperback ISBN-10: 0-86547-724-8

Designed by Debbie Glasserman

www.fsgbooks.com

3   5   7   9   10   8   6   4   2

CONTENTS

Foreword • vii

Acknowledgements • xvii

1. *"Parole, Parole, Parole" • 3*
2. *"The Mother of All Slaughters" • 32*
3. *Penalties and Impunity • 71*
4. *The Sofri Case • 106*
5. *The Means of Seduction • 136*
6. *Pietra and Parola • 166*
7. *"Fewer Taxes for Everyone" • 198*
8. *Forzismo • 240*
9. *Penisola Felice • 281*

Notes • 301

Index • 307

FOREWORD

"Travellers, without exception," wrote Stendhal in 1824, "are wont to confine their descriptions of Italy to the realm of the inanimate; their portraits concern only the monuments, the sites, the sublime manifestations of nature in that happy land." Even today, this is still very much the case. People talk or write about Italy because they are obsessed by the age, the beauty, and the hedonism of the country, by the Roman ruins, the Renaissance art, by a favourite duomo or *palazzo*. Visitors flock towards cathedrals and canals. They are over-awed by the great historical cities Venice and Florence, and by the stunning countryside of Tuscany and Umbria. Holiday-makers head for the beautiful beaches, there to enjoy pizza and ice-cream and Chianti. The Grand Tour path to those "sites" and "sublime manifestations" is so well trodden that I decided to take a different route, to write about the "animate" Italy, about its livelier and stranger sides.

Someone once wrote that "history begins when memory ends." This book is on the cusp between the two. I moved to Italy at a time when the country was engaged in a strange sort of collective historical debate as people tried to remember or forget what had gone on in Italy only a few years, or decades, before. Something called the "Slaughter Commission" was, after thirteen years of investigations, beginning to reach conclusions about some of the country's intermittent terrorist "slaughters" (which were one part of the country's *anni di piombo*, its "years of lead," from the late 1960s until the early 1980s). Simultaneously a series of acutely politicised trials were drawing controversial conclusions about that era of political terrorism. It was a unique opportunity to watch "terrorists"—politicians, academics, or militarists—defending and explaining themselves and their pasts. Extravagant accusations were made, indignant defences mounted. As one of the defendants, Adriano Sofri, wrote:

> I had to overcome a resistance to fighting on an old battle-ground I had abandoned a long time ago. I couldn't defend myself as I am today, with my more rounded thoughts . . . my good manners and my old books. I had to defend the person I was then, sharp-tongued, vituperative, constantly on the move. I was faced with the alternative of confounding time and identifying absolutely with the person I was or denouncing that person and losing my relationship to my own past.

As I attended the trials and interviewed the protagonists, it often felt as if I were watching the country's history through a kaleidoscope; every few weeks the lens was twisted, and the

colours spilt into new and disconcertingly different arrange-
ments.

Meanwhile, the historiography of Italy's "revolution," its
"Clean Hands" initiative against corruption during the early
1990s, was hurriedly being rewritten. "Corruption," according to the "restoration" rhetoric, wasn't really in business and
politics but rather embedded deep within the Italian judiciary.
That "revolution" (which caused the ignominious end of the
First Republic and heralded the beginning of the Second) was
suddenly being portrayed not as a noble clean-up of public
life but as a bloody *coup d'état* hatched by "Jacobin judges."

Many of the threads from those historical debates, and the
scandals which surrounded them, seemed to lead in the direction of one man: Silvio Berlusconi (since May 2001 the Italian Prime Minister). Each time there was a big news story—a
scandal or success story, or usually a strange combination of
the two—Berlusconi or members of his political coalition
seemed somehow involved. As I watched the nation's historical debate (the furious arguments between "Fascists" and
"Communists," between "corrupt" businessmen and "corrupt" judges), I realised that what was at stake wasn't simply
an interpretation of Italy's tragic past. Rather, political careers
were on the line. The debate, I realised, was so furious precisely because many of the players were on the brink of political power and were keen to present themselves as part of the
"New Italy" rather than stalwarts of the old. Berlusconi and
his bizarre coalition were particularly compromised: their
winning electoral line had always been that they were naive
newcomers to Italian politics and public life, whilst in reality
they slowly began to appear very familiar players from the
past. As one observer remarked, Berlusconi seemed nothing
more than the "butterfly" which had, since the early 1990s,
emerged from the Christian Democratic caterpillar: more
colourful, nimbler, but essentially the same beast.

Thus I began writing about Berlusconi almost by accident. I had wanted to write about the country's recent history, about all those aspects of Italy ignored by tourists. And yet each time I wrote about the history, contemporary politics imposed itself. I tried writing about other things—about the nuances of the language, about the football, the television, the Catholicism—and Berlusconi and his coalition reappeared. Thus Berlusconi's career became the thread which links the following chapters because he is, I realised, the "owner" of Italy. In the words of one famous song, he seems to own everything from *Padrenostro* (Our Father) to Cosa Nostra (the Mafia). Living in Italy, one finds it impossible to move without, inadvertently, coming up against his influence. If you watch football matches or television, try to buy a house or a book or a newspaper, rent a video, or simply shop in a supermarket, the chances are you're somehow filling the coffers of Il Cavaliere (last estimated to be worth $7 billion). When you lie on any beach during the summer months, one of his planes is likely to fly overhead with a banner trailing behind: "Liberty," it reads, or "Forza Italia!"

Berlusconi is, without doubt, the most unconventional and controversial political leader on the world stage. The consistent accusation against his government (from both Italy and abroad) is that it's made up of "Blackshirts" and "white collars": that is, former Fascists and white-collar criminals. Moral indignation is the standard response, because from every angle the government really does seem contrary to normal, democratic discourse. But the indignation does little to explain the phenomenon of Forza Italia. It doesn't begin to explain who Berlusconi is; nor does it explain why he is loved and has been elected by millions of Italians. Italy and its Prime Minister are two sides of the same democratic coin, and I've spent four years travelling in Italy trying to understand "both sides," both the country and its Cavaliere. I'm aware that I have often conflated the two, identifying Berlusconi entirely with Italy, and I'm aware that the result can tend (depending on political opinion) to portray a beautiful country in an unfairly ugly light. I have taken this approach because the electoral landslide of 2001 showed just how intimate is the marriage between the two. It would have been perverse to divorce Berlusconi from his electorate, or vice versa.

Of the following chapters, " 'Parole, Parole, Parole' " is a "long glossary," a description of learning the language and all its implications. " 'The Mother of All Slaughters' " examines the work of the parliamentary Slaughter Commission and the tortuous, politicised trial with which it overlapped. "Penalities and Impunity" is an induction into the beautiful game and the ugly business of Italian football. "The Sofri Case" is a prison interview with the country's most famous "murderer." "The Means of Seduction" is about Italian aesthetics, about the country's visual culture, from the heights of its cinema to the depths of its televisual "videocracy." "*Pietra* and *Parola*" is a pilgrimage to the Catholic and Protestant extremes of the peninsula and traces the wafer-thin line between the Vatican and Italian politics. " 'Fewer Taxes for Everyone' "—the central electoral slogan used by Berlusconi in 2001—is an analysis of the anomalies of Italian capitalism. "Forzismo" is an attempt to understand the iconography and implications of Berlusconi's post-democratic politics, an attempt to understand a political party which appears both incredibly new and eerily familiar. Finally, "*Penisola Felice*" describes why living in Italy is still, despite everything, an idyllic experience.

This book was published last year in Britain. The critics were very generous, and sales—for what it's worth—were gratifying. But what happened in Italy was really fascinating. To coincide with the British publication I had written an article for the *Financial Times* about the depravity of Italian television. The piece appeared on the front page under the mildly provocative headline "My Italian TV Hell." Overnight, I was catapulted from near-anonymity in Italy to being a household name. Berlusconi's Minister of Communications went on prime-time news to denounce me: my writing, he screamed angrily, was "a mixture of bigotry and Marxism, typical of a country in which a branch of the Parliament still wears a wig." A whole host of anchormen from Berlusconi's Mediaset channels were lined up over the weekend; they all furiously attacked the "foreign Trotskyist," urging their millions of viewers that this was all part of the worldwide left-wing conspiracy against Silvio. It was, in footballing terms, an unpleasant foul: they were taking the man, not the ball, attacking the writer and not what he had written.

The English-language version of the book was available in Italian bookshops. Under that other mildly provocative title—*The Dark Heart of Italy*—there was, on the cover, a photograph of Silvio Berlusconi: standing on a balcony in Milan, smiling at his adulatory supporters, looking uncannily like Benito Mussolini. In the space of a few months, it became the best-selling foreign-language book in the history of Italian retail. People were carrying the book on buses and trains almost as if it were a badge, a lapel pin against a particular politician. Views on the book were the inverse of views about Berlusconi: it was loved or loathed according to one's politics. I was invited onto almost every TV show in Italy. I politely refused each time for the simple reason that I had the distinct impression that very, very few people had actually opened the book.

Then, a few months ago, a revised version was published in Italian. Once again there were furious attacks and corrosive criticisms. I watched in dismay as an army of old men were wheeled into television studios: in their faux-professorial tones, they pontificated about why the book was "blasphemous." I remember, a few days after the Italian edition came out, ordering a pizza over the telephone. When I gave my name to the boss (so that his delivery kid could buzz the right flat), there was silence on the other end.

Then: "Are you that writer?" The tone was surly to say the least.

"Erm, well, yes, I am."

"Then you can look elsewhere for your pizza." And he hung up. It felt as if I had been punched in the stomach. In a twenty-second conversation with a *pizzaiolo* I had run the gamut of emotions: the writer's dream of recognition to the writer's nightmare of critical contempt. I flopped into a chair and just stared into space. Maybe, I thought, it's true; maybe I really have—as they say here—"spat in the plate in which I eat." Maybe I have written a terrible book, and their disdain is the correct reaction.

A few days after publication, however, letters began to arrive. First only one or two, then dozens every day. I began receiving letters from all ages, from all walks of life. After a while, the postman jokingly asked me for a tip because he was, literally, having to lug a bin-liner of letters to my door each morning. Many of them were very moving. One eighty-year-old man from Benevento wrote: "I have lived in Italy all my life. I love this country. It is very obvious from reading your book that you do too. I write to express my gratitude to you because you have been very courageous. You have described, with calm and ironic prose, precisely what is happening in Italy in these terribly turbulent times." That was the tone of hundreds of the letters. Others, with that refined, exquisitely polite way Italians have, pointed out small errors of interpretation or blind spots in my analysis.

I went on a book tour all over the country, visiting about fifteen cities on the peninsula. In each bookshop or theatre there would be hundreds of people and, invariably, TV cameras. Time and time again, as I was signing copies at the end of the evening, a reader would say something along the lines of: "Everyone on TV said that this book was a corrosive attack on Italy. But it's not; it's not that at all." Umberto Eco wrote an article saying I was a "likeable eulogiser." I was invited to the literary festival in Mantua and, on entering the Palazzo Ducale, found myself in front of an audience of a thousand people all offering enthusiastic support.

A week after that evening in Mantua I was in a restaurant back in Parma. We had eaten magnificently and indulgently. It was one of those entirely unpretentious places where the waiter wears an apron because he doubles as the chef. At the end of the evening I presented my credit card, and he looked at it, then looked back at me.

"You're the writer?" he asked, looking at me as if he were taking aim.

"Yes."

"Then you're not paying." He smiled broadly and reached under the counter. There was a copy of the book, clearly well thumbed. In the margins there were what looked like the black smears of mushrooms, the maroon smudges of red wine. "Just sign here," said the old man, still smiling, holding open the book. He called into the kitchen, and two young guys came out. "Grande Jones!" said one of them, slapping me on the shoulder. "You've got a lot of friends round here."

I recount all this not for solipsism but to underline the astonishing warmth and generosity of the Italian public, to underline the fact that—outside the TV studios—there were people who understood and appreciated what I had written.

The most common reaction to the book in England was: "Come, come, it's surely not that complicated?" One of the most common reactions in Italy was: "*Attento*, Tobia. I don't think it's that simple." Trying to explain one country to another is, obviously, an excruciating task. It's similar to being a tightrope walker, tottering nervously from one side to the other. Amidst that bewilderment, the only balance you've got comes from you, the writer. That, in the end, is why I have used the first person throughout: "not," as Stendhal wrote, "for egotism, but because there's no other way to tell the story."

Tobias Jones
February 2004

ACKNOWLEDGEMENTS

Parts of this book first appeared in the *London Review of Books*, in *Prospect*, and in *Diario*. I am very grateful to the respective editors, Mary-Kay Wilmers, David Goodhart, Enrico Deaglio, and all their colleagues.

My agent, Georgina Capel at Capel and Land, has kept me fed and clothed. I'm hugely grateful to her and to Jonathan Galassi at Farrar, Straus and Giroux. Thanks also to Robert Caskie, Philippa Brewster, and Annie Wedekind. I have had the immense fortune, over many years, of picking the large brains of Professors Diego Saglia, Jeremy Elston, Hugh Jones, and Niall Ferguson. The sharing of their wisdom in times of need has been invaluable. Filippo Ziveri has accom-

xviiiACKNOWLEDGEMENTS

panied me on various journeys, and has always been very generous and judicious. I've also been exceptionally lucky to share the company, contacts, and Catholicism of Glenn Alessi, an outsider with the inside track. Without the *moschettieri* from the summer of 1998 I would never have stayed here: "L'Albe," "Il Davo," and "Il Gallo" have been very, very *grandi*.

The following have all helped me out when it really counted: Stephanie Berry, Paolo Zaninoni, Massimo Birattari, Chicca Galli, Duncan Boothby, Milton and Edith Hyman, Lucia Sbravati, Carlo Torinesi, David Pines and Hilary Branch, Philip Purchase, Gloria Saccò, Maurino Levati, Steven Lukes, Giovanni De Mauro, Jacopo Zanchini, John Lloyd, Paolo Garimberti, Jeff Biggers, Mary Money, Sue Rocky Jordan, Rebecca Nicolson, Pino Colombi, Betta Salvini, Richard Beecham, Katharine Fogarty, Giovanni Granatiero, Norah Wallace, Marco Mazzoli, Mette Rudvin, John Foot, Giuseppe Lavagetto, Marcello Ziveri, Mario Casartelli, Stefano Mercurio, Livio Lacchini, Joe McGinniss, Luca Fontana, Nicola Clerici, Anthony Fernandez, Anna Pallai, Manu Dazzi, Erica Scroppo, Richard Newbury, Pierleone Ottolenghi, and Giovanni Camattini.

I am enormously indebted to my Italian family. Heartfelt thanks to Francesca Lenzi, to Raul Lenzi and Daniela Calebich, to all the sisters Calebich, to the Diena family and Enrico Basaglia. I've benefited from extraordinary back-up from Britain. The generosity of my parents, Bob and Jane, and of my siblings, David and Vandana and Paul, defies description. Thanks to them, and to all the other Joneses, Wallaces, and Ramrakhas.

Unless otherwise stated, I take responsibility for the translations of Italian texts. Any errors, of translation or otherwise, are obviously entirely mine.

THE DARK HEART OF ITALY

1

"PAROLE, PAROLE, PAROLE"

The Latin is attentive, sensitive to the perfection of form. Italian literature is, from this point of view, exemplary for its academic, formal character, concerned with the perfection of expression and of language. Italian life, particularly political life, is difficult to understand if one overlooks this point. The declarations of political men, and parliamentary debate, are invariably aimed not towards the setting out and resolution of concrete problems, the reaching of useful ends, but towards creating images . . . and Ciceronian rhetoric, its formal perfection, its taste for the elaborate, its dream of a universe made up of perfect equilibrium, accompanies the entirety of Italian literature like a shadow.

—GIORGIO TOURN

I arrived in Parma knowing only a few Italian words culled from classical music and from menus (*adagio, allegro, prosciutto*, and so on), and I found myself in the infantile position of trying to understand my surroundings at the same time as I learnt how to describe them. At the beginning, not knowing what was being said, I only heard the noise of the language, which sounds like coins fired out of a machine-gun: quick *clinks*, long, long words made up of short, rhythmic syllables. Conversations were also visual: words were underlined by hands which worked overtime, the fingers moving into strange shapes as if the speaker were working on some invisible origami creation in his palms.

When you do begin to understand the words, you quickly appreciate the beauty of the language. Every worthy person or object or place is given an evocative nickname. Football players, the princes of society, are called "the Swan" (the tall Marco van Basten) or "the Little Pendulum" (the Brazilian Cafu, who races up and down Roma's right wing). Venice is La Serenissima. The south of the country is *il mezzogiorno*, the "midday." The road which leads there is called the Autostrada del Sole, "the Motorway of the Sun." The little pleasures of daily life have suggestive names. A *cappuccino*, with its frothy milk and cocoa powder, is so called because it resembles the brown hood of a Capuchin friar. A hair-drier is called a *fon* because the warm wind which blows over northern Italy from the Austrian Alps is called the *föhn*. Even words relating to sexual matters seem more imaginative, more amusing: "to key," "to sweep," "to saw," and, my favourite, "to trombone."

Another difference is simply the decibel level. Italians, I didn't need to be told, are loud. The *palazzo* in which I live is a square medieval building. It is now divided into flats, each with windows and crumbling balconies onto our little courtyard. It's hard to explain the implications of that simple architecture. I had always seen Italian paintings of sun-drenched courtyards lined with laundry and loggias but never quite realised what they're like to live in. It's not that there's particularly a sense of community (most of the flats are now legal offices, since the courtroom is only a few hundred metres away; there's a restaurant on one side, a gymnasium on another). It's that you live in very close proximity to your neighbours and, above all, to their noise. Instead of answering the modern speaker-phones which double as doorbells, most lean out the open windows and shout to their friends four floors below. The whole *palazzo*, naturally, hears the conversation. I frequently hear arguments from the lawyers' offices. There's pop music permanently blaring out of the gym, and twice a week an aggressive aerobics instructor rolls up to bark instructions which can be heard at the other end of the building. At precisely five every evening the lady in the flat opposite mine, on the west wing of the building, starts singing her arpeggios and arias. The noise, always mingled with the roar of a nearby moped, takes some getting used to, but after a while other countries begin to seem eerily quiet, even dull.

The next, obvious difference from English was that conversations sometimes sounded like excerpts from intelligent discussions in a museum. It's hard to explain, but the past seemed ever present: not just in the endless ancient buildings, but also in conversation. Even in cheery chats at the pub, people started heated arguments about some incident from the seicento (the seventeenth century) or began discussing the merits of some baron or artist from the Middle Ages. It was never done boastfully, but rather casually, as if they were gossiping about a neighbour: just sitting in a pub, people would explain the history of the Farnese family (the dukes of Parma, who produced their own Pope) or the importance of Maria Luigia, Napoleon's widow who was Duchess here for three decades. They would explain the origin of the word "Parma" (the name for the circular Roman shield), and since the city is the epicentre of Italian cuisine and opera (home to Parma ham and Parmesan cheese, birthplace of Giuseppe Verdi and Arturo Toscanini), conversation often revolved around food or opera. That intelligence, an intelligence which never verged on arrogance, was astonishing. Listen to the old men in the squares who swig wine and play cards all day, and you sense that same easy familiarity with subjects which would, in England, appear effete: prosciutto, opera, grapes, and so on. And they're discussed in the most earthy terms: "I swear it, when I heard the orchestra my balls rolled out of the auditorium."

The blissful creativity of the language is most obvious in the insults and arguments. The humbling effects of one-liners and put-downs were incredible, and in the course of time I received my fair share: "Holy pig!" screamed one old woman as I inadvertently blocked her exit from a parking space. "If you screw like you park, don't be surprised when you become a cuckold!" All that verbal jousting is hard to take at first, but once you can respond in kind, arguing becomes a normal, enjoyable pastime, a refreshing burst of sincerity.

Those, at least, were my early impressions: the happy noise and creativity of the language, the intelligence, and the carefree chaos. Gradually, though, something very different became obvious. Having read E. M. Forster and D. H. Lawrence, I had always imagined Italy as a place where reserve and reticence fall away, and where the polite hypocrisies of Britain could be thrown off. For those Edwardian writers, Italy was a country so vivacious and sensuous that it became a theatre for sexual awakening and for carnal knowledge. It's what Lawrence called the Italians' "blood-knowledge":

> My great religion is a belief in the blood, the flesh, as being wiser than the intellect. We can go wrong in our minds. But what our blood feels and believes and says, is always true . . . That is why I like to live in Italy. The people are so unconscious. They only feel and want: they don't know.[1]

The more words I learnt, though, and the more I understood their origins, the more the country seemed not chaotic but incredibly hierarchical and formal. Even *ciao* was a greeting, I discovered, derived from the word *schiavo*, "slave." The cheery *ciao*, Italian's most famous word, originally implied subservience and order, as in "I am your slave." (In the Veneto, when you go into a shop, you're often greeted with *comandi*, which is again rigidly hierarchical: saying *comandi* is a plea by the shop assistant to "be commanded.") In Italy one endlessly has to obtain "permission": all foreigners—even those from the European Union—have to have a *permesso,* a "permit," to stay in the country. It's also the word used when crossing the threshold of someone else's house: "permission" to enter?

The next word which recurred again and again was vaguely related: *sistemare,* which means to order or sort out. A situation was invariably *sistemato,* "systematised," be it a bill, a problem, a relationship. It can also mean a murderous "sorting out," as in *lui è stato sistemato,* "he's been sorted." The rigidity, the search for orderliness, was everywhere. "All's well" is *tutt'a posto:* "everything in its place." Randomness is a recent, imported concept (the English is used, as in the neologism *randomizzare*). Rules are, at least on the surface, very important in Italy. Since eccentricity is frowned upon, one of the most frequent phrases one hears is *non si fa,* "it's not the done thing" (which invariably refers to dietary habits or dress codes, where the rules are most rigid). Other words which sent shivers down my spine were *in regola* and *le norme.* Rather than excitingly chaotic, Italy began to appear incredibly conservative and obedient.

I had moved to Italy because I was in love, and I thought that a relationship would be, if not casual, then at least outside cast-iron conformity. But this, too, came as a rude shock. It was an example of "systematisation" which I had never expected. About three or four months after I had arrived in Parma, friends (from southern Italy, where things are even more formal) started talking about someone called my *fidanzata.* Until that time they had usually referred to the person in question as my *ragazza,* my "girl." Then, almost overnight, this new word was apparently more apt. I went to the dictionary and found *fidanzata* translated as "betrothed." Strange, I thought, I'm sure I would have remembered if I had proposed to her, or even discussed an engagement with her family or our friends.

"No, no," I said, wagging my finger in imitation of their usual admonition, "she's my *ragazza*." The amused faces were unforgettable. My friends slapped me on the back, enjoying having to explain exactly why I was now "betrothed." "And you've done it all so quickly," Ciccio said with a laugh.

There was something else, though. When I went into shops, people would call me *giovanotto* or *ragazzino*. Even though they mean "young man" and "little boy," respectively, I heard the descriptions used to refer to people who looked like forty-year-olds. Maybe it was a compliment, I didn't know; to me, it instinctively felt very condescending. The attitude towards twenty-year-olds, even thirty- or forty-year-olds, was incredibly patronising. It's hard to describe, but in Britain someone who's, say, twenty-five has probably bought his own house, lives on his own or with friends, has a job. If anyone calls you "young boy" in Britain, you think it's almost an insult. Here, though, it seemed that one is "young" for a very, very long time. Until you're thirty-five, your career doesn't really start. It's unlikely you'll have a real promotion until you're fifty.

I had begun listening to the gravelly voice of a stunning singer-songwriter, the man the Italians call their Bob Dylan: Fabrizio De André. One of his interviews summed up precisely the excruciating geriatric structure of the country: "We're living in a society built for rich, old people, not for willing youngsters," he wrote. There was no "generational change-over," he said, because old people remained

clinging until death to any type of activity which could be better executed by young people. The young remain unemployed, facing the impossibility of being able to form and maintain a family: and to those few who manage to find work, it's absolutely forbidden even to think about buying a house . . . if all goes well, they'll buy it towards the age of fifty, on the edge of old age.[2]

Interestingly, the word for hierarchy in Italian is *gerarchia*; the etymologial root is the same (from the Greek *hieros*, implying sacred or divine), but the Italian contains an implicit sense that superiority is based upon age.

Thus, after a few months, I saw that the country wasn't only happily chaotic but also rather "systematised" and rigidly hierarchical. Any approach towards authority had to involve a startling degree of grovelling. *Garbo*, I was told, was a quality which even an Englishman would need to work on. It means "courtesy," or the ability to smooth over contradiction, betrayal, or rudeness. The other quality required of an Italian speaker, and especially a journalist, is *salamelecco*, which implies obsequiousness and flattery (from the Arabic *salaam aleikum*). As I spent weeks and then months in police stations and post offices trying to get the correct "permission" to live or work in Italy, I realised that it wasn't enough to bluster in and demand the necessary form. I had to deploy a contorted, formal language full of *svolazzi* (embellishments), or else the sun-glassed officer reviewing my case might be offended and want to flex his bureaucratic muscles. To request interviews, I had to write sentences of such sycophancy it was almost embarrassing: "Given one's noted fame as a political thinker, and notwithstanding the busy timetable which one has, I would be honoured if one felt able to consent to a courteous interview."

Then, the more I watched and understood TV, I realised that credibility in Italian is often based upon *la parlantina* (pomposity). Nowhere else are words so often spoken just for their idyllic sound rather than their meaning. To be *logorroico*, "incredibly wordy," is esteemed more than anything that's actually being said. *Accademico* doesn't have the pejorative meaning which it does in English, the sense that "academic" is precipitously close to irrelevance. Invariably, the only way to get a conversational look-in was to interrupt. The only way to be taken seriously (especially as a journalist) was to hold forth with contorted clauses and forget any pretence of concision. There was one song which, for me, came to appear like Italy's alternative anthem (partly because it's so often aired, and also because it's so appropriate): Mina's "Parole, parole, parole" (Words, words, words). It's beautifully sung with resignation at all the yakking, all the inconsequential talk.

The stereotype of German speakers in Britain, that they're brutally to the point, is exactly what Italians think of English speakers, and especially journalists. "You can't be so direct," said my girlfriend, correcting my idiosyncratic style of writing Italian; "you need to dress it up a bit." So each time I wrote a letter (usually a letter of complaint to Telecom Italia), I had to have my prose turned into an august essay, as if it were written by a rather cocky, over-erudite schoolboy. Every letter is opened by the word *egregio*, which in English implies flagrant or foolish (egregious), but in Italian is an honorific, as in *"Egregio Signor Jones."* And honorifics are the all-important sweeteners of the language—every graduate is called "doctor," the football manager of the national side is called a "technical commissioner," a weather forecaster has to be at least a lieutenant colonel.

I became fascinated by the different registers within Italian, by the way in which the same people could be beautifully expressive one moment, then painfully baroque and Byzantine the next. The latter is what Italo Calvino called the *antilingua*, a sort of bureaucratic, formulaic language which creates "semantic terror." It was, he wrote, a "mortal contagion" in which the actual meaning gets lost along the way: "In the anti-language the meanings are constantly distanced, relegated to the background of the words, which in themselves don't mean anything or mean something vague and elusive."[3] I used to read four or five newspapers a day to brush up on my slowly improving Italian. At the end of hours of diligent reading, with a doorstop dictionary at my elbow, I knew nothing more about current affairs at lunch than I had before breakfast. I had been informed about absolutely nothing. It was a case not of incomprehension but of bewilderment. There were so many words, pages and pages of comment and opinion and surveys, which said absolutely nothing. Everything had to be qualified and contradicted. It was, I was told, a famous rhetorical device called *anacoluto* (anacoluthon), inconsistency of grammar or argument.

All of this does, strangely, have an important bearing on political discourse. There is, as Calvino wrote, a different Italian which is used to control and command. The political importance of that smokescreen of words is that no one can ever penetrate to the core of an issue or fully understand what's going on. More important, there was an obvious, dangerous divergence between the everyday and the official modes of linguistic communication. On the one hand, the country appeared serenely *alla mano*, which is to say entirely unpretentious: noisy, vivacious, never pulling its linguistic punches. But when confronted by any incarnation of authority, that directness gave way to deference, chaos gave way to conformity. I had seen friends who, in their homes, were the epitome of the carefree; when they had to go to the post office, though, they would put aside a whole morning to practise the long, imploring speeches they would have to use.

Whilst I was trying to learn Italian, everybody else was desperate to speak English. It became very obvious that the chic thing to do in Italian is to drop in English words—rather like showing *savoir faire* in English. Almost all the advertising slogans, on TV or on billboards, are in English. Many DJs speak half in English, or have American interns who do various chat shows. Sometimes the news on radio stations is read in both languages. Even though Italy's fashion industry is superior to all others, if you walk down any street, you will see dozens of Italians wearing clothes covered in English writing, often superimposed on a Union Jack or the Stars and Stripes. It's called *esterofilia*, a liking for all things foreign.

Even football, which like food and classical music is one of the bastions of Italian pride, has been thoroughly anglicised, such as "corner *di Totti*, dribbling *di Delvecchio*, cross, *però Montella è in* offside"; a football manager is also *il mister*. The importations are often hilariously inaccurate. The many billboards for sex-shops on the ring roads around cities advertise what are called *sexy shops*. I've often tried—and always failed— to explain why it's so funny: it would mean that the actual bricks and mortar of the shop are provocative, "you know, maybe in a G-string." Victimisation in the workplace is called *mobbing*. A morning suit is called *il tight*. A tuxedo is *lo smoking*. *Petting*, it's as well to know, doesn't mean petting in the English sense, but a type of foreplay at the extremely advanced stages. *Flirting* means flirting. *Slip* means "slip" only in the Y-front sense, not as in "slip-up." Politicians, too, are keen to show that they're cosmopolitan and drop in all sorts of English words, even titling their rallies *Security Day* or their conferences *I Care*.

Sometimes that importation of English is nothing other than *snobismo*, a bit of easy showing off when an Italian phrase could just as well have been used. At other times, though, there are fissures in the Italian, conceptual cracks where there is no alternative to an English notion. Soon after I arrived, I spent an enjoyable night sampling a friend's grandmother's home-made *nocino*, walnut liqueur. (Anything *della nonna*, "of the granny," be it a restaurant dessert or a fiery liqueur, implies family and therefore *bontà*, "goodness.") The following morning I discovered that "hangover" simply has no equivalent in Italian. (Drinking habits are infinitely more civilised than in Britain, and even when they're not, it's a transgression to which no one's going to admit.) There's no word to express "condescending" or "patronising," which are, I suppose, the flip sides of subservience. "Self-control" is also absent in Italian, so the English is used.

Esterofilia, the liking for all things foreign, extends to names. Friends despair of my taste, but one of my favourite Italian actors is Bud Spencer, a bullish former Olympic swimmer whose real name is Carlo Pedersoli. During the 1970s he went to America with Terence Hill to make B movies which pretended to be American but starred Italians mouthing English; the films were then dubbed into Italian for Italian audiences. Slapstick but touching, these films deliberately put a bit of hamburger beef into the spaghetti western, thus catering to the yearning for all things American. Christian names often follow the lead. I had found a job teaching English at Parma University, and in my classes, next to Maria Immacolata (Mary Immaculate) and Gian Battista (John the Baptist), there were a William, a Tommy, and a Gladys. Other favourites are Jessica, JR (thanks to *Dallas*), and Deborah. Italy's most famous televisual personalities are called Gerry and Mike.

More surprising was that Russia has also been—especially for those from "red" Parma or the Communist bastion of Reggio Emilia—the inspiration for non-Italian names. Amongst people my age (those born during the *anni di piombo*, the "years of lead" of the Cold War), Yuri is certainly more common than Tobia, and much less laughed at. (The first of many nicknames I was given was Zio Tobia, Uncle Tobias, which is the Italian for that famous farmer Old MacDonald.)

The difficulties of learning the language were compounded by the fact that Italian still hasn't entirely percolated into Italy's city-states. Until the advent of radio and then TV, few people spoke correct Italian as their first language. Children of Italians who emigrated in the first half of the century often return to Italy thinking that they know Italian, only to discover that their parents only spoke and taught them their dialect. The results are still obvious today. When I asked students to translate an English word into Italian, I was normally offered a dozen alternatives, and long arguments ensued amongst the Sicilian, Venetian, and Lombard students as to what was the proper Italian translation. TV and radio are dominated by quiz shows which ask contestants what a fairly ordinary Italian word means, or question them about some long-forgotten piece of grammar. I would occasionally ask a simple linguistic question at the dinner table (the "remote past," say, of a particular verb), only to be offered three or four alternatives before my fellow diners started laughing and admitted they weren't quite sure.

It was, I was informed, a problem of the piazza. *Piazza*, which I had always assumed meant simply "square," had other connotations, as in "the team should start playing better soon because Reggio is *una piazza calda*" ("a hot square," which, it was explained, implies volatile fans or a politically engaged population). The piazza is the "city," its symbolic centre where people (for political or footballing reasons) "descend" to celebrate or protest. The piazza is the soul of local pride, a concept which is close to *campanilismo* (the affection for one's own bell-tower). It's also, sometimes, the place of resistance to outside, even Italian national, influence. If Italians spend much time deriding Italy, doing the same to their (truly) beautiful home town is unthinkable. There's a provincialism (in the proudest, least pejorative sense) in Italy which is unthinkable elsewhere. The word for "country"—

paese—even doubles as the word for "town," suggesting that solidarity exists as much on a local as on a national level. City-states are still city-states, with their own cuisine, culture, and dialect.

It became very obvious that Italy and Italian were notions which had been somewhat superimposed on city-states, and which still hadn't been entirely accepted or absorbed. The country was really what Carlo Levi called "thousands of countries," in which inhabitants enjoy the best of both worlds: the cosiness of provincialism mixed with urbane cosmopolitanism. The result is the most beautiful aspect of Italian life. People invariably live and work where they were born rather than flocking to some far-off capital. Cousins and uncles and grandparents live in the same town, and very often under the same roof. (Although the following figures are from 1988–89, they have changed little in the last decade: 15.2 per cent of married Italian children live either in the same house or in the same *palazzo* as their mother; 50.3 per cent live in the same *comune*; only 13.2 per cent live farther than fifty kilometres from the maternal nest.)

The notion of community, of society's cement, had become something which interested me because it seemed to describe all the differences between Britain and Italy. "Here it's just so civilised," I would say to Italian friends. "In Britain, many nights, a lot of people will be drunk, fighting, and shouting. The country's rude and rushed. Here, well, it's just so much more civilised." And I meant it: Italy really is much, much more civilised than Britain. At sunset, young men will walk arm in arm through the city with their grandmothers. Lunches last for hours, and the conversation, without ever being pretentious, will always be amazingly sophisticated. The politeness, the gentility of Italians, is astonishing. But civility in Italy is always understood in private terms: house, family, community, *campanile*. In Britain, it's the opposite: it may be the result of exaggerated patriotism, but "belonging" in Britain is conceived in public terms: the state, the Crown, the Commons, and so on.

In Italy, that notion of citizenship is entirely absent. Here, the notion of the state is almost always pejorative. The word *stato*, referring to the state at a national level, is almost always used as a criticism. The *stato* is the cause of all complaints and grudges. There is, as is well known, no patriotism in Italy. Nobody feels much affection for anything national (the only exception being the *azzurri*, the national football team). The unification of Italy was so recent that many people still feel that the Italian flag is only a "heraldic symbol . . . crude and out-of-place—the red shameless and the green absurd."[4] Every Italian I met spoke about his country, at the national level, as exactly the opposite of what I had been told in Britain: instead of describing a land of pastoral bliss, Italians told me, with disparaging sneers, that their country was "a mess," "a nightmare," and, most often, "a brothel." Italy, they said, was a "banana republic" or, since the advent of Berlusconi, a "banana dictatorship." Everyone was very welcoming, but there was always, after a few hours, a warning. No one could understand why I had left Britain. A few told me to go back as soon as possible. They all, without exception, said Italy was *bella*, before explaining to me why it's not at all what it seems.

There was an obvious, inexplicable inferiority complex about being Italian. The first time I went to browse through a bookshop, a host of indignant titles were on display: *Italy, the Country We Don't Like*, *The Italian Disaster*, *The Abnormal Country*. Watching TV, I realised that a large percentage of the Italian film industry seemed to rely on the "indignant" genre. Countless films have honest men taking on the dark, unknown forces of Italy and meeting their inevitable, early death: *An Everyday Hero*, *The Honest Man*, *A Good Man*. If I listened to musicians, I would hear them singing songs like "Non mi sento Italiano" (I don't feel Italian) or "You Wanna Be Americano." I would sit down and watch films—especially those starring Alberto Sordi—and see that same sense of unease about Italian identity (though Sordi, of course, satirised the obsession with America and made the *esterofilo* appear much more daft than the Italian underneath).

The discrepancy between my drooling friends in Britain and the dismayed locals was even more evident reading Italian classics. One metaphor was always used to describe Italy: "whore," "harlot," "brothel." For Dante, Italy was an "inn of woe, slavish and base . . . a brothel's space." For Boccaccio, it was "the woman of the world," once regal but now fallen (*"fuggit'è ogni virtù, spent'è il valore"*). Italy was, for Machiavelli, a woman disfigured and nude: "without head, without order, beaten undressed, lacerated, coarse." So much for the sunny, celestial land I had, having read Shelley and Byron, been expecting: "a plane of light between two heavens of azure," or a place "whose ever-golden fields" were "ploughed by the sunbeams solely."

I tried to find the origin of the use of "whore" as a metaphor, and found that it was coined because of the perception that Italy had, as it were, been through so many hands. Bourbons, Habsburgs, rival popes, and other external dynasties had so regularly conquered and "possessed" her that a weary, common expression became *"O Franza o Spagna, purchè se magna"*—it didn't matter who the political "pimp" was as long as there was food to eat. Since Italy wasn't united until 1861, it remained for centuries a sort of bargaining chip in the balance of European power. Long before imperialism reached the East and West Indies, Italy was a colonised country, becoming rather like what India would be for the British: a "jewel" in the imperial crown, esteemed for its age and cultural inheritance. There were, of course, indigenous dukedoms and independent republics on the peninsula, but they remained squeezed between strongholds of Habsburgs and Bourbons in the "race for Italy." (Even the "mythological conception" of Italy was thanks to outside influence: Saturn, ousted from Olympia by his son Jupiter, became the first of Latium's many "foreign rulers.") As a result, even now the metaphor of prostitution is endlessly invoked and reiterated. It's become like Albion for the English: an intuitive image of what, for Italians, Italy has been (with the difference that it is invariably a negative image, and one which hints at the uncertainty about what "Italy" really is or whom it belongs to).

The metaphor is also used because the word for brothel (*casino*) also means "mess" or "confusion." The very *modus operandi* of Italy is confusion. That's how Italy's power and secrecy work. Any investigator simply gets tied up in knots with all the facts and words and documents, with the convictions and contradictions. As a result, their investigations invariably end up with such an unbelievable story that, even if it's true, people are already bewildered beyond the point of no return. By far the most common expression heard to describe Italy is *bel casino*, which is rather like Laurel and Hardy's "fine mess." It means "beautiful confusion" or (originally) "beautiful brothel."

I quickly understood the reason for Italians' dismay about their state. Italy isn't a religious country; it's a clerical one. The fourth estate isn't really the press but a power which is much slower, more ponderous, and invariably faceless: bureaucracy. Its clerics are the modern incarnations of priests. They are the people who classify and authorise, the people whose signature or stamp is vital to survival. Like priests, they're the intermediaries who usher you along the yellow-brick road towards the blessed paradise of "legitimacy."

Here post offices and banks are like large, emptied churches. They're sacred, communal places with the same shafts of oblique sunlight falling from high windows. There's a sense of people meekly approaching authority as they queue like communicants—waiting not to receive the Eucharist but to impart large portions of their earnings to one faceless monopoly or another. Hours pass and you get closer to the counter, closer to your brush with institutionalised usury. Then, because nothing—but for driving—is done with anything resembling speed, and because the queuing system is unorthodox, you will find yourself further back than you were an hour ago. I used to get infuriated in such situations when I first arrived, but now I rather enjoy them. I've realised that, as the British go to the pub, the Italians go to the post office. You meet and make friends, read a paper, or just pass the time.

"Bureaucracy" means "office power" (*bureau-kratos*), and nowhere are offices as "powerful" as in Italy. One recent study suggested that two weeks of every working year are lost to Italians in queues and bureaucratic procedures.[5] The calculation went that since Italians need, on average, twenty-five visits to various offices each year, the equivalent of almost seven thousand minutes each year is spent queuing. That would be in a normal year; if you want to apply for a job, it's best to put aside a week or ten days in order to gather the correct documents, pay for them to be stamped, and so on. It's like trying to catch confetti: racing from one office to another, filling in forms and requests, trying to grab pieces of paper which always just elude your grasp. As much as 2,000 billion lire ($1 billion) is spent annually by Italians just to "certify" their status (car owner, divorced, resident at a particular address, and so on). It's not just expensive; it's exceptionally slow. It's been nicknamed the *lentocrazia*, the "slowocracy."

For many reasons, the importance of the bureaucracy lies in its politicisation. The civil service has often been so slow to implement laws and legislation that they are superseded before they're in place. Funds offered by the government often, in the past, never arrived, and they became *residui passivi* (funds beyond their application date) which were duly returned to the Treasury. Time-wasting, the greatest skill of a politicised civil servant, became in the postwar period an art form, whereby civil servants could delay reforms through their obstinate slowness. Endless historians have written of the clerical class as a shadow Parliament: hostile to change, servile only to its insider clientele. The bureaucracy is also acutely politicised because "clerical" jobs are so precious that thousands, millions, of Italians compete for a *posto*, a "place." The jobs are particularly precious because they offer contracts for *tempo indeterminato*, "time immemorial." Thus politicians are lobbied by ambitious parents who long for their child to enjoy the comfortable, cosy world of a clerical job. When I went to buy my morning newspapers, I would see the little pavilions which sold papers covered with magazines dedicated to advertising the latest important competition for public-sector jobs. It's an example of another keyword of Italian politics: *clientelismo*, the culture of looking after your friends and family and thereby keeping outsiders and unknowns out of the loop. I'm told the whole set-up is much more meritocratic than it was a few years ago, especially in the north, but it's still unlikely that you'll ever get a job without "contacts"; you need to know the right local politician, or have the backing, the *raccomandazione*, of—a phrase you frequently hear—a *famiglia importante*.

If you're outside the clerical class, though, you begin to understand the contempt Italians feel for their own state. You have to be painfully deferential to the clerics; you have to plead or lobby for the simplest things in the most wordy, sycophantic way. Or you have to have *conoscenze*, "acquaintances," have to know people "with their hands in the pasta." It all comes with wonderful opportunities and dangers: everything works brilliantly on a personal, private footing; but from anything institutional you can expect only headaches and queues.

After about a year in Italy, I was queuing at the post office; I was furious because I had to pay the former state monopoly Telecom Italia vast amounts of money for two phone lines which, for complicated reasons, hadn't been operative for months. I met one of my middle-aged students, "Lucky" Luciano, and started grumbling to him. He laughed and shook his head as if that were nothing. He was, he said, still waiting for a 28-million-lira refund from the state because he had paid too much tax back in the 1980s. Most of his friends had dodged the tax because they knew it was about to be revoked; he, having been honest, had paid a hefty price. Then someone next to us in the queue began listing her woes, which went back to a rip-off she had suffered at the hands of the state during the 1970s. Within minutes, three parallel queues were all complaining, each person coming out with a horror story of governmental avarice and bureaucratic incompetence.

Attempting to reason, of course, is as futile as Canute's defying the tide. "We're not citizens," the mother of my "betrothed" explained, "but subjects." That distance between government and its people, and the them-and-us mentality it breeds, are central to any understanding of Italy. Because everyone feels so badly treated, because everything is so legalistic, people feel justified in being a little lawless. "Impotence in front of a blocked political system, incapable of change . . . the negation of democratic logic," was even offered in the 1970s as a central reason for Italian terrorism.[6] Italians, the argument went, felt it a "metaphysical curse" to be Italian, to be subjected to those grinding, inefficient, but very powerful "offices."

The political consequences of Italians' disdain for the Italian state are that the sense of community and of the common weal is minimal. That distancing from anything *statale* breeds individualism and an unusual attitude towards law-abiding. I have never lived in a country in which so many people think the state so criminal and in which, therefore, breaking that state's laws was so often, and so indulgently, smiled upon. Few other countries have citizens with such an "each to his own" mentality or so much *menefreghismo*, "I don't carism" (signalled with the back of the fingers thrown forwards from the throat to the chin). It often seems as if everyone were trying to beat the system instead of trying to uphold it. *"Fatta la legge trovato l'inganno"* goes a common proverb: no sooner is a law made than someone will find a way round it.

Next to the description of Italians as *brava gente* (good people), I started hearing another, less complimentary one: *furba gente* (cunning people). A *furbo*, it was explained, watches his money, and probably casts a wistful eye on his neighbours'; he doesn't worry unduly about the rules. It's a vaguely attractive trait (unless the cunning is at your own expense). Its opposite, *ingenuità*, implies gullibility. It's much better, of course, to be *furbo*, mildly dodgy, than *ingenuo*, naive (which originally implied virtue, because an *ingenuo* was one "born free" rather than into slavery).

In Italy there's a morality unlike anything I had ever come across before. It's best summed up by Jacob Burckhardt in his *Civilisation of the Renaissance in Italy*:

> Machiavelli . . . said openly, "We Italians are irreligious and corrupt above others." Another man would have perhaps said, "We are individually highly developed; we have outgrown the limits of morality and religion which were natural to us in our undeveloped state, and we despise outward law, because our rulers are illegitimate, and their judges and officers wicked

men." Machiavelli adds, "because the Church and her representatives set us the worst example."[7]

Therein lies the irony. Wrongdoing is invariably excused by the fact that political or Church leaders are, rightly or wrongly, thought to be up to much worse things and a little tax dodging or bribery by us lesser beings really isn't that important. This, of course, continues the vicious circle: everyone's up to something, and you're stupid if you're not, too. Judgements are, in fact, rarely moral. Linguistically, as in so much else, the country is based upon aesthetics rather than ethics. The judgement words most used are not "good" or "bad" but "beautiful" (*bello*) or "ugly" (*brutto*). The adjective *bello* is trotted out with such regularity that it entirely obscures a concept like "good"; it can then be trumped by *troppo bello* when something is overwhelmingly "too beautiful." Thus immorality is less frowned upon than inelegance; to be beautiful, or to be somewhere beautiful or with someone beautiful, is more of an achievement than righteousness. This obsession with outward appearance is at the root of the word *figura*, which implies the "figure" you've achieved not only physically but in the sense of creating an attractive or ugly impression. *Fare una figura*, to make a bad impression, is an error not necessarily of morals but of presentation.

Strangely, the immorality is culturally related to the Catholic Church. There's a confessionalism in which it doesn't matter what you do, whether you're good or bad, as long as you remain "in the ranks," as long as you profess your intention to be better. Catholicism is all-embracing (the origin of the word, *katholikos*, implies exactly that): everyone is included, which means that everyone's forgiven, pardoned. There's nothing that a humble nod towards the purple cassocks or judicial "togas" can't resolve. Politicians may be criminals, everyone may even acknowledge as much, but it doesn't matter: everything is whitewashed. History, personal or political, is quickly forgotten.

I met one journalist who had very strong views on the subject. "OK," he said one night as he tried to explain it to me, "imagine you've got a country which has always, throughout its entire history, said: 'These are the rules: don't break them. If I catch you, well, you'll be let off, just don't do it again.' Obviously it's not the best recipe for law-abiding. You know what the Duc de La Rochefoucauld said? 'Hypocrisy is the homage which vice pays to virtue.' Very few Italians are hypocrites. Half of them are noble, heroic, and virtuous, and the other half are so outside any moral orbit that they don't even understand the definition of 'vice' or of 'virtue.' " It sounded a bit extreme, but it certainly aroused my interest.

It's probably not related to the a-legality or amorality, but I found the attitudes towards obligation completely different from those in Britain. "Stop saying 'I must' all the time," friends said to me, nicknaming me *il calvinista*. Red lights and speed limits and no-smoking signs and queues are all fairly slavishly obeyed in Britain; here, it was obvious, they were merely suggestions. The advantage, I realised, was that life here is simply more enjoyable. The longer I stayed here, the more obvious it became that life was not lazy, just more leisurely. I noticed during the skiing season that my favourite barman had left a note outside his bar, handwritten on cardboard: "Closed because of illness. I've gone to recuperate in the Dolomites. I will be better on Monday 18." Protestantism and bad weather speed things up in Britain; here, everything seems more relaxed, including certain rules.

The more I enjoyed the leisurely beauty, the *bellezza*, of Italy, the more sophisticated (in both senses) it seemed. The purpose, I was told, of beauty in Italy, quite apart from simply "being beautiful," is that it's a form of fancy dress: an opportunity to seduce or sedate observers. Italy was a country, I read, "peerless in the art of illusionism." *"Bisogna far buon viso a cattivo gioco"* goes a proverb: appearances are important, and it's therefore "necessary to disguise a bad game with a good face." In English we say "stiff upper lip," which implies stoicism. This was subtly different: it implies not stoicism but presentation. Everything is dressed up, beautified, and embellished. An Italian writer once described that peacock syndrome in which everything becomes part of a great show and subtle disguise:

> [D]ull and insignificant moments in life must be made decorous and agreeable with suitable decorations and rituals. Ugly things must be hidden, unpleasant and tragic facts swept under the carpet whenever possible. Everything must be made to sparkle, a simple meal, an ordinary transaction, a dreary speech, a cowardly capitulation must be embellished and ennobled with euphemisms, adornments and pathos . . . [S]how is as important as, many times more important than, reality.[8]

On two occasions I began to realise how different everything was, or at least was thought to be. One Sunday afternoon I was sitting on the terrace of a house in the Apennines. A friend put on the coffee, which came to the boil like an aircraft, arriving from nowhere with a growl and receding with a hiss and a vapour trail. "You see," said the friend, smiling, "this says everything about the differences between English and Italian." He was pointing at the icing sugar on his croissant. "You call that icing 'sugar,' right? We call it 'veil sugar.' Apart from the fact that our term," he was nodding, smiling because he knew he was right, "is infinitely more elegant than yours, it's also much more subtle. 'Icing on the cake' implies ostentation, right? Ours is a veil, romantic, beautiful, concealing something within."

Then, a little later, I was in Parma's football stadium

watching a match. Everyone was sitting on personalised blue-and-yellow cushions, until the ref made a bad decision and the fans were on their feet, insinuating that he was being cheated on by his wife: *"Arbitro cornuto! Arbitro cornuto!"* It's an amusing and apt insult (in Britain the referee is just an onanist): apart from the fact that it sounds Shakespearean when translated into English, it implies that even the black shirt of authority, controlling the game, doesn't know quite what's going on (be it in the match itself or in his marital bed).

Receiving street directions in Parma is rather like leafing through a calendar at random: go down 22 July, turn left, and then right onto 20 March. All over the city there are plaques, memorials, and statues of partisans from the Resistance, guns in hand, who are sculpted to look suspiciously as if they've been shot in the back. On street corners, copies of the Socialist or Communist papers are pinned up on public boards. Often you see graffiti imploring, "Barricade Yourselves!," though I'm never sure whether it's politicking or just an advert for a nearby restaurant, The Barricades.

Before living in Italy, I had never really heard the words "Fascist" and "Communist" used. In England, such political labels are only used as critical hyperbole, or for historical debates about the early part of the last century. Here, although they are thinner on the ground than a few years ago, many politicians still earnestly and proudly describe themselves as "Fascists," "post-Fascists," or "Communists." Even the flags of the political parties maintain insignia relevant to their Fascist or Communist origins, and graffiti artists follow suit. In Parma, hammers and sickles are standard fare; elsewhere, especially in Rome, there are swastikas or Celtic crosses. "There must be a reason," an Italian academic wrote recently, "why

Italy was the fatherland of Fascism and of the largest Communist party in the Western world, why the two most important secular religions of the twentieth century had their greatest success in Italy."[9] His explanation was that Italian politics is quasi-religious, expressing the "hopes and fears" of its people. Whatever the reason, Fascism and Communism are bedded in the Italian soul, and their collision was the cause of the country's *guerra civile*, its "civil war."

The concept of civil war has been increasingly (and controversially) used to describe phases of Italian history since 1943. Two books published on the war between Italian Fascists and partisans between 1943 and 1945 are called *Una guerra civile* and *Storia della guerra civile in Italia*. Recently, though, it's come to be used also for the period of political terrorism from the late 1960s to the early 1980s: "a low-intensity civil war," a period in which there were almost fifteen thousand "terrorist attacks" and in which 491 people were killed. It was, I was told, one of the enduring features of Italian history, a sort of ongoing, costly conflict between civilians. The country has always been divided into warring halves. I was pointed towards Dante, who (having experienced another Italian "civil war"— the Guelph-Ghibelline conflict) wrote of Italy:

> . . . the living cannot, without shame
> Of war reside in you, and man wounds man
> Though guarded by one wall, one moat, the same.[10]

The more I became interested in those "civil" and "civilian" wars, in the "Fascists" and the "Communists" who were aligned against each other, the more I came across another elegant phrase: the *muro di gomma*, the impenetrable "rubber wall" off which all investigations bounce. Any research, I was told, would be futile. Nothing ever comes out into the open. There may be *intrecci* and *trame*, threads and tracks, which criss-cross the peninsula, linking politicians to the Mafia or terrorist groups, but they are all buried by *omissis* (omission) and *omertà* (the silence of the Mafioso). Investigations go on for years, sometimes decades. When someone is finally brought to court, it seems almost *de rigueur* that if he's been condemned in *primo grado*, he will be absolved in *secondo grado* (on appeal) or else in the Corte di Cassazione (the Supreme Court). No one is ever entirely guilty, no one ever simply innocent. It's part of the rewiring process of living in Italy that you can never say, even about the most crooked criminal, that he is factually, legally guilty: there's always the qualifier that he's "both innocent and guilty." Sooner or later the accusation will be dropped anyway, because the deadline for a judicial decision has been superseded.

Thus when I talk politics with Italian friends, they are always astonished by, and envious of, the way in which British politicians are held accountable. "He just took money to help a friend get a passport, and for that he's in the political wilderness? Incredible." "You mean he lied in court to protect his wife from the knowledge of his infidelity, and he's gone to prison?" After one recent British political scandal, a newspaper wrote on its front page that "if the same were to happen in Italy, there would be no parliamentarians left." The amazement of Italians is twofold: first, astonishment that such paltry infringements represent political wrongdoing and, second, incredulity and envy that powerful men (they are only ever men) can be held to account for their actions, can ever be given a conclusive "guilty" stamp.

"Think of politics like this," said Maurino one night as we were playing the Italian version of pool. "You Brits play pool where balls go down and stay down. Here, anything you knock down gets put back up again. There are no pockets. You just keep playing." He was laughing rather bitterly.

As I began studying postwar Italian history, it became obvious that surrounding any crime or political event, there are always confusion, suspicion, and "the bacillus of secrecy." So much so that *dietrologia* has become a sort of national pastime. It means literally "behindology," or the attempt to trump even the most fanciful and contorted conspiracy theory. *Dietrologia* is the "critical analysis of events in an effort to detect, behind the apparent causes, true and hidden designs."[11] *La Stampa* has called it "the science of imagination, the culture of suspicion, the philosophy of mistrust, the technique of the double, triple, quadruple hypothesis."[12] It's an indispensable sport for a society in which appearance very rarely begets reality. Stendhal wrote about it in *The Charterhouse of Parma*: "Italian hearts are much more tormented than ours by the suspicions and the wild ideas which a burning imagination presents to them."[13] As a result of the conspiracy theorising, probably the largest genre in publishing is the *misteri d'Italia* industry. Whole publishing houses, as well as film production companies, survive solely by revisiting the epic mysteries of Italian postwar history.

And the more I read, the more Italy's recent history seemed dark and intriguing. Leonardo Sciascia and his literary mentor, Luigi Pirandello, both wrote of their native Sicily and Italy as places of illusionism and secrecy where nothing can ever be understood. For Sciascia, Italy was so plagued by sophistry and deceit that it had become "a country without truth . . . there's not a criminal episode which, having some relationship with politics, has had a rational explanation or just punishment."[14] Many history books on modern Italy open with a resigned apology, suggesting that the whole thing is unfathomable. It's the same story with Pirandello's plays, which mock anyone's attempt to work out what is going on in the world. Players become puppets, pushed and pulled by unseen forces. Everything is so confusing that searching for evidence, the famous "document," becomes entirely futile:

Granted, this document you talk about might serve your purpose—that is, to relieve you of this stupid curiosity of yours.
But you don't have it, and so here you are, damned to the
marvellous torment of finding here before your eyes on the
one hand a world of fantasy and on the other a world of reality, and you are unable to distinguish one from the other.[15]

It was this side of Italy which, I slowly realised, was at the
root of those worried warnings I had received when I arrived.
Nothing, I was repeatedly assured, would ever become clear.
"If you're a journalist, forget it," they seemed to be saying.
"You can guess at what has been going on, but no one will
ever get close to the truth." One Italian historian, for example, has written of Italy's postwar history as "partly submerged, dark, not revealed because perhaps not revealable,
not mentionable, as if it were the history of a grim divinity."[16]
I realised that it was, as Pirandello wrote, impossible to
distinguish fantasy from reality. The words "history" and
"story" are the same in Italian (*storia*). Unless it's defined, or
given a definite article, *storia* could be a tale from true life or
simply make-believe. You wouldn't know unless you asked.
Even if you do, it's often hard to believe. The deeper I
delved, the more Italy's postwar history seemed a sort of
magic realism, full of symbolism and surreal touches. "Italy,"
wrote Pier Paolo Pasolini, "is a ridiculous and sinister country.
Its powers are comic masks, vaguely stained with blood."[17]
Even today, given the levels of intrigue and drama, real-
life crimes are always called *gialli* (literally "yellows," or
"thrillers"). Newscasters often excitedly introduce news of a
murder or kidnapping as *un giallo incredible*. That's probably
why, despite the huge success of Giuseppe Tomasi di Lampedusa's *The Leopard*, there are barely any other (comparatively
recent) historical novels in Italy: the factual, true-life version
simply couldn't be bettered. The best writers on Italy in the

postwar period have been well aware of that "thrilling" side to Italian life in which the divide between fact and fiction appears paper-thin. Leonardo Sciascia wrote about the "untouchable, literary perfection" of one tragic Italian "thriller" (the kidnapping and murder of Aldo Moro);[18] Umberto Eco wrote about the same event: "This would be a joke if the novel were not written with blood."[19] One British historian, commenting on another postwar *giallo*, wrote that it seemed "to come straight from a best-selling novel."[20]

As I began trying to distinguish "histories" from "stories," one image of voluptuous secrecy stuck in my mind: "Italy is really like a great, mythological artichoke . . . A single flower, green and purple, where each leaf hides another, each layer covers another layer, jealousy hidden. He who knows how to take off the outside leaves will discover unimaginable things, in a difficult voyage in time and space."[21] Despite the warnings, I decided to make that "difficult voyage," to travel "in time and space" across the country.

2

"THE MOTHER OF ALL SLAUGHTERS"

> See, in these silences where things
> give over and seem close to betraying
> their final secret,
> at times we feel we're about
> to discover an error in Nature,
> the dead point of the world, the link that won't hold,
> the thread to untangle that will finally lead
> to the midst of truth.
>
> —EUGENIO MONTALE

The first year I spent in Italy was idyllic. Any sense of melancholy melted away under so much clear blue sky, and everything seemed more serene and civilised than in Britain. I was earning money in the least arduous way, writing random articles for editors in London: I would be sent to taste the wine on the steep vineyards of the Ligurian coast, or dispatched to review the pastel colours of restored frescos in Florence. If I was ever short of money, I could sit and chat to a friend in English for a while, and he would duly pay for my ski pass in the Alps. At the end of each week, I would sit down and drink a tiny coffee in Parma's main square, getting just enough of a rush to realise how incredibly relaxed I was.

Then, each weekend, we would drive into the mountains. It was like walking into one of those famous landscape paintings: suddenly we were surrounded by the Arcadian scene of children playing in lakes or waterfalls, behind them the warm pink stone of a distant city in the sunset. We would always eat lunch amidst the rhythmic drone of cicadas and protected from the heat by a canopy of wisteria. As always, the food would be a combination of simplicity and extreme sophistication. If anyone was still hungry, or even awake, at the end of the meal, he could just wander into the orchard to collect another course.

They were blissful days, but they were, I knew, essentially escapist. Nothing I was writing was remotely connected to Italian reality: it was all cuisine and culture and nothing else. By contrast, the front-page scoops of Italian newspapers, and hours of chat shows, were dedicated to something very different. They seemed obsessed with a strange kind of news story, which wasn't properly "news" at all. Everything seemed to be about an iconic crime from decades ago. Unfamiliar with the *misteri d'Italia*, I often found the headline splashes incomprehensible: "Sisde Covered Up the Monster of Florence," for example. There's nothing the dictionary can do to help explain that sentence. And if you ask a friend what it means, he will pause for a long time before slowly sitting down and explaining, with slight embarrassment, the implications of the story. That particular headline referred to the discovery that the Monster of Florence, who decades ago had murdered copulating couples in Tuscany, allegedly enjoyed protection from the secret service because he was working on behalf of a clique of aristocratic perverts. Another front-page scoop might be about the kidnapping and murder of Aldo Moro, or something called Gladio.

It was as if a large part of Italian journalists, academics, and judges were still trying to solve whodunits from many years ago. The list of "mysteries" was endless, as were the theories they spawned. The weekly revelations surrounding such crimes—like that one about the Monster of Florence—often appeared incredible, literally unbelievable. Invariably the secret service was involved. Accusations normally ricocheted towards Parliament, where someone was suspected of being the *grande vecchio* who had pulled the hidden strings of Italy's postwar history.

It all sounds like an acute case of paranoia, especially when people try to link up the "mysteries" and end up with theories that look like something cobbled together from *The X-Files*. Yet when you start reading newspaper cuttings and books on the "mysteries," you realise that something very unusual really is going on. It's not just that there's so much murderous intrigue, or that there's such an appetite for it; it's that nothing is ever resolved. That's why the front pages of newspapers are still dominated by facts about those iconic crimes: there has never—despite the yearning to know the truth about Italy's many "illustrious corpses"—been an adequate explanation for what "really happened."

In the "mystery industry," the word *strage* is particularly emotive. It is used to refer to those bombings, from the 1960s to the 1980s, in Milan, Brescia, Bologna, and elsewhere, in which all evidence suggested the participation of Fascist terrorists, but which have rarely, if ever, seen the convictions of those responsible. At random intervals, the slaughters killed ordinary members of the public, in banks, on trains, at railway stations. If their effects were horrific, the consequences were perhaps even worse, showing that the physiology of Italy's democracy was assaulted by a "bacillus of secrecy" and mystery which "fed upon itself, degenerating and corrupting the texture of the state."[1] The sheer inscrutability of Italy's "slaughters," and the desire to understand, finally, the mysteries of those "Fascist" bombings, led to the creation in 1988 of a bizarre parliamentary commission. It's called the Commissione Stragi, the "Slaughter Commission." Its full title is the "Parliamentary Commission of Inquiry into Italian Terrorism and into the Reasons for the Failed Individuation of Those Responsible for the Slaughters." The more I read about the Slaughter Commission, the more intriguing I found it. I was fascinated not so much by the historical task the commission had been set as by something rather different. Why are there so many mysteries in Italy? Why can no journalist or historian or judge ever say what's been going on? I was interested not in finding out the truth about the slaughters (an undertaking which I suspected would be doomed from the outset) but in explaining to myself why, in Italy, truth never seems to emerge. How does that Italian "veil"—beautiful and concealing and intriguing—really work?

My first brush with the Slaughter Commission came in the summer of 2000, when I received an invitation to one of their press conferences in Rome. I spent the four-hour train journey reading newspaper cuttings from the 1960s and 1970s. Accompanying each article would be a photograph of another slaughter: a pavement peppered with blood, corpses lying with limbs at odd angles; torsos slumped over steering wheels or broken bodies found at the bottom of stairwells. Rather strangely, the venue given for the Slaughter Commission's event was Botteghe Oscure—"Dark Cellars"—the street in Rome formerly synonymous with the Communist Party and now home to its reincarnated self, the Democrats of the Left. I walked up to the first floor, where the commission's most recent report was being presented. The room was full of those politicians and judges famous for their investigations into the slaughters from 1969 to 1984. A report, coming in at a modest 326 pages, was being handed round. It was titled "Stragi e terrorismo in Italia, 1945–1976."

Of course, all was not quite as it seemed. I quickly flicked through the doorstop of paper on my lap and realised something was amiss. The work was not that of all twenty parliamentary *deputati* and twenty *senatori* supposed to make up the commission but simply of a breakaway eight members, all Democrats of the Left. Hence, I realised with sinking heart, the location. The report, which was presented as a bringing together of all the recent trials and research, certainly didn't pull its punches: "The slaughters," it said, "were organised, promoted, and supported by men within Italian institutions and by people linked to American intelligence." The central plank of the report was that American landings in Sicily in 1943 represented the beginning of "the American war against Italy, which was to impede with every means the autonomous decision of who to have govern us." Nor was the Vatican spared a swipe: the Holy See, "having maintained an ambiguous attitude, to say the least, towards Fascism, declared itself in favour of whatever intervention necessary on the part of the USA."

The Slaughter Commission was supposed to be part of an Italian "peace process," something like the South African "Truth Commission." But that day in Rome I felt rather like I was watching an arguing couple who, each time they approach each other, seemingly about to make up, suddenly realise they can't do it, can't resist the opportunity for one last verbal volley. Those who wrote the report even made explicit their disdain for the "culture of pacification." "No one wants to re-raise the Wall," said one politician from the Democrats of the Left at the press conference, "just throw some light on some pages which have been kept buried." "We don't want to use history as a cudgel," assures the commission's president, Giovanni Pellegrino.

The climax of the document is the allegation that the current parliamentary head of the National Alliance (the reincarnated Movimento Sociale Italiano, the postwar Fascist party, then in the opposition coalition with Silvio Berlusconi's Forza Italia) had "never done his accounts with the past." Senator Giulio Maceratini, the report said, was the filter between the far right and the neo-Fascists, a "reference point" for—amongst other things—"arms traffickers." "It's documented," the report went on, "that even in the years following those of the so-called strategy of tension, Senator Maceratini continued to have political links with personalities from the subversive right who have already been investigated and each time convicted with definitive sentences for terrorist episodes or for reconstituting the Fascist party."

Within minutes there was a swift response from the right. Gustavo Selva, one of Maceratini's colleagues in the National Alliance, said that the Slaughter Commission's research "seems like a document from the Red Brigades [the left-wing terrorist organisation]." Another spokesman called it "Stalinist." Another said: "Incredible, worthy of a little Maoist group from the 1970s." For his part, Senator Maceratini affirmed that he's "proud" of having "operated" in Ordine Nuovo. Asked if it was true that as recently as 1997 he had meetings with members of the extreme right, he replied, "It's possible that they happened," before slipping into the classic defence of a convenient mnemonic gap: "But I don't have a dazzling memory." The entire day felt like something from the Cold War: knee-jerk accusations and denials, visceral loathing. Low blows were aimed from moral high grounds. There was even a sense of excitement, of glee, at the opportunity to return to the fray. The Slaughter Commission, I quickly realised, was as much a part of the problem as it was the solution, raising ghosts as much as laying them to rest. It became very obvious that nothing in Italy, least of all history, isn't fiercely politicised.

"Think it's true?" I asked one of the Italian reporters next

to me, who duly put his chin in the air and shrugged his
shoulders in dramatic slow motion. *"E che ne so io?,"* "What
do I know?" He looked at me and smiled, as if the question
were rather risible. Later I went for a drink with a friend. "Of
course it's true. It's not that mud in Italy doesn't stick," he
says; "it's that there's so much of it that it doesn't even matter if it does."

One particular piazza in Milan kept being mentioned in
newspapers' front-page scoops from the past. In the centre of
the piazza is the fountain which gives the place its name: Piazza Fontana. It has the feel of a swollen side-street, leading
somewhere else. Barely a few hundred metres away, in Piazza
del Duomo, people gawp at the flying buttresses of the cathedral. Backpackers plait coloured threads into their hair and
share benches with older, more earnest sightseers with guide-
books open on their laps. But nearby, Piazza Fontana remains
untouched by tourism.

Historians, though, have seen in its dreadful bombing a
pivot in Italian postwar history. The epic enigma of that
bomb on 12 December 1969 has become emblematic of the
country's subterfuge, and the slaughter is endlessly revisited
in the hope of finding, as Corrado Stajano wrote, "the key to
understanding the history of the last twenty [now thirty]
years."[2] Understand Piazza Fontana, the theory goes, and
you can uncover the sinister truth of modern Italy. It has
become a sort of historical Holy Grail which, if located,
could prove a source of beatific, and horrific, revelations. The
bomb has hung over the country like a fatal contagion. Many
who might have come close to explaining what happened on
12 December 1969, and in the days and years immediately
after, have become themselves additions to Italy's long list
of "illustrious corpses." Suspects, witnesses, *carabinieri*, and

magistrates all became additional, indirect casualties of the Piazza Fontana bomb ("the mother of all slaughters"), victims of an escalating cycle of recrimination. With each subsequent death, the imperative for an explanation for Piazza Fontana became both more pressing and more improbable.

If you approach Milan in the spring, the air in the suburbs will be full of white *piumini*—pollen from the poplar trees—which waft in the air like overgrown, ethereal snowflakes in the sun. In the city, squeezed between chic boutiques at regular intervals, are narrow bars, full of mirrors and curling chrome. Men and women are drinking thimbles of coffee. If you walk along the city's wide boulevards or its narrow canals, the place feels more Teutonic than Latin: bustling, businesslike. Sparks fall like rain from scaffolding overhead, and trams clatter past. The city is industrious and wealthy. It's home to two of the country's most famous industries, fashion and football. It's also home to the Borsa, the country's stock exchange, and you can often see small crowds gather on the pavements outside banks, from where big screens project to the outside world the latest stock-market quotations. Milan, many proud Lombards will tell you, is the real capital of Italy.

I'm standing in the square reading the imposing marble tribute to the victims of the bomb on the wall of the bank. It was erected on the tenth anniversary of the bomb and condemns the "subversive attack" (no mention of an ideological motivation) in the name of "liberty and justice." It lists the names of the sixteen people killed in the bombing. Another, much smaller and now rusting plaque was put on the lawn opposite the bank two years earlier, in 1977: "To Giuseppe Pinelli, anarchist railwayman. An innocent killed in the grounds of the police headquarters, 16.12.1969. The Students and Democrats of Milan." Despite the attempts of the Socialist mayor to have the second plaque removed in the 1980s, it still stands, testimony to a country's unhealed wound.

Now, more than three decades after the original explosion, a new trial (the eighth) has started. Cynics within the press have denounced it as at best a chasing of shadows which left the scene a long, long time ago or at worst an irresponsible rearguard action by the left, still bearing unfounded grudges against former Fascists who have now reincarnated themselves as serious, mainstream politicians. The trial, say the cynics, has come too late to be of either relevance or consolation. By now the events of 1969 have become so distant that they are like fossilised ancestors, to be regarded with nostalgia or ridicule, or else ignored. For others, though, Piazza Fontana contains a Shoah-like symbolism, such an obscene departure from normality that they are compelled to "bear witness," repeatedly retelling the events and the accusations. Some of the weary campaigners on the left even suggest that there is an active, historical denial of the truth, and that Piazza Fontana has deliberately been turned into a distant event—Piazza Lontana, or Piazza "Far Away."

The Piazza Fontana trial was, like the Slaughter Commission, an opportunity to watch history being written and rewritten, squabbled over by those politicians who were under accusation or defending the accused. The extraordinary thing was that nowhere was there anything resembling a consensus about the most simple facts. Everyone agrees that the Piazza Fontana bomb changed forever the direction of Italian history, but thereafter the country's left and right diverge irreconcilably. Even in debating an event from 1969, any compromise is impossible. The very mention of Piazza Fontana only serves to antagonise the country's right and left and to set off snarling from both sides of Parliament. I couldn't understand why, so long after the event happened, it still meant so much to so many people. After all, the number of victims, in a crude mathematical count, looked small compared with other atrocities all over the globe.

Only one phrase from the Slaughter Commission hinted at why Piazza Fontana was so important. During the entire postwar period (in the words of the president of the commission) neither of Italy's warring halves ever quite "took their fingers off the trigger." It was a melodramatic sentence, but it was exactly what I had been told by endless Italians. Ever since 8 September 1943, they said, there had been (if only between the most extreme halves of the country) a "civil war." Piazza Fontana was, I realised, Italy's version of Bloody Sunday (when, in January 1972, British troops opened fire on civil rights protesters in Northern Ireland): a terrible event in which civilians were the victims of a wider but hidden war. I decided to delve deeper into the history, to try to understand better the implications of 8 September 1943.

On 10 July 1943 the Allied powers landed in Sicily, from there to begin the bombardment of Rome on the nineteenth. Within a week, Benito Mussolini's twenty-one-year rule was over: a meeting of the Gran Consiglio del Fascismo in Rome had passed a motion critical of Il Duce by nineteen votes to seven, and the next day, 25 July, King Vittorio Emanuele III forced Mussolini's resignation. After the so-called Forty-five Days of limbo between opposing powers, and as Eisenhower was disembarking his troops south of Rome in Salerno, Italy signed an armistice of unconditional surrender to the Allies. On the same day, 8 September, Marshal Pietro Badoglio announced the armistice to the Italian people, urging them no longer to fight the Allies. The voltafaccia *was completed on 30 October, the date on which the King declared war on Italy's former ally Germany.*

For the next eighteen months, until the liberation day proper of 25 April 1945, the country experienced the full throes of civil war. Mussolini had been arrested and imprisoned on the Gran Sasso mountain in the Abruzzi. In a glider-and-parachute operation headed by the SS commander Otto Skorzeny, he had been rescued and established at the head of the Repubblica Sociale Italiana (also called the Republic of Salò), based near Italy's northern border on the shores of Lake Garda. Its dominion reached as far south as Rome (which had fallen to the Germans) and Naples and was defended by the so-called Gothic Line. Farther to the south were the Allies, beginning their tortuous advance up the peninsula.

*The country was caught between the Allies in the south and Germany in the north: given the side swapping of Vittorio Emanuele and Marshal Badoglio, it was difficult for the Italian populace—both civilian and military—to be sure which was now the legitimate regime. It was in this almost-existentialist vacuum that the civil war was born: a sense of uncertainty as to what or who represented the real "Italy." The poignancy of the conflict was guaranteed by the fact that each side, those faithful to the German regime and the partisans aligned against them, could present the other as the party guilty of betrayal. For the former, the partisans were classic turncoats (*voltagabbane*), simply opportunists who betrayed both Mussolini and Italy; for those partisans, however, the supporters of the Republic of Salò had betrayed King and country, preferring to side with Hitler's Nazi-Fascists.*

As many as eighty-two thousand people took a direct part in the partisan war in the north. The Comitati di Liberazione Nazionale established a few independent republics in the north of the country. The pockets of resistance were recognised by the Allies in the "Protocols of Rome" in December 1944, granting the Resistance a subsidy of 160 million lire a month; the CLNAI, for its part, became subject to the orders of the Supreme Allied Command. The ferocity of the Nazi reprisals in Italy is well documented and succinctly epitomised in the German commander Major Walter Reder's "March of Death." Beginning on 12 August 1944 at Sant'Anna di Stazzema, where 560 men, women, and children were massacred, it continued until 1 Oc-

tober at Marzabotto, which lost 1,830 of its population. Nor were the atrocities simply committed by the one side; on 6 July 1945 (almost three months after the Italian liberazione*) a group of former Resistance fighters executed fifty-one Fascist prisoners at Schio. Long after the armistice, even years afterwards, reprisals continued between the two sides.*

Those two years of civil war are central to any understanding of Piazza Fontana and of the subsequent era of "civil war" (the terrorism of the anni di piombo*). In both periods northern Italy was the battleground for the political soul of the country. The periods even shared some of the same protagonists, as many of the Fascists agitating for an alternative politics in the postwar years (Prince Junio Valerio Borghese or Pino Rauti) had been "blooded" during Mussolini's Republic of Salò. Moreover, the knee-jerk resort to violence between 1943 and 1945 left "the country with a residue of political terrorism, inspired by Anarchist, Fascist and Communist doctrines, as well as some scores to be settled by the adherents of those doctrines."[3] Also, and vitally, the civil war offered a precedent of civilians taking up arms against a rotten body politic, beginning a debate about the morality of resistance. It was a debate invoked decades later as people began to ask "how and why violence is legitimate when it has to be practised without an obvious institutional cover."[4]*

For many on the left, Italy's postwar politics was the perfect example that there was unfinished business from the civil war. So quickly was Italian and German Fascism replaced by Russian Communism as the international bête noire, *so keen were the Allies to check Italy's partisan "wind of the north," that immediately after the war "the social groups which had supported the Fascist regime . . . managed to climb back into their former positions of influence."[5] The vast cracks in Italian society were swiftly papered over. An amnesty for forty thousand Fascists who had committed horrors during the civil war was announced in 1946; only those guilty of "especially heinous crimes" were ex-*

cluded from the amnesty. In one infamous example, the gang rape by "Black Brigadiers" of a partisan woman wasn't considered sufficiently heinous; in the words of the judge, "such a beastly act is not torture, but only the worst offence that can be made against a woman's honour and modesty, even if she was somewhat 'free,' having been a partisan messenger."[6]

The theory was colpire in alto, indulgere in basso, *to indict Fascist leaders but indulge the foot-soldiers. Rarely, however, were even those in the highest military and political ranks indicted. Studies of the postwar period revealed a continuity of personnel between Mussolini's* ventennio *(twenty years) and Italy's First Republic: in 1960, for example, of the 64 first-class provincial prefects, all but 2 had served under Fascism, as had all 241 deputy prefects and 135* questori *(provincial chiefs of the state police). As late as 1973, 95 per cent of senior civil servants had been appointed to the service before the fall of Mussolini.*[7] *In another example, a former officer of OVRA, Mussolini's secret police, was given a post at the Ministry of the Interior.*

The stumbling-block of Italy's postwar democracy was thus a widespread sense that there had been a tradimento, *that Italy had "betrayed" the partisan members of its population. There was also a belief, one historian has it, that "the ideals of the Resistance were excluded from the so-called democratic and parliamentary compromise, which had even reached a pact with the neo-Fascist right, represented by the Movimento Sociale Italiano."*[8] *The MSI was for more than fifty years the symbol of the Italian state still flirting with Fascism. To many, its very existence was an obvious example of Italy's inability to remember its dark past. In July 1960, for example, the party organised a conference in Genoa and announced that it would be chaired by Carlo Emanuele Basile, who had been the Fascist prefect of the city during the Republic of Salò and was responsible for the executions of partisans and anti-Fascists.*

Since the country still hadn't been purged of its Fascist con-

tingent, the myths and symbolism of the Resistance were endlessly invoked by those who later took part in the lotta armata, *the armed struggle. Renato Curcio, founder of the Red Brigades, lost an uncle who had fought against the Fascists. Years later, in November 1974, he wrote to his mother from prison at Casale Monferrato, recalling the uncle*

> *who carried me astride his shoulders. His limpid and ever-smiling eyes that peered far into the distance towards a society of free and equal men. And I loved him like a father. And I have picked up the rifle that only death, arriving through the murderous hand of the Nazi-Fascists, had wrested from him.*[9]

Remembered and romanticised, Italian partisans became role models for the next generation. The ranks of the left (be they armed or artistic) were swelled in the 1960s and 1970s by those from northern Italy who had either fought themselves or lost relatives in the Resistance. It became a proud point of reference; when, in the early 1970s, a new left-wing guerrilla force (the Partisan Action Group) was formed, it published a magazine appropriately called New Resistance. *Another member of the Red Brigades, Alberto Franceschini (whose grandfather had fought as a partisan), spoke of the "red thread that tied us to the partisans."*[10]

The years after the Second World War, though, were initially ones of bonaccia—*what Calvino called the years of calm before another storm. The referendum on the monarchy in 1946 had narrowly decided in favour of a republic, and when the new Italian constitution was ratified two years later, the male members of the royalist family of Savoia were barred from re-entering the country. The following decades saw a lightning transition of Italian society from one founded predominantly on agriculture to one based on industry: between 1950 and 1970, agriculture's share of the workforce fell from 42 to 17 per cent. In 1961 the ab-*

rogation of a Fascist law against internal immigration meant that within years millions of Italians had migrated either from the countryside to the cities or from the mezzogiorno *(the agricultural south) to the industrialised north. The Christian Democrats engineered an economic miracle, relying, largely, on steel, cars, and concrete and a massive web of para-statal companies.*

Traditionalists, however, began "clinking the sabres." It was an apt description of the threatening noises and rumours with which the far right reminded the country of its presence. As early as 1964, there had been a confused gambit to take power, a sort of crawling coup by the secret service and its leader. Since Italy's most obvious Mediterranean paragons—Greece, Portugal, and Spain—were in the late 1960s and early 1970s under military Fascist regimes, there was an almost permanent hysteria on the Italian left regarding the possibility of a right-wing coup. (The film Vogliamo i colonnelli, *literally "We Want the Colonels," was its most obvious, ironic expression.) That noise of clinking sabres and the hysteria it produced were the permanent backdrop to the* anni di piombo, *a perception from both sides that the country was on the brink of a violent turnaround and had to be defended.*

In December 1969, the Italian correspondent for Britain's Observer *coined a phrase which was to become standard usage in reference to the far right: "the strategy of tension," implying a sustained campaign of destabilisation by Fascists to promote a coup, the so-called Greek—or later Chilean—solution. "Elements from the far right and from officialdom," the* Observer *journalist wrote, "are plotting a military coup d'état in Italy, with the encouragement and support of the Greek government." Twenty-four hours before the Piazza Fontana bomb had exploded, one magazine had emblazoned its cover with the Italian tricolour, accompanied inside by the reassurance that "the armed forces could be called upon to restablise immediately the Republic's legality. This wouldn't be a coup d'état, but an act of*

political will . . . [I]sn't the confusion we are now witnessing,"
posed the rhetorical journalist, "due to the fact that the institu-
tions are by now insufficient and out-moded?"[11] *The head of the*
Confindustria, an alliance of industrialists, had already ex-
claimed that "the parliamentary system isn't made for Ital-
ians," and went on to invoke "a mythical faith in order."[12]

The months preceding the bomb had been dubbed the autunno
caldo, *the "hot autumn," because of endless industrial disputes.*
During 1969, the number of workers involved in strike action
rose to over 7.5 million, the hours duly lost increasing to over
300 million. At the same time, the country had witnessed, be-
tween 3 January and 12 December 1969, some 145 explosions.
Stand-offs between the forces of order and protesters of various
guises had already established the symbology and rhetoric of the
1970s: students (for example at Valle Giulia) and striking
workers (engineering workers at Fiat and Montedison) con-
fronting captains of industry and carabinieri. *Just one month*
before the Piazza Fontana bomb, a policeman had been killed in
Milan during a union meeting. On the fifteenth of that month,
one colonel announced, "Given the present situation of disorder
in the factories and in the schools, the army has the job of de-
fending the internal frontiers of the country: by now the army
has become the only bulwark against disorder and anarchy."[13]
Italy seemed to have reached an impasse, a confrontation be-
tween irreconcilables: a liberal country modernising at an expo-
nential rate, and those traditionalists and "forces of order"
who—after two decades—were still struggling to come to terms
with democracy. The climate, suggested both left-wingers and
foreign journalists, was self-evidently ripe for a coup, and—so
the theory went—Piazza Fontana was to have been its tragic
starting gun.

Much is known about what happened that Friday afternoon
in 1969. The bomb had been placed in a black bag under a
round table on the ground floor of the bank. At the time the

bank was crowded with merchants from the rural suburbs. Seven kilograms of trinitrotoluene, or TNT, exploded, leaving in their aftermath what someone later described as a scent of bitter almonds. One eyewitness, a client of the bank, described what happened: "I saw that everything was collapsing around and in front of me. The wooden counters of the bankers had literally jumped into the air while the room was filled with shards of glass. Many around me had fallen. Some were certainly dead, others were wailing." One newspaper the following day wrote of "a hell of screams, of shouts, of desperation, of panic, of lamentation."[14] Shoes were found with severed feet still inside. In all, sixteen people died, fourteen of them on the actual day. Eighty-eight were injured. On the same day, an explosion at Milan's Banca Commerciale Italiana injured six people. In Rome, bombs planted in the underground walkway of the Banca Nazionale del Lavoro and at the Altare della Patria (the "Altar of the Fatherland," the spiritual centrepiece of the Italian state) caused further injury.

Butterfly-net techniques of arrest were carried out, bringing in a haul of anarchists in Milan. Improbably, when one of their number, Pino Pinelli, was asked in for questioning, he rode behind the police escort on his scooter. At around midnight on the Monday after the bomb, a journalist in the courtyard of the police headquarters heard a thud. The body of Pinelli had fallen from the fourth floor of the building, hitting the corner of a wall and bouncing off another before coming to rest on the ground. He had been held in custody for seventy-two inconclusive hours. Marcello Guida, the questore *coordinating the Piazza Fontana bomb investigation, claimed that Pinelli's alibi had collapsed and that his suicide jump had been "a desperate gesture, a sort of self-accusation."[15]*

February 2000. The first day of the trial for the Piazza Fontana bombing, and there's a big "presence" outside the courtroom. Not just camera crews and journalists, but also a few hundred students in grunge uniform who are playing loud drum and bass, mixing their tracks with interludes of cod history over the PA. Most are smoking grass, ignored by the insouciant *carabinieri*.

Given the ferocity and indignation of the prosecution, and given the age and evasiveness of the defendants, the atmosphere of the court is like a Nazi war-crimes trial conducted decades after the war. When I first started attending the trial, it seemed as if amazing revelations from the past were finally about to come out into the open, as if some long-absent truth had finally been found. That's certainly how it was presented in the left-wing press, which spoke of decades of *omissis* (omissions) and *depistaggi* (the deliberate derailing of investigations) finally coming to an end. The famous *muro di gomma* (the "rubber wall" against which all previous investigations inevitably, impotently bounced) had been scaled, the *omertà* was at an end. The epic *segreto di stato* of Piazza Fontana was about to be revealed in all its grotesquerie.

Inside, the courtroom is an oval bunker. Lining the walls to the left and right are eight enormous and barred prison pens, a reminder of the "maxi-trials" that took place here against entire terrorist organisations in the 1970s. Two judges sit below an imposing crucifix. To their left and right on the dais are the so-called popular judges, or jurists, wearing tricolour sashes. They in turn are flanked by other jurists without the gaudy sash (each juror has to have a possible replacement, because the trial is expected to be so long). Accordingly, the start of the trial is delayed by a lawyers' strike. It begins a week later.

The first decision of the court is whether to move the trial to Catanzaro, over a thousand miles to the south in Calabria. It was on the basis of a law about "public order" dating from the era of Il Duce that various Piazza Fontana trials were removed to Catanzaro during the 1970s. There accusations were blurred and confused, witnesses whisked abroad. "You see," explains one journalist next to me in the press gallery, "nothing south of Rome is left to chance." In a portent of things to come, the judge speaks for hours on the subject—a judgement described the next day by even the most sober newspapers as "very tedious." The request for a transfer to Calabria is turned down.

The apparent trouble with the trial is that nobody (neither Amnesty International, nor the European Court of Human Rights, nor the Italian populace in general) maintains much faith in the "togas," the judiciary. For its snail's pace and contrary decisions, the Italian judiciary has recently been blacklisted by Amnesty International, and in 1999 the country topped the list of condemnations from the European Court of Human Rights. At the end of that year, the European Court still had almost seven thousand cases to deal with from Italy, making up over 20 per cent of its impending workload. Moreover, since the judiciary is politicised to a degree unthinkable in most modern democracies, Italian "justice" often looks more like "revolutionary justice," like Robespierre and his sansculottes dispatching a whimsical terror in all directions. Political enemies can be laid low not by ideological debate but by a timely accusation, thereby subjecting them to the near-stagnant waters of the legal system (there's no habeas corpus, very rarely a jury). That habit of sordid smear and political finger-pointing is called *giustizialismo*, and is one reason why there's such a breezy attitude towards the fact that many politicians have lengthy criminal records: if you point out that the Italian Parliament (of 950 senators or deputies) currently has fifty politicians *inquisiti* (under investigation), people simply shrug: "The magistrates must be out to get them, that's all." Most people I spoke to, especially with regard to the Piazza Fontana trial, said that it was probably a case of a grudge and that magistrates didn't know the difference between *perseguire* and *perseguitare* (between "to pursue" and "to persecute").

Moreover, it became obvious that the courts, like the Slaughter Commission, are acutely politicised. No one pretends to believe that the judiciary is separate from the legislature; so if someone receives a conviction, it's often treated not as a moral indictment but rather, say, like an electoral defeat: it's a temporary setback. He hasn't committed a crime, just had a decision go against him. People will forget about it. Increasingly, the Piazza Fontana trial seemed less a historical reconstruction, less a "righting of historical wrongs," and more simply a continuation of politics by legal means. Perhaps it was coincidental, maybe not, that the case arrived in court at a time when Italy had its first left-wing government since the war. The right, too, had obvious interests in the outcome of the trial. Despite the acute political sensitivity of the trial, two of Berlusconi's Forza Italia parliamentarians were acting as defence lawyers in the case. One proudly donned his Forza Italia lapel pin each day. There was no sense of a conflict of interest, no need to separate judiciary and legislature.

The other reason anything emerging from the togas is taken with a spoonful of salt is the culture of *pentitismo*. Originally intended to break the silence of left-wing terrorists by allowing them the opportunity to "repent" and to point the finger, *pentitismo* has by now become a simple mechanism to stitch up enemies. There are, at the time of writing, 1,171 *pentiti*, suddenly turned from poachers into the judiciary's most revered gamekeepers, and many have produced convictions which are little short of staggering. In the south, the smear normally used is involvement with Cosa Nostra; in the north, it's the suggestion that the accused participated in the *lotta armata*, the armed struggle of the 1970s. In one infamous case in the 1980s, a *pentito* pointed the finger at a famous television presenter, Enzo Tortora, whom he accused of being involved in dealing cocaine along with the Camorra, the Neapolitan Mafia. The case became another absurd show trial, and Tortora was sentenced to ten years' imprisonment. He was later absolved, but died soon afterwards. On his urn were written the words of Leonardo Sciascia: "*Che non sia un illusione*," "Don't let it be an illusion."

In between hearings I watch a documentary from the late 1980s. The journalist is asking an anarchist, the "monster" first accused of planting the bomb who was absolved in 1975, where or when the truth got lost. Pietro Valpreda, with a shock of grey hair at each temple, looks stern and says: "Immediately after the slaughter, as soon as the judges arrived from the powers in Rome . . . I believe that since then, the truth has totally disappeared . . . even though something continues to emerge, not in an active form, but in a negative form . . . not 'I did' but 'I don't remember,' 'I couldn't have done.' "[16]

The prosecution in the new trial alleges that the slaughter at the bank in Piazza Fontana was part of the programmatic terrorism of Italian Fascists. "It's probable," wrote Guido Salvini in his *istruttoria*, the lengthy prosecution document which proceeds any trial, "that the bombs of 12 December 1969 had the end of promoting a coup which was already planned for the end of 1969 on a wave of fear and disorientation which, as with the bombs on trains and in banks, affected ordinary citizens." Salvini identified Ordine Nuovo, the Fascist party then led by Pino Rauti, as "the prevalent structure responsible in terms of material execution for the attacks of 12 December 1969, and for those which preceded them and continued to operate . . . causing . . . the slaughter outside Milan's *questura* on 17.5.1973, very probably the slaughter

of Piazza della Loggia in Brescia, and the chain of major
and minor attempts, including some near-slaughters on trains
from the beginning of the 1980s." A more catch-all accusation could hardly have been hoped for: over a decade of
bombings laid at the door of the avowedly Fascist organisation Ordine Nuovo and, indirectly, its leader, Pino Rauti.

Two of the accused, Delfo Zorzi and Carlo Maria Maggi,
come from the ranks of Ordine Nuovo in the Veneto, the
north-east of the country. Zorzi, having avoided extradition
by virtue of being a Japanese citizen, is absent throughout the
trial. Zorzi—or Roi Hagen, as he is now called, in deference
to his assumed nationality—is now a wealthy businessman in
Tokyo, having spent the 1980s and 1990s importing and selling Italian designer labels to the Japanese. In 1969, he was
twenty-two. One of his school friends described him to
Salvini as "a person of very strong character, often hard, very
brutal, and without those reactions which arose in many of us
at the sight of blood during beatings . . . [H]e had a closed
character, introverted and very reserved, carried almost to a
type of mysticism."[17] He had studied Oriental languages in
Naples, and afterwards opened the first karate salon in the
Veneto. During one police raid on his house, a significant arsenal had been unearthed: a P38, a Beretta, and a Smith &
Wesson, as well as explosives. His was a perfect emulation of
the writings of Julius Evola, Italy's postwar Fascist philoso-
pher *par excellence*: a heady blend of neo-Nazism and Oriental spiritualism. "Six million Jews aren't enough" he once
plastered across walls in the Veneto.

Although Zorzi is absent from the trial, another of the accused—Carlo Maria Maggi—is ever present, sitting impas-
sively in the front row of the court in a cream suit and dark
glasses. In 1969 he was thirty-five, already qualified as a doctor, and working in one of Venice's hospitals. Outside his
working life, however, Maggi was the leader of the Veneto di-

vision of Ordine Nuovo. He was a regular presence on the firing range in the Lido and was a member of the so-called Children of the Sun, an organisation which at the solstices used to burn wooden swastikas on hilltops. In November 1991, Maggi was sentenced to six years' imprisonment for "reconstituting the Fascist Party" between 1969 and 1982.

The accusation rests, of course, on the testimonies of two *pentiti*. Carlo Digilio, nicknamed Zio Otto ("Uncle Eight," because of his love of the Lebel 8 handgun), was for years an informer for the CIA in the Veneto. His contact—one "David Carret"—is constantly invoked throughout the trial, though he has never been identified or located. As an explosives expert used by Ordine Nuovo in the Veneto, Digilio claims to have brokered a deal for gelignite from a deep-sea recovery expert in Venice. Having taken possession of the consignment, Zorzi apparently showed Digilio three military cases stashed in the back of Maggi's car days before the Piazza Fontana bomb: inside each were wired explosives, "at least a kilo in the small ones, a bit more in the larger one." Later, Zorzi is said to have boasted to Digilio: "I participated directly in the placing of the bomb in the Banca Nazionale dell'Agricoltura." The other *pentito* in the case is Martino Siciliano, one of Zorzi's peers at the Raimondo Franchetti school. "It was us who did that stuff, us as an organisation," Zorzi apparently boasted to Siciliano days after the Milan bombing.

The accusations go much further, however. The prosecution and various historians suggest that the Piazza Fontana bombing was actually organised from within the Ministry of the Interior: "The Piazza Fontana bomb," one army general has written, "was in some way organised by the 'Office for Reserved Affairs' of the Minister of the Interior. SID [the secret service] took over to cover everything up."[18] The allegations centre on Elvio Catenacci, a man from that same Office

for Reserved Affairs. Catenacci had, according to the accusations, recruited Delfo Zorzi; he had immediately dispatched
one of his men to Milan after the bombing and had systemat-
ically interfered with evidence. The allegation that the secret
service was somehow involved recurred throughout the
1970s: two of the Fascists originally accused of the bombing,
Franco Freda and Giovanni Ventura, were close friends of
Guido Giannettini, a colonel in SID. All three were sentenced
to life imprisonment in 1981; all three were later absolved.

Put simply, the new accusations suggest not only that Fascists from Ordine Nuovo planted the bomb (subsequently
blamed on anarchists) but also that they were nudged by men
from the Ministry of the Interior and the secret services and
by a mysterious CIA agent in the Veneto. With no sense of
sub judice, the Slaughter Commission has echoed the findings
of the initial investigation, describing with its usually robust
rhetoric the bombing as a *strage atlantica di Stato*, more or
less a "slaughter by the Atlantic [that is, American] state." In
the words of the president of the Slaughter Commission, Piazza Fontana's bomb wasn't an obscure incident of extremist
terrorism but a shrewd prompt for a political turnaround:

> What happened in 1969 was a phenomenon . . . which for
> many years was assumed to be extremist neo-Fascism. But . . .
> there appeared, if not one director, at least a centre of fomen-
> tation, instigation, finance, and partial coordination. The mu-
> tation of radicalism of the right was a phenomenon induced
> by sectors of the security services . . . belonging to a strategic
> dimension of international inspiration.[19]

George Bush Sr. was even on the wish-list of witnesses presented by the prosecution. It was a great story, but I—
like everyone else—had no idea if it really represented *La
storia*.

The "suicide" of Pino Pinelli, the anarchist in police custody, became "an awkward death," his name "like a collective remorse." That was how Camilla Cederna, author of A Window on the Slaughter, *described his death in 1971. As the police account of events became increasingly inconsistent throughout that year, a handful of journalists began interrogating the official line of the anarchist bomb and its allegedly repentant perpetrator who had fallen from the fourth floor of the police station. The* controinformazione *began to portray Pinelli's as the suicide that never was, to hint heavily that he had, rather, been* suicidato *and quickly made the scapegoat for much darker political forces. The previously anonymous railway worker was immortalised as the anarchist who had suffered an awful, "accidental death" (the phrase, famously borrowed by Dario Fo, came from the coroner's report of July 1970). Walls began to be daubed with* "Calabresi è assassino" *(Calabresi was the police commissioner in charge of Pinelli's interrogation) or* "Valpreda è innocente, la strage è di stato, unico giudice il proletariato" *(Valpreda is innocent, the slaughter is by the state, the only judge is the proletariat).*

Whilst investigations into the Piazza Fontana bombing were continuing, two overlapping court cases began in an attempt to resolve the riddle of what exactly had happened to the anarchist suspect. In the first, starting in October 1970, Luigi Calabresi sued Pio Baldelli, editor of the left-wing magazine Lotta Continua *(Continuing Struggle). The magazine had repeatedly insinuated that the police had "suicided" their suspect. In the second case, the mother and the widow of Pinelli presented an accusation of murder against the police officials who had been in charge of the interrogation. What emerged from those trials was a disconcerting tangle of confusion and contradiction. When Pinelli's body was exhumed, evidence emerged which suggested that his had been a "passive" rather than an "active" suicide leap: there were no injuries to his arms, even though suicides in-*

stinctively protect their head in a fall. Nobody had heard a scream as he fell. There was evidence of a blow to the back of the neck (a possible cause for the police request for an ambulance two minutes before the "suicide" jump). No one could explain why the window was open in winter, or why four policemen were unable to impede Pinelli's alleged action. One policeman claimed to have grabbed one of Pinelli's shoes when he was at the window, although the victim had shoes on both feet when he was found. The cases brought by or against Calabresi were abruptly halted, however, when, in May 1972, he was murdered with five shots on the pavement outside his house.

I begin to get used to the commute to the courtroom in Milan. The same trains, thoroughly spray-painted and looking like the rainbow colour of spilt petrol. Inside, columns of cigarette smoke pirouetting upwards before being sucked out the windows. Percussive confusion: everyone staring into mobiles, laboriously writing and receiving messages, experimenting with ring tones, so that the whole carriage becomes an atonal electronic chorus. As the train rattles across the *pianura padana*, the basin of the Po, single rows of poplar trees loom into view, looking like the upturned teeth of a comb on an empty table. Facing Milan, one sees the Apennines to the left, the Alps to the right, but for most of the year they're hidden by the gypsum sky, by the blanket fog of the plain.

The courtroom has the same sense of bathos as a modern church, unable to capture the import or solemnity of its subject matter. Journalists tap their short bulletins into laptops; lawyers nip out for cigarette breaks. TV cameras from Japan are permanently rolling, since Delfo Zorzi is still a fugitive from justice in Tokyo. Today is the first day of the deposition of the *pentito* Carlo Digilio. He has recently suffered a stroke, and so his deposition is relayed by video from a clinic in Lake Garda. It's hard to know whether the resulting fiasco is a result of technical incompetence or a deliberate attempt to undermine any credibility in the witness. The courtroom becomes an echo chamber of *"Pronto, pronto"* as the video stalls. The picture frozen on the screens shows a balding man slumped in a wheelchair in a cramped room.

When the connection is fixed, the relay of question-and-answer is punctuated with long pauses. The prosecuting lawyer reads out long, fluent phrases apparently given by Digilio years ago and asks him to confirm them. Digilio breathes heavily into his microphone before finally slurring his assent. He confuses dates and names, and at mid-afternoon he complains about "the humid, sweltering heat," and the court is adjourned until the next day. Everyone retires to the nearby bar, and lawyers leave their indiscretions. "As a first run, it was frankly embarrassing, for the prosecution obviously," says Gaetano Pecorella, the Forza Italia deputy defending Zorzi. (Pecorella had previously, in the 1970s, been the lawyer of the *parte civile*, representing the victims of the slaughter; during the closing months of the trial, in 2001, he would also become president of the Commissione Giustizia alla Camera, the political head of the judiciary.) The left-wing press concedes the next day that it was a "difficult hearing."

During the ensuing days and weeks, Digilio's version of events, tortuously told, begins to emerge. "Mine was neither an ideological nor a political adhesion," says Digilio. "I entered Ordine Nuovo at the suggestion of David Carret on behalf of the Americans. I am a nationalist, nothing more than a man of the centre right . . . A few days before 12 December 1969, the day of the *Immacolata*, Zorzi . . . asked me to examine the explosives closed in three metal boxes with English writing. They were those [used to contain] the belt-feeds for machine-guns used by the Italian army, inherited from the United States. The explosives were placed in the boot of

Dr. Maggi's [Fiat] 1100. I asked Zorzi: 'But where are you going with all this load?' The reply was: 'To Milan.' "

"It was the right thing to do" are the words Digilio claims Zorzi used in the aftermath of the bombing. "He spoke of the Piazza Fontana slaughter," continued Digilio, "as a war report. He spoke of it as if he had been the head of the command. He said that he had had the courage to do it, the others were weak."

A few weeks later, on the witness chair in front of the horse-shoe of judges, Pino Rauti is rubbing his hands in a scholastic manner. He's a short man, wearing a cheap blue suit. He's got slicked-back white hair, and eyes which seem to fall away at the edges. One Italian journalist tells me Rauti is playing the "Andreotti gambit": the important, cultured man dragged through the courts by spiteful lesser beings. Rauti was, in the 1960s, the leader of Ordine Nuovo. "The motto of Ordine Nuovo is the same as that of the SS: 'Our honour is called faith,'" he wrote back in the 1960s. His is a cantankerous performance. He frequently calls the prosecution lawyer by a lesser title and is each time corrected. During his deposition one journalist from the "Communist daily" (*Il Manifesto*) guffaws melodramatically, rocking her hands—pressed together in praying position—backwards and forwards (the gesture usually used by imploring footballers). The judge suddenly interrupts Rauti and asks for the journalist to be ejected from the court.

In 1956, Rauti and his followers left the Fascist party the Movimento Sociale Italiano and formed their own "study centre," Ordine Nuovo. The move had been precipitated by a perceived softening of the MSI, and Rauti remained outside the party until 1969. During that time, the new movement made its position explicit: "The Aryan blood of the SS is still warm and so is that of the kamikaze and of the Black Legionnaires and those of the Iron Guard who fell in the name of and for the eternal Ordine Nuovo." At a conference in 1965, Rauti presented a paper in which Communists were described as "some sort of an alien presence, like the extraterrestrial races of science fiction."

Although Rauti denies chairing a meeting of Ordine Nuovo in Padua in April 1969, shortly before the spring bombing campaign, it's certain that he went on an "educational" tour of Papadopoulos's Greece in the summer of that year. When an electrician came forward as a witness, claiming that he had unknowingly supplied the timers for Ordine Nuovo's bombs, Rauti (identified by the electrician's wife) apparently visited the shop to counsel silence. (Asked about this in court, Rauti indignantly replies that it's inconceivable that a respected politician would do such a thing.) The strange fact—if it's true—emerging from the trial is that Rauti and his Fascists weren't isolated extremists but pawns of a very clear strategic plan. Salvini, in his *istruttoria*, wrote of Ordine Nuovo as "one of the organisations of the right characterised by the most extensive collusion with the apparatuses of the state." Rauti is cantankerous in the witness stand not because he denies his Fascism (which he proudly admits) but because, after years of appearing the most threatening extremist in Italian politics, he now seems little more than a man manipulated by much greater forces. During his deposition, newspapers report that in the early 1970s, Rauti was receiving cheques from the US embassy.

It gets even stranger, though. As I emerge into the hazy Milan sun of the June evening, I watch Rauti chatting amiably with journalists, talking about his bridge building towards Berlusconi's right-wing coalition. It's half wishful thinking on his part, but they have been in alliance in the past (Rauti claims to have swung the European elections the way of Berlusconi's Pole of Liberties when they shared the electoral ticket in Abruzzi, Caserta, and Calabria). I'm amazed not because Rauti might be on the fringes of a rather dark right-wing coalition but simply because he's still there. A man whose organisation has been accused of almost every Italian "slaughter" is still in politics: smiling, suited, flirting with the female journalists. I join the huddle around him and ask for an interview. He courteously invites me to Rome.

Rome is a city full of august classicism. The manhole covers are still initialled with SPQR, *Senatus Populusque Romanus*. Palm trees stand outside embassies and governmental palaces. Here the graffiti is very different from that in Parma: swastikas and Celtic crosses, obscene phrases against "the blacks" and the Jews. It's a strange, beautiful place, almost knowingly theatrical. It has the perfect balance of modernity and antiquity. The seat of the Tricolour Flame, Rauti's political party, is a short walk from the Vatican. Rauti, the secretary of the party, sits mock-presidential between threadbare flags and ageing posters.

In 1943, at the age of seventeen, he volunteered to serve under Mussolini during what he calls "the civil war." He was captured by the British in Algeria in 1945 while trying to reach Spain to "continue the fight." Ironically, he graduated in law from inside a prison in Reggio Calabria. "I've been in prison a dozen times," he says proudly. "I consider myself something of an anomaly as a politician. One Russian publication once said that Rauti, with his glasses, seems like an ordinary accountant, but he's actually a dangerous revolutionary." He prides himself on being, to Communists, "a black beast."

He revels in using the words "Communists" and "Russia," just as much as the left in general jeers "Fascist" each time his name is mentioned.

"The *anni di piombo*," he says, "were ugly, dramatic, numbing, bloody years in the history of this country. But I have no regrets. We had so many youngsters killed by the Communists. There was never any tranquillity. Hundreds of our young people from the right were put in prison. They were terribly dramatic years, in which our youngsters responded to violence with violence." The only thing dangerous about Rauti now is his charm, his steely politeness, his ability to brush off any question with amiable, sometimes barbed banter. What, I wonder, does he make of the wave of trials trying to resolve the many riddles of those years. "There will be no legal truth," he says confidently. "There have been court cases and counter-cases, absolutions, inquiries, new prosecutions. The current thinking seems to be suggesting that what happened to, and because of, the right was in some way connected to the CIA. There was a sort of goading of opposing extremes, at the centre of which was the power system of the Christian Democratic party. One day there would be something from the left, then something from the other side, and all the while the Christian Democrats appeared as the saviour of governmental stability. It was precisely in that period that party received its maximum franchise."

"So Fascists were inadvertently the puppets of the Christian Democrats?"

He becomes impenetrable, simply staring at me, waiting for the next question. "Listen," he says eventually, "about some things there have been partial conclusions, but about the darkest incidents there are only question marks."

"And your own personal involvement?"

"It's true that I was involved in some things thirty years ago, but I have always been absolved. We should turn the page. All these cases are just attempts by the Communists to demonize me and the right. Times change," he goes on, "no one wears the clothes they did thirty or fifty years ago. I might admire the Roman Empire, but I don't go around riding a chariot, right? But I'll tell you this, we haven't as a political party renounced our history; we haven't renounced the ideals which are generally called 'Fascism.' Italians are at risk of physical extinction. We have the lowest birth rate in the world, bar none. I'm not racist, but there's a limit to tolerance. There has been such a rapid influx of immigrants, from Morocco, from Algeria, from China. These people have different colours, smells, flavours, climates. Why should they be on the peripheries of our society instead of back home amongst their own?"

That evening, sitting in a bare hotel room in Via Venezia, I finally find the perfect description of Italian politics. It comes from a columnist for *Espresso* magazine: "In Italy, as in chemistry, nothing is created, nothing is destroyed, everything is transformed." In other words, given the catalyst of time, appearances might change, but the elements involved remain exactly the same. In either side of the equation, past and present, the same personalities exist, only configured slightly differently, arranged in new, confusing coalitions. That's what causes the surrealism and sensitivity when writing, decades later, about the slaughters or the *anni di piombo*: some of those names which recur throughout the history books or in the court cases are still highly active in contemporary politics. It seems there's no crime or conviction sufficient to end an Italian politician's career, no historical event which can't be *smemorizzato*, conveniently forgotten.

It would be understandable if Italy had undergone its own peace process. But, unlike in Northern Ireland or South Africa, the past isn't faced before being forgotten; it is simply never faced. Nothing is ever, ever resolved. "The one con-

stant of Italian schools," writes Giorgio Bocca, "is that of re-
moving the history of the previous half century . . . [T]he fear
of history seems congenital, ordinary people have somehow
understood that to talk about history, to interrogate history,
isn't prudent, that there's something inconvenient in history."[20] As a result, Italy is better than any other place in the
world at reinvention or rehabilitation. It's called *gattopar-
dismo*, the "leopardism" of Lampedusa, in which everything
pretends to change but remains exactly as it was: "If things
are going to stay the same around here, they've got to
change." It's similar to the notion of *trasformismo*, which is
usually used to describe the revolving-door image of Italian
governments (hinting that the doorman, and those going in
and out of the lobby, remain for decades the same people simply in rotation). Another slightly bewildered British journalist
once called it the Italian version of musical chairs, in which no
chair is ever removed. The political music might change, and
people will shuffle into other chairs, but basically the same
players always remain in the game.

*By the time investigators, in the early 1970s, identified Rauti
and members of Ordine Nuovo as the probable perpetrators of
the Piazza Fontana bomb, the bombing of 12 December 1969
had already begun to seem not simply an isolated, tragic act of
terrorism but a reflection of the entire "strategy of tension."
Suspicions regarding a strategy were increased by the long list
of illustrious corpses which began to be added to the original
victims of the bombing: adequate evidence, it seemed, that
Piazza Fontana wasn't the inspiration of a few fanatic delin-
quents but the product of a well-drilled organisation. (Illustrious Corpses—the title of Francesco Rosi's 1975 film based on a
work by Leonardo Sciascia—was fictional, but the atmosphere
was similar: mysterious murders which seem anything but coin-*

cidental.) As the president of the Corte d'Assise di Roma wrote in 1971: "It's necessary immediately to fix a date for the trial. I have received a list of the witnesses who have died mysteriously, and public opinion is worried."

Pasquale Juliano, a Paduan policeman investigating Franco Freda, another Fascist suspect, was accused of irregular conduct and suspended; the only witness in his defence, himself a former policeman, was found by his wife at the bottom of a stairwell. (He had predicted his own violent death, saying to a friend: "You'll find me in the basement with a blow to my head, or in the lift shaft.") Other strange deaths followed. Armando Calzolari, a treasurer for the Fronte Nazionale of the "Black Prince," Junio Valerio Borghese, went missing in December 1969. His body was found over a month later, on 28 January 1970, at the bottom of a well on the outskirts of Rome. Left-wing journalists suggested at the time that he had been killed because he was about to make revelations regarding the Milan slaughter. Another victim, Vittorio Ambrosini, a sixty-eight-year-old lawyer and brother of the president of the Corte Costituzionale, had hinted that he knew the names of those involved in the bombing. In October 1971, he fell from the seventh-storey window of a hospital. (It was intended "to be passed off as suicide," claimed one former Fascist to Guido Salvini in April 1995.)

The problem with the trial is that at every turn, the subject appears deliberately confusing. Working out, decades later, what really happened is like trying to write on water: impossible. The more confusing it becomes, of course, the more paranoid the casual or academic observer is. Giovanni Pellegrino writes of the secret services of the time, of Gladio and the Office for Reserved Affairs and the Nuclei di Difesa dello Stato (Nuclei of State Defence), as component parts of "a large occult structure . . . a polymorphous reality . . . an infinite series of Chinese boxes." Understanding anything is impossible. Speculation and hearsay (from *pentiti*) are the only inadequate guides.

The other problem with the Piazza Fontana trial is that it seems entirely divorced from reality. There are so many words. Words everywhere, and not a shred of common sense. Documents multiply amongst themselves, which sire new pieces of paper, loosed from all logic. The longer I spent following the trial, the more it seemed like something out of Kafka. Legalese which promises clarity only ushers in confusion. One English academic often sitting beside me in the press gallery says with a sigh: "You know that the bill simply to photocopy the documents of this case would be about 16 million lire? That's eight thousand dollars of photocopying!" The transcripts of another recent case (in which the seven-time Prime Minister Giulio Andreotti was accused, absolved, and then sentenced to twenty-four years for involvement in the murder of the journalist Mino Pecorelli) came to 650,000 pages. The number of documents gathered by the Slaughter Commission is now well over 1 million. Inevitably, after the first, spectacular accusations, media interest in the Piazza Fontana trial is ebbing away because it's all so mind-boggling, increasingly impossible to see the wood for the trees.

I'm finally beginning to understand why so much scandal, even murderous, is simply ignored in Italy. It's too confusing to find the truth. It takes so much time. There is so much legalese and mystification that it's impossible to say explicitly, concisely, what happened. The way that mystification and confusion occur is very simple. Italy has more laws than any other European country. The oldest university in the world, in Bologna, was founded for precisely that reason: to decipher and recipher the Justinian codes, the *Corpus iuris civilis*, the *Digesto*, and the rest of the Roman laws. What's important is not the principle but the points of law. Codify, recodify, encrypt. *Quod non est in actis non est in mundo*: anything not written down, documented, simply doesn't exist. The standard compliment for a history book here isn't that the argument seems convincing; it's simply that the book is *documentato*, that it's based on documentary evidence. The Codice Rocco from 1931 even demanded a *certificato di esistenza in vita*: it wasn't sufficient to be alive; you had to prove it with a document.

Italy's great novel of the nineteenth century Alessandro Manzoni's *I promessi sposi* has a lawyer who is appropriately called Azzeccagarbugli, "pettifogger" or "bamboozler." Debate relies not upon common sense or precedents but upon producing alternative documents which trump the others in their intricate absurdity. To be convincing, you have to deploy impenetrable pomp. That is how Italian power works, by bamboozling the listener. "Using erudite law, which is by its very nature inaccessible to the many," one Italian academic has written:

> Italian power became something naturally distant from the population, as the language of command was distant and diverse from ordinary language. Law detached itself from life. It became something for specialists, intellectually refined . . . abstract. The use of something as coarse and democratic as an Anglo-Saxon jury would be unthinkable . . . [T]he law will remain always a thing of bamboozlers, of cryptic language, which is of liars, a power used only to take in and deprive the weak.[21]

The irony is that Italy, so painfully legalistic, is as a result almost lawless. If you've got so many laws, they can do anything for you. You can twist them, rearrange them, rewrite them. Here, laws or facts are like playing cards: you simply have to shuffle them and fan them out to suit yourself. It's true in all the world, but especially in Italy: the innocent are those with the best lawyers.

On 28 September 2000, there's a *colpo di scena* in the court-room—a show-stopper. Martino Siciliano, the other *pentito* on whom the Piazza Fontana trial pivots, is due to start his deposition. Siciliano was at the same school as Zorzi in the 1960s, and is described in one paper as a "controversial char-acter, psychologically flawed, divided among collaboration with justice, the need for money, [and] fear of his ex-boss Delfo Zorzi." In recent years, Siciliano has more or less auc-tioned himself to the highest bidder, accepting employment and money from Zorzi before taking a wage and a modest protective escort from the Italian state. Zorzi calls his former friend a "Falstaff," "an alcoholised megalomaniac" serving "Communist justice."

Then the *colpo di scena*. Siciliano goes missing. Since his ar-rival from Colombia, he had been staying in a hotel on the outskirts of Milan. All that's left in his hotel room is a book titled *Little Money, Much Honour*. His brother claims that Si-ciliano, who had previously provided hundreds of pages of in-terviews, had lost faith in the state, having been "treated like a tramp." It's unlikely that those interviews, conducted by Salvini, will now be admissible as evidence. None of this goes reported in the press. During the weekend following Sicil-iano's disappearance, journalists are on strike. By the follow-ing Monday, the press has become more preoccupied with Italian gold medals in the Sydney Olympics and the weekend exploits of the Ferrari cars in the Grand Prix race than with the disappearance of another witness.

A little later *Panorama*, a weekly magazine owned by Silvio Berlusconi, finds a bizarre scoop. Martino Siciliano, the

AWOL *pentito*, hadn't been receiving millions of lire from the official slush fund for that purpose. He had been receiving money directly from Guido Salvini, the investigating magistrate to whom he had made his confessions—a financial collaboration which seems at best unwise, and certain to cast doubt on the veracity of the *pentito*'s confessions. Another scoop for the defence is that Carlo Digilio, the infirm *pentito* in a Lake Garda clinic, has identified a photograph of the man he claims was his CIA contact. Defence lawyers, though, track down the man, claim the CIA agent is actually an old American in a small town in Kansas, and reveal that he wasn't even in Italy when the alleged meetings with Digilio, in Venice's Piazza San Marco, took place.

The case against the Fascists seemed to be collapsing. I wasn't even particularly disappointed. By then, my flat had been strewn with thousands of documents, each one promising amazing revelations but in reality only referring me to another document. I had begun to understand why the mysteries sire endless court cases and scoops but never reach convincing conclusions. I had begun to understand why "understanding" in Italy is often impossible: everything is too politicised; there's no objectivity anywhere; and there's no difference, in terms of personnel, between the past and the present. I decided to give up on my commuting to Milan. Piazza Fontana, which had fascinated me for months, was becoming too exasperating.

There were other reasons, though, to leave the court case behind. Writing about Italy's long list of illustrious corpses gives a sense of the country as nothing more than an arena of murderous intrigue, whereas in reality I had never felt, since moving to Parma, either happier or safer. If the country does occasionally appear incredibly violent, it's more often blissfully peaceful.

A few days after deciding to give up on the Piazza Fontana

trial, I was in a trattoria with Filippo. For months he had been a kind of cerebral tour guide, pointing me towards interesting places or people. We were sitting at a bare wooden table with a chipped jug of wine between us. He was squeezing lemon juice onto his mince of raw horse meat and capers. I had a plate of steaming polenta topped with wild boar.

"So now you understand why we say Italy is a 'brothel'?" he asked at the end of our conversation about Piazza Fontana.

"I think so," I said. "Or at least I'm beginning to get the idea. But . . ." I was trying to explain why I wasn't convinced by the metaphor anymore. "But it seems all too pejorative. I'm blissfully happy here. I don't feel like I'm in a 'brothel.' I want to write about something simpler. I want to write about . . ." I was looking over his shoulder, searching for inspiration. I saw the row of garish yellow-and-blue Parma shirts hanging up behind the bar. "That's it. I must write about football."

Filippo began to laugh. He put down his fork and guffawed for about a minute. When he had finished, he leant towards the next-door table and shared the joke. "He says," he was pointing at me, "he says he wants to write about something simpler, something more complimentary about our country . . ." He paused for dramatic effect. "So he's going to write about football!" They, too, started laughing. For another minute there were yelps of amusement all round.

"Zio Tobia," he said eventually, slapping me on the back, "if you write about football, you just find another *bel casino*!"

3

PENALTIES AND IMPUNITY

The ball is caressed, tamed, hit according to laws which, despite being spontaneous, obey a sublime, abstract, fantastic geometry whose form expresses the best intentions of man: generosity, a sense of togetherness, of altruism, of friendship, of courage, of trust, of hope, of gullibility, of fantasy, of shrewdness, of faked naivety, of timing, of ferocity, of open-mindedness . . .

—GIANNI BRERA

When the sun shines on the Cittadella, it's an idyllic sight. It's a squat, pentagonal castle about two hundred metres from my house. It's covered with trees and hedges and hiding couples. Up top, around the turrets, men jog in their smart tracksuits and try to pace themselves perfectly to catch up with beautiful women. The central bench above the main entrance is reserved for the regulars: the middle-aged men who spend all day there gossiping. Below, in one corner, is a playground where *parmigiani* bring their grandchildren. In another corner there's a basketball court where everyone dresses like he's been watching too much MTV.

Most of all, around dusk as people get out of work and libraries, there are always those looking for a game. They wander round in the shadows of the warm pink brick walls, just waiting for enough people to roll up. And invariably they do. Often they're not from Parma, often not even from Italy: Moroccans, Senegalese, Albanians. Once there are a dozen of us, someone will get bossy, organise the teams, and we'll play until sunset.

It's funny the way that national stereotypes are most obvious when you play football. The Africans who come to the Cittadella are always brilliantly unpredictable, lanky, and loping. The Albanians are muscular. Occasionally English students on a study year abroad will brave their luck, and they're normally very English: fast, good passers, but technically not up to much. The Italians are the most interesting, though. Instinctively they welcome you. Then, once they realise you're English, they will pretend to be having second thoughts: "Mamma mia, not an English footballer!" The seriousness with which they play, whispering advice to each other as they sprint across the grass or signalling where you should put the ball just by moving their eyes, is incredible. They hardly ever foul; if, by accident, they do, they will pick you up, bow, and apologise. Often they'll stop halfway through a game and tell you, in a very nice but firm way, what exactly you're doing wrong: "Tobia, your balls jump into your throat every time you're one-on-one with the keeper. Stay calm, just pass the ball into the net, don't try to kill the keeper, OK?" Afterwards, once you're in a bar with them all, it's normally impossible—thanks to their hospitality and generosity—to buy even one drink. Forget, for a minute, all the glistening, flag-filled stadia: when you go play in the parks, you see the real nobility of Italian football.

At the other end of the scale, of course, at the top level, Italian football is endlessly criticised. Everyone seems to say it isn't as good as it once was. "It's no longer a great *spettacolo*."

They play better in Spain and England, everyone says. Over there they're more attacking, people say, more daring and inventive. This is exactly what everyone in England says: they play better in Italy and Spain. The grass is always greener. Every country—except, probably, Brazil and Spain—grumbles about its football. If in England they do play better now than ten years ago, it's largely thanks to brilliant Italians like Paolo Di Canio, Gianluca Vialli, and, above all, Gianfranco Zola. If English footballers no longer go to the pub on Friday night before a Saturday match, it's largely because coaches like Arsene Wenger and Claudio Ranieri have taught us the basics of dietary discipline. English football, without the influx of foreigners, would still be in the Dark Ages.

When I first moved here in 1999, I was astonished by the beauty and elegance of Italian football. That first spring in Parma I went to two semifinals. One was the Coppa Italia against Inter Milan, the other the Coppa Uefa against Bordeaux. Now, bear in mind that I'm an Everton fan. I've followed Everton all over Britain for twenty years, and—but for a couple of years of glory in the mid-1980s—the team is famous for one thing: miraculously avoiding relegation to a lower division every year by just one point. Look at the league tables at the end of every Premiership season, and you'll see Everton hanging on by its fingernails. The team used to be nicknamed "the school of science," but our striker—until Wayne Rooney's arrival—was a two-metre-tall Scot called Duncan Ferguson, who was recently put into Scotland's hardest prison for head-butting. It was his speciality. Now I think about it, I don't believe I've ever seen him score with his feet.

So arriving in Parma, and watching back-to-back semifinals, was like emerging into the light after years of darkness. Comparing Italian and British football was like comparing snooker with darts. One is cerebral, stylish, slipping the ball across the smooth green felt; the other is a bit overweight, slightly raucous, throwing the occasional arrow in the right direction. To put it in musical terms: British football is like the brass section of an orchestra—noisy, boisterous, occasionally impressive but normally unsophisticated. Italian football is the string section—soaring elegantly, providing the melody and emotion. That Parma team contained Gianluigi Buffon, Lilian Thuram, Nestor Sensini, Dino Baggio, Suan Sebastian Veron, Enrico Chiesa, and Hernán Crespo: the very best players in Italy. It was an astonishing side; they never seemed to lose the ball. They were imperious, imposing. Inter Milan came and went, having conceded four goals. Bordeaux—and this was the semifinal of the Eufa cup—leaked six.

As I spent months and then years in the Curva Nord, I realised that there are two vital ingredients to Italian football which we don't have in Britain: *fantasia* and *furbizia*. Fantasy is the ability to do something entirely unpredictable with the ball. The British will always try to pass through a defence, or run past it, but they never outwit it (David Beckham, afterall, is a great crosser and passer, but one-on-one he's nothing special). Italian fantasists produce that nanosecond of surprise which springs open a defence. It can be a back-heel, a dummy, a pretence of being off balance. It's the one aspect of football which can't be taught. It has to be instinctive, suddenly inspired, which is why the Italian players in Britain are so admired: they are touched by an indefinable genius which is in very short supply. In the last decade in Britain, the number of fantasists could be counted on the fingers of one hand: Paul Gascoigne, Paul Scholes (sort of), Ryan Giggs (Welsh), and possibly now Wayne Rooney.

The other ingredient lacking in Britain is *furbizia*, "cunning." It's the ability to tilt the game in your favour through slightly sly, but perfectly legitimate, tactics. Watch young amateur Italians and they will already have learnt all the guile from their favourite players. I sometimes go watch a teenage student of mine who plays in a semi-professional league. He's a tall central defender called Francesco. Towards the end of one game, when his team was hanging on to a one-goal lead, he doubled up and raised his hand just as an attack was on its way. The game stopped for five minutes as Francesco wobbled around, staring at the grass. He was pointing at his eyes. The parents around me started muttering: "Good old Francesco, always such a professional."

As the seconds ticked away, it slowly dawned on me that he was looking for his contact lenses. The game eventually restarted, but only for a couple of seconds before the final whistle. At the end, I congratulated him on the win. "I didn't know you wore lenses," I said.

"Of course I don't," he said with a laugh.

Watch any game and you see the *furbizia*. Here, when a player falls over, he instinctively grabs the ball with his hands, as if to force the referee into giving him a free kick. It seems natural in Italy, but Fabrizio Ravanelli was whistled by his own supporters in England for showing a little too much *furbizia*: diving as soon as he was in the penalty area or, something which is decidedly disdained, begging the referee to book opponents. There are other traits of "sly" football: a goal is never, ever scored without a handful of defenders raising their arms in hopeful protest to the linesman or referee. Players will shuffle forwards when a free kick is being lined up. Any important refereeing decision is accompanied by five minutes of arguing. It is, perhaps, the aspect of Italian football which looks strangest to a foreigner. In England, people often say the national side doesn't know how to win; in Italy, as Giorgio Tosatti recently said, they don't know how to lose (which probably accounts for that withering quip from Winston Churchill: "The Italians lose wars as if they were games of football; and lose games of football as if they were wars").

The players are, though, often very dignified. No one in England would ever kiss cheeks before or after a game—in Scotland they would be laughed out of the stadium—but seeing it done here, I found, strangely, that it seemed to add to the dignity of the occasion. If one scores against his old team in Italy (cause for exultation in Britain), he often refuses to celebrate. To do so would be an affront to his former employers and fans. Sometimes they don't only not celebrate a goal against their former team; they actually break down and have a little weep (like Gabriel Batistuta after his glorious goal for Roma against Fiorentina, a goal whose symbolism only became clear later as Fiorentina began bankruptcy proceedings). All of this is described by gushing commentators as *un gesto bellissimo*.

I once met the Parma and sometime Italian national captain, Fabio Cannavaro, after a game. He was an example of pure class and politeness. He stood up when I came to the table and pulled out a chair for me. He wanted to know what the game looked like from the stands. The whole game was dissected as if it were a game of chess: the opening gambits, exposed flanks, the end-game, and so on. You quickly realise that the national stereotypes of Britain and Italy (the one reserved, the other impetuous) are actually reversed when it comes to football. Italians play such a calculated game that they are usually astonished by the unregulated passion of British football.

And the attention to tactics here is incredible. I once had a chat with a guy in a billiard hall. The conversation, for some reason, had taken a religious turn. "But what are you?" the friend asked me.

"I suppose I'm a Methodist," I said, probably a little pompously. I assumed he knew what I meant: a Nonconformist Protestant.

"Ah, *fantastico*." His face lit up. "That's great." He suddenly seemed animated. He grabbed the balls from the pockets, placed them on the felt, and asked me to explain. He had cleared a space on the table. I wasn't quite sure how I was supposed to explain John Wesley's theology with these implements. Only after ten minutes of misunderstanding did I figure out that he thought I was talking about my tactical approach to playing football. Methodism, I realised, was a tried-and-trusted tactic back in the 1950s. By contrast, tactics in British football didn't exist until foreign coaches like Arsene Wenger and Sven-Göran Erikson arrived; before then, the only innovative technique had been pioneered by Graham Taylor, who, amazingly, became England's national coach. It was called "route one" and consisted in kicking the ball upfield as quickly as possible to a striker who was tall, aggressive, and fearless: Duncan Ferguson, John Fashanu, or Mark Hateley.

And the reason the Italians can be so tactical is the other keyword of the football vocabulary: *tecnica*. No one ever needs to hoof a ball into the stands, as they often do in England, because the players have the skill to put it exactly where they want: they can juggle it, dribble it, spin it. They can trap a speedy ball dead on the spot, or lay it off with a perfectly weighted pass using their collar-bone or their studs. And like the white ball in snooker, in Italy the ball only leaves the green when absolutely necessary, when a defence needs to be prised apart. Watch a game in England, any game involving Everton between 1890 and 2003, and you'll see the difference.

The nobility of the players is often reflected by the fans. When someone who is a genuine footballing legend plays against your team, he's as likely to be applauded as whistled. When, after two years of injuries, the Brazilian star Ronaldo finally returned to the Inter Milan line-up, and moreover scored a goal, the Lazio supporters (seeing his goal announced on the big screen of their stadium hundreds of miles to the south, in Rome) instinctively applauded for a minute. Thus the theatricality of the pitch is matched by the grand gestures of the fans: fantasists are occasionally given a minute's standing ovation, and the stadium suddenly feels, rather than thuggish, like a large theatre at the end of a moving scene. (Enrico Chiesa and Francesco Totti are the usual candidates for such adulation.) When players do head off to pastures and pitches new, they're not greeted with hatred and sneers by their former fans (as in England) but given standing ovations—again, for what they've achieved.

Compared with that of their British equivalents, the intelligence of Italian fans is often extraordinary. Watching a game on television, or even with friends, is like listening in on some serious literary criticism. I've spent hours on the terraces listening to fans arguing heatedly about the adjectives which could best capture the beauty of particular players: "He's so rococo!" someone will say about a long-haired midfielder with muddy knees. "Rubbish, he's more pugnacious than that. He's rustic, a noble savage." "No, I repeat, he's rococo. So deft, slightly one-sided." Even the best English players from years ago are still lovingly recalled: David Platt, Ray Wilkins, above all Graeme Souness. Talk football with any fan of Juventus (the team from Turin, called the "old lady" of Italian football), and he will recall the best goals scored by John Charles, the Welshman the Italians nicknamed the "Gentle Giant."

In between matches I would study the sports journalism, and I realised it is—like the football—just about the best in the world. It's withering and straight-talking. No one is pardoned anything. There's even something called the *pagella*, where each player is given a mark out of ten for his performance. (The only 10 I've ever seen awarded was for a player who gave mouth-to-mouth to a collapsed colleague; an 8 is normally considered the top conceivable mark even for a fantasist.) Football journalists are almost as famous as the players; one of the country's longest-running TV programmes is called *Biscardi's Trial*, where three or four men shout simultaneously at one another in an atmosphere of epic indignation. It sounds ridiculous but is actually riveting. There are highbrow programmes hosted by the country's "philosophers of football." Hours of television are dedicated each week not just to the matches but to long documentaries about the history and culture of *calcio*. Some people complain that there's too much football on TV, or rather, not football, but football talk. I can't get enough of it, though. On these programmes, if you didn't know they were talking about football, you would think it was a war documentary: weeping men poring over sepia photographs, unfolding letters from fifty years ago. Football, it's very obvious, is more than just a sport; it's an inheritance, the nation's sacred heirloom.

Most of all, though, the quality of print journalism is astonishing. Take, for example, Antonio Ghirelli's description of the troubled Argentinian genius Diego Maradona: "a champion capable of all the prowess and all the madness, capricious, moody, irreducible to the most elementary criteria of discipline . . . greedy as a moneylender, splendid as a sheik, surrounded by a miraculous court of bag carriers and businessmen, he was courted by women and idolised by an entire city . . ."[1] Or Gianni Brera on Peppìn Meazza: "He had sloping shoulders and cow-like knees, but dozing inside him was a juggler's feline cunning, which suddenly burst out, astonishing both the opposition and the public."[2] Such poetic descriptions are much harder to find in British newspapers because football isn't invested with that glow of deep, metaphorical meaning. Cricket, not football, is where British journalism is at its best. (I often wonder what Italy would be like if the Genovese had made a different sporting choice in the 1890s: British sailors in the port had formed their "cricket and football" club, hoping, I suspect, to introduce the first rather than the second.)

Only one aspect of the sports coverage was insufferable. It was an element of football coverage which I had never seen before: the *moviola*. Actions are analysed in slow motion, backwards and forwards as experts discuss whether a supporting leg has been clipped, a shirt tugged, the offside line overstepped. Computer graphics are set up, and the discussion goes on for hour after hour. Now, whenever I hear those terrible words—"There might have been the extremities for a penalty"—my heart sinks. It's the ultimate in counter-factual speculation. You would need a time machine to make such observations of any relevance. It creates suspicion and resentment and futile polemic. Most of all, it gives everyone an excuse to get upset about what, in the end, are the most irrelevant things. As two of football's sociologists write, it creates "fans ready to threaten a popular revolt for a refereeing injustice, but resigned to suffer the abuse of a powerful local politician."[3] That, in fact, was the central irony, because most humans have only a finite amount of indignation and using up the reserves for football probably prolongs many political careers. In Italy, thanks to the *pagella*, that brutal mark out of ten for performance, footballers or referees are forgiven nothing; politicians are forgiven everything.

Only slowly did I begin to realise why the *moviola* was so important: there's always the lingering suspicion that football isn't entirely "limpid." As with everything else, there's suspicion, conspiracy theorising, *dietrologia*. Part of the paranoia comes from the fact that the referee is a much more important figure in Italy than in Britain because players, as well as displaying an imperious grace on the ball, are full of guile. By a rough personal estimate, there are about three times the number of penalty appeals in Italy—not because the Italian game has more fouls (it actually has a lot fewer) but because players know instinctively when and how to fall over. As a result, of course, refereeing becomes acutely sensitive, and suspicions about the referees' interpretations, and about the motivations for those interpretations, become ever more exaggerated. Nobody in Britain could name a single referee; in Italy, they are household names.

Presidents of the football teams almost behave as if they wanted to increase those suspicions. In 1999 the president of Roma sent Serie A's referees pristine Rolexes for Christmas. Other investigations have revealed that referees have enjoyed holidays paid for, very indirectly, by Juventus; referees have also enjoyed the company of what's called in Italian a *sexy-hostess* courtesy of various clubs. The importance of having a referee "on your side" is shown by the fact that the leading clubs vehemently oppose what's called the *sorteggio integrale*, the practice of pulling the names of match referees from a hat. That, of course, would be too random. Instead, only "reliable" refs are allowed to be responsible for the big games of the big clubs.

As a result, there is always a merry-go-round of accusations, of conspiracy theorists and their deny-all adversaries arguing about whether it's all a stitch-up. I've often spent long evenings in old wine cellars as someone explains in intricate detail a vital goal from the 1950s which was scored from off-side, or a referee who suddenly became very wealthy upon his retirement from the game. If you ever appear sceptical about such paranoia, you're told that you're naive and that, even though you understand football, you don't understand Italy. The extraordinary thing is how much the football-fixing debates mirror, almost word for word, discussions about Mafia or terrorist association: Some brave observer puts his head above the parapet, suggesting that all is not quite as it seems, that there's something dodgy going on. To this the reply is first a dismissive ridiculing of the idea, followed by increasingly threatening noises if the accuser continues with his accusations. By far the most intriguing personality in Italian football is the man whose job is exactly that: to defend Juventus against weekly "paranoid" accusers. His name is Luciano Moggi, a man with drooping, reptilian eyelids who seems like something straight out of a *Godfather* film. He's always sardonic and unruffled, but he's often (especially when he smiles) ferocious. He cut his very sharp teeth at Napoli during the glory days with Diego Maradona, since when—at Torino and Juventus—he has become the *éminence grise* of Italian football. (The TV parody of Moggi is a man who, when he captures an opponent's chess piece, calmly crushes it with a hammer.)

The more I watched football, the more I began to suspect that the real game is not on the grass but in the boardrooms, corridors, and presidential suites. It's hard to put into words, but I had an imperceptible feeling that there was much more to calcio *than just kicking a football. It was partly because I was used to Britain, where owners of football clubs are anonymous. In Italy, though, they appeared like medieval barons who countenance no dissent. They were part of a family dynasty which, invariably, didn't stop at football but bled into politics and the media.*

I began to get the impression from watching football that the country is based upon a few very powerful oligarchies. It's not dissimilar to the Renaissance, with a dozen important families who have carved up the spoils of the country, because it is, invariably, a "family thing." The same surnames recur again and again, regardless of whether you're talking about politics, television, or football, regardless of whether you're reading a contemporary newspaper or one from the 1960s. The sons and brothers (occasionally a sister or a mother) become part of the footballing entourage, which is often an apprenticeship before they enter Parliament or start editing the family's newspaper. Many of the sons of famous club bosses are "agents," which means that they take a percentage on every deal done by their fathers. There's no notion of a conflict of interest, due to the desperation, the absolute determination, for strapotere, *all-encompassing power.*

When I first moved here, I was living in a flat in the part of the city the other side of the river ("di là dall'acqua," as they say in dialect). I was living with three students from Matera, from the deepest south, and they would explain, each night as we watched the news, who the various people were. "This," Gino would explain, pointing at the TV, "is Vittorio Cecchi Gori. He is the owner of Fiorentina; he's a cinema impresario and owns the TV channel we're currently watching. He also produced the film which is on after the news." Or, "This is Massimo Moratti, a petrol magnate and owner of Inter Milan. His cousin Letizia is former head of RAI [the state broadcaster]. Ten per cent of Inter," Gino would explain with precision, laughing at my disbelief, "is owned by Marco Tronchetti Provera, who also sponsors the team." (A few months later, my mobile phone network provider and Cecchi Gori's football team and TV channel would fall into Tronchetti Provera's hands.) Over the next few weeks Gino described the careers of Gianni Agnelli and Silvio Berlusconi (both mega-rich magnates of team owners), and my sense of a very bizarre, oligarchical power structure was reinforced. Take, for example, the career of Franco Carraro: he was president of AC Milan in the late 1960s before becoming president of the football league—Legacalcio—before becoming president of the Italian football federation, FIGC. Then he became government Minister of Tourism, then mayor of Rome, then he returned to be president of Legacalcio, and so on. It's not, of course, that there's anything illegal going on; it's simply that there's no separation of powers, no sense of a conflict of interest.

Even in the duchy of Parma, the football team is owned and sponsored, filmed and broadcast, by different organs of the Parmalat empire, which is owned by the Tanzi family.

I've tried to explain the situation to English friends: "Just imagine Prince Charles and Tony Blair both own football teams, a few newspapers, and probably the odd television channel, and you'll begin to get the idea. Or imagine that the head of Arsenal becomes a government minister for a while." Here there seems to be an endless swapping between jobs without embarrassment. It's such a small world the same surnames kept coming up. The consequences of that power structure, of the proximity of football to politics and high finance, are many. First, it feeds suspicion because many people perceive football as prey to obscure powers. Calcio is so intricately tied to powerful men that referees, it's argued, feel a sudditanza psicologica, *a "psychological subjection," when they are in charge of certain games. Thus, when teams win titles, it's almost obligatory for the losers to claim that "the powers that be" had penalised them.*

Massimo D'Alema, when he was the country's Prime Minister in the late 1990s, bemoaned the prejudice against his team, AC Roma, blaming the cartel of northern powers for the fact that, throughout the 1990s, only Juventus and AC Milan won the scudetto (the championship). *A scudetto for Rome, he said, would be worth three championships, such was the prejudice against any team from the capital. He referred to what, for any Romanista, is the open wound of 1981: It was another crucial match for the championship, three days before its conclusion. As usual it involved Juventus, this time against Roma. Once again it was being played in Turin, and the visitors had a legitimate goal by Ramon Turone disallowed for a phantom offside. Had they won that match, Roma would almost certainly have won the championship. But the goal was disallowed, and Juventus took the title. Another example, for many, of the "old lady's" uncanny ability to benefit from glaring refereeing errors. "The ball might be round," as a famous saying against Juventus goes, "but it always seems to roll in the same direction."*

That atmosphere of suspicion and speculation leads to something else that I've only ever witnessed in Italy: long, formal meetings between referees and coaches to iron out differences. Every now and again you see them on the news: all retiring to a plush hotel to shake hands, talk about past disputes, and make future resolutions. Of course, it's supposed to promote transparency but appears like an unwise proximity between the objective umpire and the partisan coach.

More important than speculating about referees, however, is the fact that Italy's oligarchs seem to recognise no boundaries, no areas of objectivity. It was the first time I realised that in Italy a conflict of interest is seen as a positive, not a negative, thing. Luciano Gaucci, I discovered with disbelief, owns not only the Perugia football team but also the Catania and Sambenedettese teams; Franco Sensi, until recently, owned both AC Roma and Palermo; Franco Cimminelli used to own both Torino and Lecco. The real reason for suspicion, I began to think, has nothing to do with referees and everything to do with oligarchies. Take, for example, the case of the Geronzi family. Cesare is the head of Capitalia-Banca di Roma, which is one of Lazio's big creditors; it also holds shares in three different football teams, and Franco Carraro—whose CV was described above—is, of course, a board member. One daughter of Cesare Geronzi, Benedetta, works at Federcalcio, while the other works as an agent at Gea, a group of football agents. One of the members of Gea, and a leading light of the Football Management agency, is Alessandro Moggi, son of Luciano, the rather frightening boss of Juventus. The son of the current coach at Juventus, Marcello Lippi, is also a member of the agency. Meanwhile, Adriano Galliani, the president of the Milan football team—owned by Silvio Berlusconi—is simultaneously head of Legacalcio and a TV entrepreneur in his own right.

Perhaps it's the sporting equivalent of trasformismo: *although there is, on the surface, an out-and-out competition between two teams, in reality everything seems to overlap. What at first appears confrontational is actually compromise. Even players are "shared" between different teams. Financially it makes perfect sense, but in sporting terms it's absurd. It's like having a politician who sits in Parliament for both left and right. Adriano, the brilliant Brazilian striker, said recently that playing for Parma against Milan was a "derby" (a game between two teams from the same city) for him (because he's half-owned by Inter). What, one wonders, does he feel when he plays against Inter? Sometimes players are owned by one team but loaned, for months or years, to another. It must surely make loyalty to a cause difficult. If you did the same in poker—sharing useful cards or swapping them when holes needed to be plugged—you would be laughed out of the casino. In football, though, anything goes.*

Another consequence of the oligarchical power structure of football is that the sport has become seamlessly linked to the demands of the modern media. Since so many club owners are, first and foremost, media magnates, they both epitomise and encourage the conflation of sport and television. Throughout the 1990s, the face of football was completely changed by pay-per-view and extravagant television deals: games were deferred to suit scheduling or advertising. Sponsors litter not only the shirts but the pitch and the hoardings and the dugouts. As a percentage of overall income, the money from the turnstiles has plummeted; meanwhile, the income from television has exponentially increased. It now represents 54 per cent of the income of Serie A teams. As Vittorio Malagutti wrote recently, "This mountain of money has ended up drugging the world of football."[4] Football comes second to scheduling. I remember a few years ago standing in Parma's Tardini stadium. The atmosphere was one of anger and dismay because the match was being played during Sunday lunchtime. Parmigiani were being forced to make a choice be-

*tween their favourite hobbies: eating with family or watching
football with friends. Slowly, as the players emerged onto the
pitch, a huge banner was unfurled:* "La nostra sofferenza, la
vostra prepotenza," *"Our suffering, your arrogance."*

*The other side of football finance is the market created by buy-
ing and selling players. When I spend the long summer months
in the Apennines, eagerly awaiting the next football season, I'm
always interested in the* calciomercato. *In Britain there's no
such thing. Teams remain the same for years on end. Sometimes
the managers will buy a new player or sell an old one, but basically not much changes. Here, I'm astonished at the number of
players bought and sold. Often they have barely arrived in one
team before they are shipped to the next. The promiscuity of presidents seems insatiable. Sometimes teams are completely unrecog-
nisable from one year to the next. If you don't pay attention for
a couple of weeks, you could go to the stadium and discover that
half your idols have been sold to the opposition. It's an integral
part of the football economy. The quickest way to make money is
to sell a player, or buy a player and hope against all economic
laws that the inflation will continue for eternity and that you
will be able to make a profit a few months, or matches, down the
line. "As with all bubbles," the country's financial paper* Il Sole
24 Ore *wrote recently, "profits have been made only on paper,
capable of feeding on themselves in order that the volume of exchange and the relative prices continually increase." Sooner or
later, everyone knew, even if no one wanted to admit it, the bubble would burst.*

*The final part of the financial equation was, again, very
strange to foreign eyes. The British love betting. Every village,
town, and city has its own bookmakers, either an independent
businessman or part of a national chain. They offer odds, and
you look for the longest so that if you win, you make the most
money. Here, though, it's very different. The betting system is
simply bizarre. It's almost exclusively state-run, and it's very,*

very difficult to win anything. The money paid to totocalcio *or* totosei *or* totogol *is like a tax on stupidity because the odds are so incredibly long. What most amazed me about the betting system was that every time I went into a tobacconist, I would see entire walls covered by betting slips; and yet each time I tried to play poker or pool for money at home, I was told I was breaking the law. It was, I was told, only legal to bet if the state was the bookmaker.*

It is, then, only a suspicion. There's nothing to go on in terms of evidence. But it's enough to look at the facts to know the score: it's 1-0 to Juventus, and it's quite obviously going to stay that way. Nothing's going to change that scoreline, not even a goal. And sure enough, in the dying minutes of the crucial penultimate game of the 1999–2000 championship, Parma's Fabio Cannavaro jumps, almost folds his body in half at the waist as he heads the ball. It bounces against the inside of the bottom of the post and into the net. In the caged pen for away supporters, Parma fans go berserk, waving blue-and-yellow flags and letting off smoke flares.

But, strangely, the score remains 1-0. The goal is disallowed. All around me indignant *parmigiani* start screaming abuse at the referee: "You've earned it today, all right," "You've been bought, cuckold!" Not allowing the goal seems particularly perverse since the action began with a corner, and thus there could have been no offside. Cannavaro had a free header and clearly hadn't elbowed any defender. The referee, examined after the game, can't remember or recall why he didn't allow the goal. There's no explanation, except perhaps the fact that he had wrongly awarded a corner in the first place and was—having realised his mistake—making amends. Fans of Lazio, chasing Juventus for the title, duly riot in Rome. A mock street funeral is held for Italian football, and the cover of *Corriere dello Sport* announces on its front page: "Sorry, but this is a scandal."

It's not the first time something of the sort has happened. At the end of the 1997–98 season, Inter Milan were denied a blatant penalty against Juventus which could have given them the title. A few minutes later the referee awarded Juventus a penalty. They duly won their twenty-fifth *scudetto*, the league title. Talk to statisticians about that season and they'll tell you, with eyebrows raised, that Juventus had been the most "fouling" team all year (814 fouls) but with the fewest yellow (sixty-five) and red (three) cards. The referees are obviously, the rhetoric goes, on the side of Juventus.

In most places such criticisms could be dismissed as the whinings of bad losers. Here, though, there is serious suspicion that referees aren't always as independent as they should be. After all, if all the magistrates, news readers, newspaper editors, and industrialists are obviously politically aligned, why shouldn't referees throw in their lot with one side or the other? Even the normally sober *Stampa* remarked that the 1997–98 title would be a bitter trophy given the lack of credibility the club now had: "One can't remain indifferent when confronted with certain coincidences which are so singular and, let's say it, so 'nutritious' . . . [T]here's the suspicion that the rules aren't the same for everyone." The editor of the *Gazzetta dello Sport* even wrote that it was "an open disgrace" and that the refereeing had been "one-way."

During another Juventus-Parma encounter (at the Tardini during that 1999–2000 season) there was, again, an extraordinary refereeing display. I am standing on the terraces next to Ciccio, who, like most Juventus supporters, is from the south, about a thousand miles from Turin. He's very short, coming up to chest height, but makes up for it with his aggressive defence of anyone in a Juventus shirt. We are drink-

ing slugs of the coffee liqueur sold underneath the stands, enjoying the partisan banter of the terraces. All around us fans
are lighting up large joints, doubtless another reason for the
rampant paranoia surrounding Italian football. It's an incredible scene: smoke mixing with coloured flares, flags flapping
between banners, the weak winter sunshine of a Parma January. A lot of southerners from Sicily and Puglia are in bomber
jackets supporting the team from Turin. Most of them, students from Parma University, have bought tickets for the terrace for home fans and so mingle with the sedate, muted
Parma crowd, who are dressed as if they were going to the
opera.

"Listen, it's all a fix," I say to Ciccio before kick-off, repeating what I've heard for months on television debates
about football fixing. "Everyone knows that the referee will
have been given a script by Juventus."

"Why do you have to show your lack of intelligence, speaking like that?" says Ciccio, smiling.

Juventus are gifted a penalty (the Parma defender is sent
off). Ciccio wants no talk of a fix. Alessandro Del Piero steps
up and slots home the penalty. "You see, Zio Tobia, you seem
like a sore and stupid loser when you talk like that!" He's
laughing, jumping up and down celebrating the goal as he
slaps me on the back.

"Better a sore loser than a crooked winner," I say, trying to
wind him up.

"You really are so naive. You're simply up against a better
team."

"Right, starting with Agnelli," says an old *parmigiano* in
front of us, turning round to scrutinise the southerner. He's
banging his blue-and-yellow cushion on his knees in despair.

The strange thing, and it might just be an impression, is
that the longer the game goes on, the more desperate the referee appears to "seal" the result. Having already awarded a

penalty, the referee then sends off another Parma player, re-ducing the "yellow-blues" to nine men. The second player to be sent off, Dino Baggio, makes his feelings perfectly clear as a red card is raised above his head: he rubs his fingers and thumbs together, an obvious-enough sign that he thinks the referee has been bought (a gesture for which he would subsequently serve a lengthy suspension). The accumulation of injustices (not just sendings off but bizarre offsides, non-existent corners) is so relentless that it's hard not to detect a conspiracy, especially where Juventus is concerned. On this occasion, though, Parma somehow pull a result out of the bag. The last minute of the game: a through ball to Hernan Crespo, who feints and then fires with his famous left foot. The stadium goes berserk; the Parma coach, in his cashmere overcoat, rushes onto the pitch and throws himself on top of the now-prostrate Crespo. Delirium: nine men against eleven, and Parma manage to pull off a draw. "Bet that wasn't in the script," I whisper to Ciccio, who is now on the verge of tears.

As years went by, I realised that Juventus was simply very, very lucky. If I was watching a game in which the *bianconeri* (the "black-and-whites" of Juventus) were losing 2-0 with ten minutes to go, I could normally guarantee that the game would finish with a 2-2 draw. It happened against both Parma and Bologna during the 2002–3 season. There's an old joke about Manchester United which is equally applicable to Ju-ventus: "What's their greatest quality? Playing the full ninety-eight minutes." (A regular game lasts ninety minutes; the point is that many suspect that referees allow play to continue for the most important teams until the scoreline suits them.)

There's so much smoke that it's hard to know if there re-ally is any fire, whether there's any truth to the rumours about Italian football being played on an unlevel playing field. During the fateful 2000–1 season, though, the true workings of football finally came out into the open. On the pitch it was going rather badly: no Italian team managed to reach the quarter-finals of the Champions' League or the Uefa cup. There was much hand-wringing as fans and commentators realised that the traditionally shrewd Italian game had been surpassed by quick, cavalier sides from Spain, England, and Turkey—teams in which many of the superstars were home-grown rather than imported from Rio. Nervous presidents began sacking their managers: eight of Serie A's eighteen teams changed "technical commissioner," and one team (Parma) had three different managers during the season.

Off the pitch, things were even worse. It was revealed that a match between Atalanta and Pistoiese had been subject to strange betting patterns: large amounts, placed by relatives of the respective players, had been bet on an Atalanta advantage at half-time but an eventual draw at full-time (which was, of course, exactly what happened). Six players were suspended, not for having bet themselves, but for having failed to "de-nounce" exactly what was going on (there was later a blanket absolution). That was just the tip of the iceberg: the Perugia coach, Serse Cosmi, was then caught on camera describing what had happened in Serie C (the third division). The year before, he said, one team was happily mid-table: it had failed to make the play-offs and yet was mathematically safe from relegation. So "it began gifting games." One striker from an-other team, Cosmi continued, was supposed to win the league's top-scorer award: his previous seasonal highest tally was eight goals, but that year he scored twenty-eight. "They came to an agreement," said Cosmi. "They lost 4-3; it was enough that he scored three goals. Things from another world. Penalties were showered around, games finished 5-4. The south is like that, if they want someone to win the top-scorer award." Cosmi had been caught by surprise, thinking that the cameras weren't rolling, but he had only revealed what everyone had long suspected. *"Honi soit qui mal y*

pense," Filippo said to me, laughing bitterly: "It's a sin to suspect sinning, but here, in football, it's never wrong."

More serious revelations were yet to come. Juan Sebastian
Veron was probably the best player in Serie A. He had won
the European and Italian cups with Parma, and the *scudetto*
with Lazio. An Argentinian with a goatee and a shaved head,
he plays in the hole between midfield and strikers and often
scores from very long range. If defenders then close him
down, he invariably, casually, slips the ball to an attacker. It
was suggested that Veron had been playing under a false passport. As the season went on, more and more names came out,
mostly South Americans, accused of the same thing: of having
forged passports, inventing fictitious Italian grandparents to
adopt them and ease their passage into Serie A. There is a
ceiling to the number of "extra-community" players a team is
allowed to field, so once a player is Italianised, he's automatically more attractive and his market value rises by some 30 per
cent. The "crime" itself wasn't particularly serious, but in
footballing terms the scandal was seismic. Not for the first
time, it appeared that Italian football was slightly crooked.
Whilst some teams had been adhering to the rules, others had
been wilfully importing and fielding players who had no right
to play. Clubs, it emerged, had either forged passports or not
even bothered to look at them. Accusations and libel writs
flew in all directions. Fabio Capello, coach of Roma and
therefore sworn rival of the other Roman team, Lazio, suggested that Lazio's historic *scudetto* of 1999–2000 was therefore a con. More subtly, the fact that some thirty players were
caught up in the scandal added to the already-fragile sense of
the superiority of football *all'italiana*: Serie A, it was obvious,
was reliant not on native play makers but on imported stars.

Since so many teams had fielded illegitimate players, apply-
ing the law and its sporting penalties (deducting points from
offending teams, banning players, or imposing hefty fines)

would have meant invalidating many results from Serie A. The problem was so widespread that no one quite knew what to do: whether to go to the civil, rather than sporting, magistrates; whether to penalise teams or blame and ban the players themselves. Veron himself, at the centre of the row, began to get increasingly petulant, and the engine of the Lazio team suddenly found himself unable to get out of second gear on the pitch (he was later absolved of any personal involvement in the crime). The irritating law, it was obvious, was making life difficult for everyone, so a solution was found. It was a solution I was to see used frequently in Italy. The reasoning goes something like this: "If so many people are guilty, let's change the law and play people 'onside.' To prosecute the ocean of offenders would lead to utter collapse, because there are simply so many of them. So let's not prosecute." The solution, as always, was to fudge right and wrong, to change the rules suddenly to suit the rulers. Thus, mid-season, the law limiting the number of foreign players allowed to play was wiped out, allowing teams to field whomever they wanted. Those who had been honest were penalised for not having been more *furbi*, more "cunning"; anyone who had played by the book, buying Italian players and checking foreigners' passports, was suddenly at a disadvantage. It would have been fairer literally to have moved the goalposts.

Of course, days after the rule was changed, a foreigner scored a vital goal. Roma were visiting Juventus and being thoroughly outplayed by the "old lady." Capello, knowing about the rule change about extra-community players, sent on Hidetoshi Nakata, his Japanese star, who promptly scored one goal and set up another. Roma had clawed their way back into the game and, reversing the normal tendency, scraped a 2-2 draw.

Then another type of dependency emerged. Italian football, it became clear, was being fuelled by banned substances.

During the 2000–1 season, players began testing *non-negativo*, then confirmed as *positivo*, for the anabolic steroid nandrolone. They weren't simply the journeymen players but the stars: Fernando Couto at Lazio; Edgar Davids, the Juventus midfielder. A few years earlier, the chain-smoking Czech coach, Zdenek Zeman, had alleged that many of the Juventus players had quickly become suspiciously muscular. He was ridiculed, then threatened and sued, and his career in Italy was effectively at an end. As the new crisis deepened, journalists queued up to talk to the unemployed coach (still living in Rome), who confidently repeated his accusations: "At the time, they made me seem like a madman, but they knew very well that what I was saying wasn't madness. The fact is they didn't listen to me or anyone else. I'm very sad, because it's a very sad time for football."[5]

On the day the non-negativity of Edgar Davids was leaked (fifty days after the actual test), I was back on the terraces watching Parma-Juventus with Ciccio. When Davids's name was read out over the PA, the stadium erupted into a chorus of *"Drogato,"* "drugged." Even the most partisan Parma supporter, though, would admit that Davids was the best on the pitch, increasingly powerful as the game went on: strong and subtle, able to boss the midfield with sudden changes of direction and speed. The game finished nil-nil. That evening, and for the weeks which followed, there were endless debates about Italy's crisis of *frode sportiva*, "sporting fraud." There were partial confessions, veiled accusations. It never quite came out explicitly, but a very clear tension was emerging between players and their respective clubs. Players claimed to be totally innocent ("My body is the house of my soul," said Davids) and hinted that they had been slipped substances unawares. The club doctors were mentioned as possible sources of the contamination. One medical expert claimed that since nandrolone and other integrators are available commercially from England and America, it might be difficult always to understand what was contained in the imported substances. Moggi, the Juventus troubleshooter, distanced himself from the affair, underlining that Davids had been playing with the Dutch national team on the week of the positive test (as had Frank de Boer and Japp Stam, both of whom were later to test positive for nandrolone). As ever, the accused cast themselves as victims, citing the usual extraordinary slowness of the justice system: one player had waited eighty-eight days between his test and the non-negative result. Another player, a midfielder from Milan, almost admitted that everyone was taking performance-enhancing drugs and publicly pleaded that players be given more guidelines not about which substances were legal but about what were the accepted levels of illegal drugs. (The clubs duly attempted to increase the legal level of nandrolone permitted, though the action was overturned by Federcalcio.)

But the best response to the crisis was, of course, not moral but aesthetic. Italian football, more than any other, prides itself on its beauty. To put that in jeopardy is infinitely more serious than allegations of match fixing or drug use. The real complaint, then, against the steroid use was not that it was wrong but that it promoted ugly football. One newscaster (a Juventus supporter) said in a debate that the game had become too "physical, antagonistic," rather too much like the English version. Tackles flew in, players were too aggressive, there was no longer any room on the pitch for the golden boys of Italian football, the *fantasisti*. Strength and speed, the argument went, had become more important than silky skills. Steroids were wrong not per se but because they threatened the *bellezza*, the "beauty," of Italian football and made it more like its vulgar Anglo-Saxon incarnation.

As with the false-passport fiasco, the doping scandal was quickly brushed under the carpet. At the beginning of the fol-

lowing season, the term of Edgar Davids's ban from football
was reduced. Nobody really noticed. In short paragraphs at
the back of the sports pages, it was reported that the magistrature had decided to reduce the Juventus midfielder's ban
to just four months. Since a large part of the ban had been
served during the summer, he would be allowed to return to
football almost immediately (17 September). All the other
sentences were reduced or annulled, be they for forging passports, match fixing, or using nandrolone. Newspapers found
other things to write about, and the fact that two of the leading lights of Juventus—the *amministratore delegato*, Antonio
Giraudo, and the doctor Riccardo Agricola—were to be tried
for *frode sportiva* for administering illegal pills and illicit sy-
ringes to Juventus players was hardly mentioned. Raffaele
Guariniello has spent years investigating drugs in football, but
his research, too, is largely ignored. Despite the tragic, inexplicable death of Gianluca Signorini from Lou Gehrig's
disease (amyotrophic lateral sclerosis), despite the similar ill-
nesses of Guido Vincenzi and Giorgio Rognoni, the show
must go on.

There were other unattractive sides to the beautiful game.
It started when Arsenal visited Lazio in the Champions'
League. As the Lazio fans, traditionally from the far right,
barracked Arsenal's Patrick Vieira with choruses of "Boo,
boo," the Lazio defender Sinisa Mihajlovic repeatedly called
him "nigger." At the following match the Serb was forced to
apologise and denounce his own racism over the stadium's PA
system. And yet the racist fans clearly enjoyed the collusion of
the club and the *carabinieri* lined up outside the stadia. Anyone who has ever been to a football stadium in Italy knows
that it's impossible to get into the place with a cigarette
lighter, coins, and sometimes even keys. They will almost certainly be confiscated when you're dusted down by the hoards
of *carabinieri* on the gates. And yet, despite such stringent

checks, the following banners (both about fifty metres long) had recently appeared in Lazio's stadium: "Jews: Auschwitz Is Your Town, the Ovens Your Houses" and, a tribute to Mihajlovic and his fellow Serbs, "Honour to the Arkan Tiger." In another instance of incompetent policing, a motor bike was ridden up the spiral walkway which takes fans to the upper tiers of the San Siro and thrown onto fans to the tier below. How a motor bike was able to get there, when no one's ever managed to take even a hip-flask into a stadium, baffled the embarrassed commentators.

Watching football matches became like watching newsreels of matches in Britain from the 1970s: fans goading the police or other fans into close-quarter fights, train stations vandalised, cars repeatedly set on fire. Every Sunday evening there seemed to be new pictures of looted shops seen through the haze of police tear-gas. In one post-match incident, a player from Como, Massimo Ferrigno, punched his former team-mate Francesco Bertolotti into a coma which lasted over a week. A month later, a bomb was thrown into the home of the Napoli co-owner Corrado Ferlaino because the club was performing badly. (The same reason was given for the calf's head sent in the post to the president of Reggina.) Worse was the volley of smoke flares which, at almost every match, went to and fro between fans like a gently lobbed tennis ball. It looked quite picturesque unless you saw it up close: one policeman had to have a finger amputated. In an even more tragic incident, a fan was killed when a "paper bomb" was thrown by opposing fans during a play-off in Sicily.

In Italy, political power has always been intimately linked to football, and there's nothing new in the conflation of the two. Mussolini was probably the first politician who fully understood the political implications of the sport. Physical perfection and sporting finesse became metaphors for the virility of Fascism as athletic organisations drilled millions of Italians in gymnasiums. Local governments were forced to build Lictorian (Fascist) sports grounds; by 1930 over three thousand had sprung up across the country. Bologna's was inaugurated in 1926, followed by the Berta stadium in Florence, the Mussolini stadium in Turin, and the Vittoria stadium in Bari. Footballing triumphs came to be exploited as examples of the "strength" or "superiority" of Fascism (Italy won the World Cup twice during the 1930s).

Silvio Berlusconi's populism, of course, is based on his ownership of a football team. He became owner of AC Milan in 1986, saving the club from the threat of bankruptcy. In the official hagiography of Il Cavaliere, it was the fulfilment of a childhood dream: every Sunday—after "the liturgy of the Mass . . . the comments and reflections on the sermon"—Berlusconi would go with his father to the stadium. Even that official version describes the baby Silvio learning to bend the rules: at the turnstiles he used to "make myself tiny tiny to use one ticket for two people."[6] During the first year of his ownership, two of his television channels, Canale 5 and Italia 1, ran long montages of Milan glory, with a persuasive voice-over: "Make yourself a present of a new Sunday with the azure sky, the green of the lawn, and the red and black of the new Milan." A record number of fans, almost sixty thousand, quickly snapped up season tickets.

The achievements of Berlusconi's Milan are amazing. In fifteen years under his leadership, Milan have won a total of twenty trophies: scudetti, European cups, Supercups, Intercontinental cups. He brought together three of the greatest Dutch stars—Marco van Basten, Ruud Gullit, and Frank Rijkaard—and blended them with stylish, faultless Italian defenders like Franco Baresi and Paolo Maldini. Arrigo Sacchi, a little-known coach who was then manager of Parma, was picked as the new coach of Milan. Sacchi introduced what was then a revolutionary new style of "total football" in which players paid little

*attention to traditional positions in an all-out siege on the oppo-
nent's goal. Gone were the days in which Italian teams played*
catenaccio, *"lock-out," defensive football. (Before then, the
mantra of Italian football had come from Annibale Frossi, who
claimed that the perfect game of football was the artistic and
philosophical equivalent of a blank canvas: a no-score draw.)
Later, Fabio Capello became coach, and the Liberian George
Weah inherited the mantle of prolific goal scorer. Talking about
those years in his* Una storia italiana, *Berlusconi says: "Ours
wasn't only the victory of a football team but also a victory for
those values in which we strongly believed: dedication to a communal cause, altruism and perseverance, the capacity for sacrifice, loyalty towards opponents, agonising attention to every
detail. We had to win but also to convince with a great style, re-
specting the opponents and enthusing our fans."*[7]

As ever, though, the success story is mixed with scandal, and
Milan's trophy cupboard contains skeletons as well as trophies.
The club, indeed, is the reason for one of Berlusconi's many legal
prosecutions. In the summer of 1992, Milan paid Torino the
then-extraordinary sum of 18.5 billion lire ($9.25 million) for
a young footballer called Gianluigi Lentini. It later emerged
that the Lentini transfer had been the subject of shady financial
deals. The president of the Torino football club (who doubled, of
course, as a member of Parliament) alleged that 6.5 billion lire
of the transfer fee were paid* sottobanco—*without receipts or
contract—to a Swiss bank account, an obvious way to avoid
taxes; the actual player, Lentini, had his proposed annual salary
slashed from 4 billion lire ($2 million) to little more than
1.5 billion (with the obvious suspicion, according to the Torino
president, that he was "topped up" in cash from Berlusconi's
slush funds in Switzerland); most damning of all, when the Milan directors had paid a 7-billion-lira deposit on the player, they
didn't ask for the usual "receipt" of payment but instead wanted
shares in Torino.*[8] *It was that, more than the financial scams,*

which incensed neutral observers, because it meant that Milan had played much of the end of the 1992 season owning control-ling shares in another club. Berlusconi's response to the scandal was to become, during the next ten years, a familiar refrain. He was, he said, the victim: "I have the sensation of living in a po-lice state . . . I feel the object of a witch-hunt."[9]

When Berlusconi burst into politics in the aftermath of Clean Hands (the judicial initiative in the early 1990s to remove cor-ruption from Italian life), voters thus had his record at Milan at the front of their minds. There were, as usual, two sides to the coin: the epic success of Berlusconi's football presidency, countered by the strange financial deals which he was accused of conduct-ing in the dark. Berlusconi gambled that people would be so daz-zled by the success that few would worry about the scandal, and thus, not for the first time in Italian history, he openly aspired to conflate politics and football: his political party was baptised Forza Italia, which is the commonest of football cheers, as in "Come On, Italy!" His parliamentarians were originally re-ferred to as his "azzurri," referring to the blue shirts of the Ital-ian national team. When he announced the formation of his new political party, and his own candidature for the post of Prime Minister, Berlusconi even spoke of the move in overtly footballing tones: "walking onto the pitch." Forza Italia's re-gional offices were often little more than the former fan clubs of the Milan football team, which were dotted up and down the peninsula. Berlusconi, it was clear, intended to run the country as he ran his club (which could—depending on whether good football is more important than correct accounting—cut both ways).

The intimate link between football and politics is, with Berlusconi, ubiquitous. When, in May 1994, his first govern-ment faced a crucial no-confidence vote in Parliament, his team, AC Milan, was simultaneously competing for the Cham-pions' Cup with Barcelona in Athens. That evening, once

Berlusconi's team was 2-0 up (it would eventually win 4-0), Parliament voted in his favour. Some people have followed the analogy between football and politics even further. Running against Berlusconi in 1996, Romano Prodi presented himself as a keen cyclist, an image which, politically, recalled the old days of proportional representation: a mass of competitors, the result announced after months of competition and difficult calculation. Berlusconi's footballing mentality meant that he was ideal for the new, first-past-the-post system which was to revolutionise Italian politics. Italian politics was suddenly more like football: a showdown between two sides. Abuse could be hurled at the opposing fans and their players, be they sporting or political. Even the diction of politics is now imbued with footballing metaphors. The opposition talks about "pressing sul governo"; *the government replies by saying the opposition is* "fuorigioco," "offside."

One of Berlusconi's first legislative acts when he came to power in 2001 (it was presented to Parliament, like so much of his dubious legislation, at the height of the summer, when people pay little attention to politics) was the "falso in bilancio," *or* "false accounting," *legislation. The law was, in fact, begun under the previous government, but new amendments were added which fitted Berlusconi like a bespoke suit. The very crime of which Berlusconi had so often been accused was, in his first foray into government, turned into a minor infringement. In the technical phraseology, it was changed from being a crime of* "danger" *to a crime of* "damage." *Cooking the books had effectively been decriminalised. Basically, in future, businessmen would face fines instead of prisons and only if denounced by their own shareholders. The actual amendments were conceived by the Judicial Affairs Committee, whose chairman, Gaetano Pecorella, and another lawyer, Niccolò Ghedini, both double as defence lawyers for Berlusconi.*

There were two major implications of the legislation. First, since false accounting was only a crime if denounced by affected parties (a shareholder or a creditor), it was obvious that something as mundane as the state, trying to impose taxes on company profits, would be impotent. Second, since prison terms were drastically reduced, the statute of limitations—the practice whereby a crime is no longer a crime after a certain period—was cut from fifteen years to seven and a half. That simple amendment meant that the Lentini case, which had taken the sheen off Berlusconi's footballing achievements, would be washed away. It happened too long ago to be taken into consideration. It had passed its "crime-by" date.

Then, a year and a half later, another piece of government legislation was tailor-made for the footballing industry. It was called, grandly, Salva-calcio. It meant, basically, that a club's debts could be deferred over a ten-year period, whereby a costly injection of cash could be legally avoided. Clubs which had been paying extravagant sums for and to players suddenly realised the bubble had burst and were being given more time to put their houses in order. It was, effectively, like saying that the game, rather than lasting ninety minutes, would now last three hours because one side was losing. Antonio Mereu wrote the next day on the front page of Gazzetta dello Sport: *"With this scandalous law, accounting irregularities have been legalised which gravely injure justice and overturn normal behaviour and good sense."[10] Not for the first time, it appeared that the rules in football were elastic.*

All of this made me think that the real problem wasn't about penalties, about whether the referees lean slightly towards the "old lady" of Italian football or the Prime Minister's team when they blow their whistles and point to the spot. The debate is really about another type of penalty, or the lack of it. It's the fact that, as Italy's moral minority always complains, *non paga nessuno*, which basically means that no one in Italy is ever, ever punished for anything: "nobody pays." Ever since I arrived, I had heard one-half of the country, the law-abiding half, complain bitterly and incessantly about the *furbi*—the "cunning ones"—who appear to bend and break the law at will, without ever facing the consequences. In Italy there are no penalties other than on the football pitch. Crime is never followed by punishment, because, at least for the powers that be, there's guaranteed impunity. You can get away with anything. As long as you play the game, you'll be played onside. Take nandrolone, field illegal players, fiddle the accounts, put up Fascist banners: *non paga nessuno*.

Nothing new in that, though. A few months ago I went to Pompeii. It was a hazy day, and you could only just see Vesuvius in the distance through the smog. We got to the far corner, to the *anfiteatro*, after hours of serious stuff. This was what I wanted to see: the ancient equivalent of a stadium. It was stunning. We consulted the *piccola guida* published by the Culture Ministry. "In AD 59," Filippo read, "Pompeii and Nocera fans sparked off a violent disturbance, and the pitch was disqualified for ten years." We laughed at the irony, and then even more at what came afterwards: "a punishment which was annulled after the earthquake of 62." Even then the fans were violent, and the punishments, initially harsh, were invariably removed.

Perhaps none of this really matters. Italian football remains the most stylish and cultured and clever incarnation of the sport. The *azzurri* will always be the hot favourites to win any international tournament because, whatever goes on in the boardrooms, the foot-soldiers are still amongst the best in the world. Also, I would rather play football in Italy—in the parks or on the beaches—than anywhere else. Perhaps it's true that if you only watch football, or only read about it, the Italian version sometimes looks a bit irregular, unusual, slightly illegal. But whenever you actually play in Italy, especially with random teams in public spaces, you see the greatness of the

Italian game: the spontaneity, the fantasy, the humour, the hospitality to all races.

And anyway, by then I had become fascinated by another subject, something I had seen on the news, something that seemed to animate everyone I spoke with. The plight of one individual had become the complete negation of my theory of Italian impunity. Almost as if to compensate for the absence of justice, one man had been sentenced to an exemplary prison term for a murder committed decades earlier, in 1972. Here, finally, was an example of that rare thing, a genuine Italian punishment (with the irony that it had been meted out to the one man millions of Italians were convinced was actually innocent). Adriano Sofri had become the country's most famous "murderer," and—since his case overlapped so intimately with that of Piazza Fontana—I travelled to Pisa prison to meet him.

4

THE SOFRI CASE

He thought about those other informers, buried under a light layer of earth and dry leaves, high in the folds of the Apennines; miserable men, a mud of fear and vice. They had played their game of death, on a thread of lies between partisans and Fascists, they had played with their lives.

—LEONARDO SCIASCIA

Heading out of Parma to the south-west, you quickly reach the Cisa pass, which takes you over the Apennines towards the Ligurian and Tuscan coasts. It's a spectacular road which lifts you above the fog of the plain: supported on concrete stilts, it struts over valleys, and its long tunnels puncture the mountains. A few hundred metres below the asphalt, pictur-esque mountain villages huddle around their bell-towers, ap-pearing from above like random piles of matchboxes. Now, in October, the mountain colours are crisp and autumnal: white wood smoke gusting between dark green pines.

I'm driving towards Pisa prison. A few days before, on 6 October 2000 in Rome, the first penal section of the Corte di Cassazione had pronounced a final judgement on a murder committed almost thirty years earlier, in May 1972. It had taken eleven hours for the court to reach its decision, which was then curtly announced to the gathered journalists at 10 p.m.: "This court rejects the appeal for a retrial."

It was the definitive, closing chapter of a case which has obsessed the country, one which had, throughout the 1990s, become every bit as politicised and emblematic as the Dreyfus affair almost a century before. The appeal to the Cassazione was the last resort: a final opportunity to reopen the case. That opportunity denied, the conviction (announced six months previously) for the "Calabresi crime" stands, and Adriano Sofri will remain in prison until 2017, almost fifty years from the date of the crime.

The Sofri case is, in many ways, the complementary inverse of the ongoing Piazza Fontana trial: a tardy and dubious attempt to apportion blame (this time to the extra-parliamentary left) for one of the iconic moments from the *anni di piombo*, to indict not only an individual but also the wider movement of which he was representative. If evidence which is belated and confused in the Piazza Fontana trial has allowed the left to point a hysterical finger against various historical nemeses, the Sofri case has offered the same opportunity for the right. The Piazza Fontana crimes were the very reason for the Calabresi crime: Calabresi was the policeman in charge of interrogating Pino Pinelli, the anarchist suspected of the bombing who subsequently fell to his death from a window of the police station. As with so much of the *anni di piombo*, Piazza Fontana appears to be the original sin from which all other crimes descend. "The *anni di piombo* started with Piazza Fontana," wrote Giorgio Galli in Genoa's newspaper *Il Secolo XIX*, "and until the truth about that beginning has been ascertained, that about Calabresi will remain partial."[1]

Responses to the Sofri case tend to be knee-jerk assertions of either his guilt or his innocence, and all commentators inevitably become *colpevolisti* or *innocentisti*, part of the guilty or the innocent camp. For the left, Sofri is a *cause célèbre* without compare, the sacrificial lamb of the right bent on judicial revenge for left-wing terrorism in the 1970s. "They've buried him alive," say his friends on the evening of the latest decision. Some hint darkly that Sofri, as a man of granite integrity (and one who knows his own symbolic value), might now resort to suicide (a speculation he denies in a press conference from Pisa prison the following morning: "There are two things I'll never do: ask for a pardon [which would imply guilt] or commit suicide"). His brother, an academic in Bologna, declares: "This is an ugly country; if I weren't an old *signore* nearing the end of my days, I would go away." An editorial in *La Repubblica* calls the decision "a monstrosity . . . the inhuman and uncivil vendetta of the state." Sofri, runs the editorial, has to suffer the "infamy of being an assassin—still worse the sender of an assassin . . . [H]e will consider this a death sentence, and will testify until martyrdom his innocence."[2] Within days, a campaign for granting Sofri a presidential pardon is begun.

Those on the right, however, were gleeful. "Justice has been done," declared one member of the National Alliance. "Let's hope that the Lotta Continua lobby [the movement of which Sofri was the leader] now shuts up and remembers their history as killers, as definitely sanctified today by the Italian judiciary." Another National Alliance spokesman says he hopes for an end to "the obsessive apologist song which has transformed Sofri into an icon which even he doesn't seem to recognise."[3]

The responses of the political spectrum were, however, even more complicated than that. Sofri had been condemned by judges who were often, in other contexts, denounced as

Communists (a political party which was, during the latter half of the 1970s, radically hostile to any extra-parliamentary left which might foment terrorism). At the same time, Sofri had been criticised in later years for his proximity to Bettino Craxi's Socialists, a party which had favoured negotiations with the Red Brigades during and after the Moro kidnapping. Indeed, many of those within Lotta Continua had gradually drifted into Craxi's orbit in the 1980s, and (in one of those strange political trajectories typical of Italian politics) by the late 1990s had found themselves at the far right of the political spectrum, rubbing shoulders with Berlusconi's Forza Italia deputies.

The road comes out at the Golfo dei Poeti. I turn left, and stop in another small town, Bocca di Magra, and approach a man selling pancakes out of the back of a van. He's got thick waves of greying hair. This is Leonardo Marino, the *pentito* whose confessions are responsible for the Sofri case. I explain that I'm a journalist and ask him a couple of questions. He repeats the phrases I've read elsewhere: religious language about repenting, about the need, after all these years, to tell the truth. Marino, once in the rank and file of Lotta Continua in the 1970s, has become a figure of ridicule for the left. He is the *pentito* who has pointed a finger at Sofri and his two "accomplices." In 1988 he confessed first to his priest, then to the police, about his involvement in the murder of Luigi Calabresi. Almost every detail he recalled was wrong: the colour of the car, the place where the murder was planned, the weather conditions. There was little evidence, other than his, on which the accused could have been convicted. There was an eerie absence of the normally all-important *documenti*. It's strange now to see him: whilst Sofri is in prison, Marino is selling pancakes on the Tuscan coast as if nothing had happened. During Sofri's first trial it was revealed that Marino had been in contact with the police long before his "official" confession in the summer of 1988, leading many (not least Dario Fo in another invective comedy, *Marino libero! Marino è innocente!*) to suggest that the whole confession was simply a put-up job by police.

An hour later I arrive in Pisa. The city is dominated by scholars and students, and the atmosphere is very left-wing. Pisa's ancient university (where Galileo Galilei once taught), and especially its Scuola Normale (founded by Napoleon in imitation of Paris's Ecole Normale), have long been the educational cradles for future presidents and prime ministers, for philosophers and scientists. During the 1930s, the city was a refuge of intellectual resistance to Mussolini: in 1937 Aldo Capitini published his *Elementi di un'esperienza religiosa*, an impassioned plea for non-cooperation with the regime, and two years later one of his colleagues published *La scuola dell'uomo*, a sort of paean to liberty. Walking around the city, back and forth across the bridges which criss-cross the river Arno, one immediately identifies the city's political affiliation. Sprayed on walls at regular intervals, with what I'm told is typically Tuscan humour, is one recurrent sentence: "Let's hunt the Fascists from the face of the earth . . . and not only!" Another piece of urban graffiti is appended to the south wall of a church: an enormous mural, a collage of colourful floating bodies, painted in Pisa by Keith Haring shortly before his death. Like Parma, the city is full of monuments, memorials, and plaques, always more provocative than reconciliatory. In the heart of the city is a small park with the sculpted bust of a young man, Franco Serantini. The inscription explains: "20-year-old anarchist mortally wounded by police at an anti-Fascist rally." On the wall of the building opposite the bust someone has (evidently recently) sprayed: "Franco, we will avenge you."

The Casa Circondariale di Don Bosco, Pisa's prison, is a squat building, almost unnoticed from the road but for the Perspex watch-tower inhabited by a bored uniformed guard.

Immediately inside the prison there's another plaque, this time commemorating the agents of "custody" killed in the line of duty: "Repose with Christian piety," it says (dated 1977). The prison guards are good-humoured and disorganised, struggling to find the flurry of faxes and photocopied documents which I have for months been sending to them and the ministry in Rome. Finally everything is miraculously in order, and I'm ushered across a courtyard and through a series of slow hydraulic doors. The interview room is cold. In the corner, plastic chairs are stacked to the damp brown ceiling. I sit down on a chair and wait for the arrival of Italy's most notorious "murderer," Adriano Sofri.

Throughout the early 1970s, the anarchist Pino Pinelli and the police commissioner Luigi Calabresi became symbolic characters in Italy's unusual morality play, invariably hero and villain, respectively. Although he had been unknown and anonymous during his lifetime, Pinelli, in death, had become, like Che Guevara, the focal point for left-wing malaise. He was invoked in slogans daubed on walls across the country: "Quando votate ricordatevi di Pino Pinelli" *("When you vote, remember Pino Pinelli"), and Lotta Continua issued a record of "The Ballad of Pinelli." Calabresi, on the other hand, became the scapegoat for all the alleged injustices of Italian society, and of Piazza Fontana in particular.*

As the libel trial continued between Calabresi and Lotta Continua, however, the process of blurring fact and fiction was well under way. A series of films and plays began to add to the symbolic accretions of the Pinelli-Calabresi case. In October 1970 Dario Fo's Accidental Death of an Anarchist *opened, with its unsubtle indictment of the police version of events:*

Do you know what people are going to think of you? That you're a bunch of bent bastards and liars . . . who do you think is ever go-

ing to believe you again? And do you know why people won't be-
lieve you . . . ? Because your version of the facts, as well as being
total bollocks, lacks humanity.[4]

In the same year, Elio Petri's film Investigation of a Citizen
above Suspicion *won an Oscar for best foreign film, portraying*
a policeman who has murdered a lover but is persuaded not to
confess. The parallels with the Calabresi case (even though the
film had been shot prior to December 1969) were obvious. As
were those drawn a year later with the release of Sacco and
Vanzetti, *a film version of innocent (Italian) anarchists put to*
death in America, in which another anarchist, Andrea Salsedo,
fell from the fourteenth floor of a New York police station. The
momentum of indignation was such that in June 1971, eight
hundred intellectuals signed a motion in L'Espresso *magazine*
describing the police as "torturers."

That polarisation of politics was underlined on 16 April
1970, when the television news was interrupted shortly after
8:30 p.m. in various cities by the announcement of a new, revo-
lutionary formation. As the images of the day's news rolled on,
an inserted voice-over announced:

A new mass resistance has been born, the workers' rebellion
against the landlord and the State of the landlords has been
born, the rebellion against foreign imperialism has been born, the
rebellion of the populations and of the working classes of the south
has been born. Born are the Red Brigades and the Brigate GAP
[Gruppi di Azione Partigiana] have been reconstituted. The
way of reforms, the way of revolutionary Communism, the way of
the definitive liberation of the proletariat and of the Italian
workers from the domination and exploitation of foreign and
Italian capital bring a long and hard war. But on this route the
partisan brigades, the workers, the cooperatives, the revolutionary
students march compact and united until the final victory.[5]

The wording reflected the character of the leader of the GAP movement, Giangiacomo Feltrinelli: melodramatic, apocalyptic, above all desperate to inherit the mantle of the partisan movement. Feltrinelli is one of the many "fallen" from the anni di piombo *whose memory has been both lionised and ridiculed, his name becoming a reflection of both the violence and the farce of those years. Feltrinelli's family was one of Italy's richest, thanks to their acres of forests in Austria's Carinthia and his grandfather's road-building projects under Mussolini. Feltrinelli escaped from his family home in Turin during the civil war to fight with the partisans, later becoming a member and generous benefactor of the Communist Party. In 1950, Feltrinelli had founded a "study centre" and subsequently opened a publishing house and a chain of bookshops across the country. It was Feltrinelli who first published Giuseppe Tomasi di Lampedusa's* The Leopard *and Boris Pasternak's* Doctor Zhivago *(a publication which soured his relationship with the Communist Party in Italy and Russia). Increasingly, he travelled to Cuba and South America, duly publishing works on guerrilla movements and on Che Guevara and—as a close friend of Castro's—commissioning the Cuban leader's autobiography.*

The musical chairs of parliamentary politics were unable to offer any degree of stability or continuity which might have counteracted the descent into guerrilla warfare. In the aftermath of the "hot autumn" of 1969, a series of union leaders had been denounced for "delinquent instigations." A general strike was called for 6 February 1970, and the following day the Prime Minister, Mariano Rumor, resigned. After a governmental vacuum lasting fifty days, Rumor formed another coalition before resigning again in July. At a time when the country cried out for a coherent leadership, the various competing factions of the Christian Democrats were engaged in futile feuding amongst themselves.

That summer, as the Italian azzurri *reached the final of* another World Cup, there was a prolonged revolt in Reggio Calabria (towards the toe of the Italian boot). It had been announced that the seat of the new regional government, having been promised to Reggio Calabria, was to be the neighbouring Catanzaro instead. In an area of abject poverty and poor housing, where more than ten thousand people were unemployed and many still lived in sheds dating from the 1908 earthquake, the removal of long-awaited and vital public-sector jobs was naturally resented. Reggio Calabria responded with a prolonged series of strikes, demonstrations, and bombings which quickly became political. Between July and September 1970, 3 people were killed, 200 wounded, and 426 charged with public order offences. In that period there had been nineteen general strikes, twelve explosions, thirty-two barricades set up on roads, and fourteen occupations of the local railway station. The area also witnessed the second "slaughter" of the "strategy of tension": on 22 July, a bomb exploded on the Freccia del Sud—the "southern arrow" train—at Gioia Tauro, killing six passengers and wounding another seventy-two.

Pasolini's documentary of the year following Piazza Fontana, 12 dicembre, shows the pulsating chaos of Reggio Calabria in those months: wide, sun-drenched streets without cars or pedestrians, only mounted police aiming bullets or water-cannon at protesters. Blockades set up on street corners, black smoke from tires and cars which have been set alight. Occasionally, an ambulance careering through the debris.

The right began by denouncing the strikers and demonstrators as "hooligans" and "scoundrels" but later exploited the unrest. The local secretary of one of the unions, Ciccio Franco, sided with the protesters, using the infamous slogan "Boia chi molla"—"The executioner for quitters." "It's our revolt," claimed Ordine Nuovo, "it's the first step in the national revolution in which this obscene democracy will be burnt." It was, indeed, a propaganda coup for the far right, which was able to

*present itself as the champion of the impoverished, marginalised
south. It later reaped rewards at the ballot-box (in 1971, in
Catania, the neo-Fascist Movimento Sociale Italiano garnered
21.5 per cent of the vote, and a year later the leader of the revolt,
Ciccio Franco, became an MSI senator). In subsequent years,
there was a concerted attempt to export the street* squadrismo
*of Reggio Calabria to the largely left-wing and more indus-
trialised north, with Fascists marching under the slogan*
"L'Aquila, Reggio, Milano sarà peggio" *(the rhyme boasting
that things would get worse in Milan). The rising toll of violence
and the presence of two increasingly extremist movements which
appeared diametrically opposed were ominous.*

*In December 1970 there was an attempt to impose on Italy
the "authoritarian solution." It was a strange* coup d'état, *so
subtle and secretive that when it failed many denied, as they still
do, that it had even taken place. Prince Junio Valerio Borghese,
the organiser of the coup, is one of the most controversial figures
of Italian postwar history. During the Second World War,
Borghese commanded the infamous Decima Mas, a body of assault troops which was responsible for raids on the British fleet in
Alexandria and which, after 1943, was savage in its treatment
of Italian partisans. Borghese was later tried as a war criminal
and sentenced to twelve years' imprisonment. On his (very early)
release, he became president of the Movimento Sociale Italiano
before founding the Fronte Nazionale, a pseudo-military organisation to "build a dam against red terror."*

*Coming in the aftermath of the Piazza Fontana bombing,
and the subsequent polarisation of society, the coup was not entirely unexpected. Nineteen seventy witnessed reforms which,
though insufficient to satisfy any but the most moderate on the
left, were adequate enough to unnerve the traditionalists on the
right: regional government had been introduced in the spring,
and in May the "Statuto dei lavoratori," a workers' charter,
guaranteed various workplace rights. Most important, days be-*

fore the Borghese coup, the bill legalising divorce (which had been passed in November 1969) became law. The coup took place on the night of 7 December 1970 (it was known as Tora-Tora, in memory of the Japanese attack on Pearl Harbor on the same date in 1941). Borghese had prepared a proclamation to read to the Italian public:

> *Italians, the hoped-for political change, the long-awaited* coup *d'état, has taken place. The political formula which has been used by governments for twenty-five years and has carried Italy to the brink of economic and moral ruin has finally been abandoned . . . The armed forces, the forces of order, the most competent and representative men of the nation are with us, and we can reassure you that the most dangerous adversaries—those who wanted to sell our homeland to the foreigner—have been rendered inoffensive . . . [W]e raise the glorious tricolour, and invite you to shout with us our irrepressible hymn of love: Italia! Italia! Viva l'Italia!*[6]

Two hundred Forest Guards left their Cittaducale base in the north-east of Rome and made for the city centre in a convoy armed with sub-machine-guns and handcuffs. Members and former members of a parachute regiment remained at their base, under the command of Sandro Saccucci (later to become a deputy for the MSI), awaiting orders. Across the country, other groups were ready for action. The Ministry of the Interior was occupied, and a stash of arms removed (counterfeit ones were later found in their place). Suddenly, however, just as the guards were about to enter the state television studios, they were met by two unknown men who ordered them to retreat. The operation was called off, with the bizarre explanation that it was raining too heavily.

The abortive coup was quickly dismissed as nothing more than the work of crackpot eccentrics, "a jolly get-together among old comrades," according to General Vito Miceli, head of SID (the secret service) and another future MSI parliamentarian. The notion that there had been an attempted coup was ridiculed; indeed, there was barely any evidence, bar those counterfeit weapons at the Ministry of the Interior, to suggest that it had even taken place. Gradually, however, the seriousness of the coup attempt became clear. General Miceli, it was revealed, had known about the coup well in advance, as had the army Chief of Staff, who was ready to provide weapons.

Indeed, within months another subversive organisation, Rosa dei Venti, had been created by veterans of Borghese's abortive coup. It was an alliance of senior army and intelligence officers again hoping to take over the reins of government. "The objective," proclaimed one of their early manifestos, "is to fight against the political, unionist, and governmental braggarts, and against all those who cooperate and sustain the chameleons of this putrid democracy."[7] Borghese died in exile in Spain in 1974, the same year Miceli was arrested for his part in that other, related organisation, Rosa dei Venti. Those who had taken part in the Borghese coup were accused of "armed insurrection against the state," but by 1984 all had been acquitted on appeal. As ever, not one conviction followed the crime. Indeed, since then the coup has been portrayed as nothing more than a left-wing hallucination.

In any other country, the coup, if that's what it was, would be a sort of historical cul-de-sac, an example of a few politicians or militarists taking a wrong turning. But in Italy, because every intrigue is so secretive, the subject was never satisfactorily resolved. Confessions and revelations emerge from dubious pentiti years and decades after the event, usually bringing confusion rather than clarity. Just as the Sofri case was reaching its conclusion, a pentito came forward claiming to have the missing link to explain one of the country's many illustrious corpses: the disappearance and assumed murder of a journalist in the *autumn of 1970. The journalist, claimed the* pentito, *had been murdered because he had discovered plans for the coup. No one, of course, knew whether the confessions of a Mafioso more than three decades after the event were reliable, but they were certainly, in the political climate then, poignant: the brother of the murdered journalist was, at the time of the new revelations, Minister of Education; at the same time, on the opposition benches, were two members of the National Alliance who had been intimate colleagues of Borghese's, posing for photographs with him before the coup.*

Nineteen seventy-one: the iconography of Pino Pinelli, the anarchist who died during questioning in the Milan police station, was becoming ever more like that of Che Guevara; his name was endlessly invoked on thousands of banners and city walls. Meanwhile, the destinies of the two men held responsible for their deaths in popular opinion (the policeman Luigi Calabresi and a former colonel of the Bolivian police, Roberto Quintanilla, respectively) became bizarrely intertwined. The latter had been killed on 1 April 1971 in Hamburg, at the residence of the Bolivian consul. The gun used by the killer, a Colt Cobra .38, had been purchased by the publisher Giangiacomo Feltrinelli in Milan in 1968. Reports in the Italian press suggested that Feltrinelli had met with the killer, a German called Monica Ertl, throughout the months preceding the murder. Others, of course, suggested it was another sophisticated put-up job by the Italian police—more precisely, by that Office for Reserved Affairs at the Ministry of the Interior which was desperate to frame the rich revolutionary. In little over a year, both Calabresi and Feltrinelli would also be dead.

In May 1971, Pinelli's body was exhumed as evidence in the libel case between Lotta Continua's *editor and Calabresi. On 4 October, an arrest warrant was issued for Calabresi (though he was, posthumously, declared innocent of all charges in 1975).*

The spring of 1972 is the twisted, intricate knot of all the threads at the beginning of the anni di piombo. *On 3 March, the Red Brigades conducted their first, highly publicised kidnapping. On the sixteenth of the same month, Enrico Berlinguer was elected leader of the Communist Party. The publisher Giangiacomo Feltrinelli was killed as he allegedly attached explosives to a pylon outside Milan. In May, a young anarchist, Franco Serantini, was killed in Pisa by police at an anti-Fascist rally. It was, crucially, at a meeting to commemorate the death of Serantini that Sofri allegedly ordered the killing of Calabresi (another policeman accused, of course, of killing another anarchist).*

The first warning of what had happened to Luigi Calabresi was a call received at the central line of the Milan police station at 9:15 on 17 May 1972: "There's a man shot in Via Cherubini . . . it's Commissioner Calabresi . . . he's bleeding from his head."[8] Calabresi was slumped on the pavement outside his house, next to his red Fiat Cinquecento, with bullet wounds to his head and left lung. One journalist who arrived at the scene recalled the "leaden atmosphere . . . the police and carabinieri *considered themselves at war against groups on the left." Calabresi was transported to the San Carlo hospital, but pronounced dead within half an hour. He was thirty-five, and left a pregnant wife and two sons. Witnesses claimed to have seen a blue Fiat 125, number-plate Mi-16802, driven by a blond woman. A man described as near six feet tall had fired the shots. The killing was, wrote* Lotta Continua *the next day, "a deed in which the exploited recognise their own yearning for justice."[9]*

In 1988, Leonardo Marino, the crêpe seller on the Tuscan coast, came forward with his version of events. Marino claimed that Sofri had ordered the killing of Calabresi after the rally to commemorate Serantini, the murdered anarchist. Sofri and his two "accomplices" were sensationally arrested in 1988, starting twelve years of trials, retrials, arrests, and releases until that final verdict in October 2000. Partly because of the paucity of evidence against the former members of Lotta Continua, the imagery of the case became vital. Sofri was endlessly described as "too intelligent," as "arrogant" and insufficiently contrite for the obscene rhetoric of the early 1970s. Just as the case was opening, Gemma Capri, Calabresi's widow, published a memoir titled Calabresi, My Husband. *Elegant and blond, she was present throughout each trial and retrial.*

From the outset, Sofri has shown an almost aesthetic disdain for the legal pontificating. Writing of his first trial, he says: "The process has been diverted by gestures and tones closer to an auto-da-fé *rather than a civil trial. Suddenly tears and sweat, imprecations and furores . . . have overpowered and replaced the confrontation of the facts." Sofri accused the judicial circus of being "in bad taste" ("demagogic and windbag-ish"). Relying on their intuition, people had, said Sofri, been taken in by the "fat cry-baby" pentito Leonardo Marino.*[10]

Sofri was, however, apologetic about the tone of his and others' writings from decades ago:

> *The articles which accompanied the Calabresi campaign were horrible . . . The articles in* Lotta Continua *are witness to a degenerative parabola which accompanied not only this case . . . The violence and the crudity and also the brutality of the things we were writing were precisely to do with the desire to obtain real justice . . . not to let what we thought had happened [to Pino Pinelli] in the Milan* questura *go unpunished . . . [I]n the course of the campaign, that position became habitual, complacent: a sort of inert taste for insults, lynchings, for threats which took control of us, and not only us.*[11]

As another witness at the trial explained it: "We were at war, it was the perverse logic of the era."

As with the Piazza Fontana trial, not just individuals but an entire diaspora of former colleagues and "extremists" were on trial. Lotta Continua was a sort of cradle for an intellectual caste in Italy which has now, years later, graduated into the media and Parliament. Former Lotta Continua members are regulars on cultural chat shows; they work as TV anchormen (for Berlusconi), as senators, and as academics. The "Lotta Continua lobby" (many of whom were also accused by Marino in 1988, before charges were dropped) have thus fought to clear not only Sofri's name but also, by association, their own. And Sofri himself is second to none in terms of media manipulation and contribution: his byline appears so regularly in newspapers and magazines that anyone who didn't know otherwise would think he was the country's most famous journalist rather than its most famous "murderer."

It would be too strong to say that Sofri has willed himself into this position, but in stubbornly and repeatedly requesting not liberty but justice, he must have been conscious that he would become a secular martyr. Sofri finds himself in prison, wrote one journalist in October 2000, the day after the closure of his case, "for not having doffed his cap to the bureaucratic caste of the judiciary."[12] Now, in the autumn of 2000, Sofri is the only one of the four accused of the crime still in prison. The pentito *Leonardo Marino was almost immediately released. Of the other accomplices, one (Giorgio Pietrostefani) escaped to exile in France after the Venice trial of 2000 (from where he has been interviewed by the press, but untroubled by extradition); and another (Ovidio Bompressi) also went into hiding, subsequently handed himself in, and was then confined to house arrest on medical grounds.*

Sofri, on the other hand, has cast himself as the niggling point of clarity and honesty, refusing the fudge of exile or illness. The case is now only Sofri's. It has become, in his words, a case not about "my future life but about the past, more dear and vulnerable . . . [T]his affair risks hijacking not only my material existence . . . but that of my own soul."[13]

Sofri has an almost boyish face: he's very relaxed, very witty. He asks me to address him with the informal *tu*. He has a loud voice, and adds *capisci?*, "understand?," to the end of every sentence, projecting himself as the earnest professor he might, in other circumstances, have been. Deprived of any recording device, I have to transcribe his polysyllabic words at the speed of light.

"There's a very strong, virulent civil violence in Italy," he says. "It's abnormal, monstrous, grotesque. Italians wallow in the fact that they are *bravi ragazzi*, 'good people,' measured and antique . . . But there's an endemic violence between neighbours which lurks like a kind of fever under the skin." The Italian words he uses to describe this atmosphere are *una disponibilità alla riscossa*, which means more or less "a disposition for revolt." "In the 1970s there was an atavistic, militant tension, a belief that there was a moral need for thought and action. Many felt that the Italy which emerged from the Second World War was divided into two parts, Catholics versus Communists, all that Don Camillo stuff. And many saw the history of anti-Fascism as a kind of incomplete emancipation, another example that everything in this country remains either half-done or betrayed.

"But that notion of a 'creeping civil war' is a beautification of the case. Both sides—the state and elements of the far right, and the blundering criminality of the left—just fed on themselves. They fatally believed their own rhetoric, so what culminated was an imagined civil war, a simulation of a civil war. The *anni di piombo* were just the usual Italian struggle, the usual fratricidal/patricidal goings-on within city-states, a sort of multiplication of opposing views from the peripheries, from the 'bell-towers.' My case, for example, is a tempest in a teacup. I'm not saying it's not horrible, but it's not part of some epic encounter between two sides. My case shows simple personal hatred, denuded, revealed in its full horror: it's nothing more than the exaltation of hate and grudge."

Sofri is blunt and cynical. I ask him about the new trial for Piazza Fontana. "The danger is that the trial might confirm an idea which I don't share, namely that there might possibly be a degree of clarity about the Piazza Fontana bombing. This late recognition of what the 'counter-information' of the left was saying at the time is strange. For the togas to talk about 'a slaughter of the state,' using exactly the same words as we did back then, sounds a little false. Those were our slogans of extremism. And the fact that it is based upon very dubious *pentiti* takes something away from the case . . . [*P*]*entitismo* is, as we all know, a very slippery mechanism."

Sofri throws out grandiose concepts in every sentence, sometimes following them up later in the conversation, sometimes leaving them hanging dislocated in the air. His range of reference is bewildering, peppered with the leitmotif of Italian cerebrality, the suggestive subjunctive. He swaps languages without pause.

Why is it, I wonder, that no historian or court or journalist ever seems able to unearth the truth, or even a convincing interpretation, about Italian history? "I think," he replies, "that things are actually much more simple than that. *Dietrologia* [conspiracy theorising] is an air that you breathe in Italy. It's the result of paranoia and jealousy, and it simply exalts an intricate intelligence. It's like Othello with Desdemona's handkerchief: one innocent object can spark off endless suspicions. It's a game which people play, almost to show off. I prefer not to see a conspiracy which exists and to see one where it doesn't.

"I don't say that there aren't many dark or dodgy things:

people always say football matches are fixed because probably very often they are!" He guffaws. "And there is a type of wretchedness about the Italian state, with its tricks and deceits and dirty businesses. But here a rationalist would cry. When one says things, with evidence and facts, you're not believed. When something's so obviously *verosimile*, it can't be the *verità*; it would be too simple: it would be too obvious, too easy, so it can't be true . . .

"Look at my case. I've never said that it's inconceivable that the far left had something to do with the murder of Calabresi. I've simply asserted with frankness that I was never, never in any way responsible. It's the stuff of madmen. When we spoke of the 'general encounter' for the autumn of 1972, we meant the possibility of renegotiating a whole host of communal contracts, not that some killing would be the spark for armed revolution."

He leaves no doubt as to his contempt for the judiciary: "full of ambition, symptomatic of the Italian delirium for omnipotence. Judges seem to think they are almost literary critics, re-evaluating novels. Or else they pretend to be the 'good guardians.' It's a monstrous deformity. We in Lotta Continua worked very much in the light of day, in fact sometimes with too much ostentation and pretension. Ours was an experimental adventure. Not an adventure in the sense of dangling yourself off a bridge with elastic tied to your ankle, not in that sense of extreme sports . . . Ours was a communal interpretation of the world, a mixing of languages, an exciting crossbreeding of cultures. It all culminated in an extraordinary mimesis, a humane, though almost virtuoso, imitation of those around us. We were social, almost becoming others."

He describes the typical trajectory of bourgeois children feeling the gravitational pull of the workers. "We could use their language, learn their customs, appreciate and participate in their struggles. In the end, we realised it almost deprived us of our own identities. We realised we had to start taking things seriously. It all changed when women suddenly declared they were feminists . . . A few people did try to continue the mimesis, a kind of psychological transvestism." He laughs again.

"I now cull my political ideas from the same places as everyone else, from television and newspapers. That's one of the strange things, that people outside live as if they were in prison, stuck in front of the television. Most of my articles I have to write from memory, because it's not like there's a massive library here. But I get fucked off when people say I'm more free than them, because I can sit here with my thoughts. Prison is abominable—a torture, a physical torment, a sexual mutilation. We're like scavengers on society's rubbish."

Leaving the prison, I go to a bar to read the day's papers. In one, it being the twenty-fifth anniversary of Franco's death, one of the Spanish dictator's maxims is quoted: "One is the master of what one doesn't say, and the slave of what one does." The phrase, despite its provenance, seems apposite for Sofri. He is a talker, a man who loves words, especially— say many—his own. In fact, Sofri is frequently accused of pompousness, of arrogance, of a yearning to be the protagonist; he's an intellectual who enjoyed the 1970s *engagé* game of cowboys and Indians, according to a friend. And yet it's very rare to meet anyone who doesn't express "reasonable doubt" about Sofri's conviction. At most some say he's guilty verbally, guilty of having been incautious with his words. He has been convicted simply for talking too much, for boasting and provoking. He is, I realise, a very literal prisoner of his own past, a "slave" of the words he has spoken.

A few months later: December 2000. With an election expected in spring, the political exchanges are getting worse. Two bombs, one allegedly anarchist, quickly followed by the Fascist "reply," have sent shivers down the spine of the body politic. "Something strange is happening," admits the secretary of the Democrats of the Left, "terrorists are shooting again . . . there's a return to a situation of tension." Everyone describes a sense of déjà vu, a sense of disbelief that, years after the anni di piombo *were thought to have petered out, these bombs are still being prepared and planted. It seems absurd and surreal. As one dismayed journalist writes:*

> *Here again are the ghosts which stink of dynamite . . . [I]n most European countries, governments of left and right alternate without any problems of public order or security. Not in Italy, where it seems [the bombs] will never finish. And the hands of the clock actually seem to have gone backwards . . .*[14]

The first device was found on 18 December, placed a few metres away from Piazza Fontana, amongst the steeples of Milan's gothic duomo. It was left in a black bag next to a public passageway, though timed to go off at 3 a.m. The anarchist trail is immediately under suspicion, particularly since the explosive used (called "Vulcan 03" or "quarry dust") was used in other recent anarchist bombs. The bomb is later claimed by a group called Solidarietà Internazionale. The response from the right is swift. On 22 December, a former "black" terrorist decided to enter the offices of Il Manifesto, *the "Communist daily," as it calls itself, in Rome. On the fourth floor, shortly after midday, he asked for directions, explaining, "I've got to deliver a package to Manifesto." His bomb, however, exploded before he reached his target, lacerating his legs and giving him multiple fractures. Doors were blown off hinges, and a photograph the next day showed a poignant image: one dusty shoe, that of Andrea Insabato, the bomber, upon a mound of glass, papers, and masonry. By chance Insabato was the only one hurt, but—as* Il Manifesto

wrote the following day—"if the bomb hadn't exploded before ex-
pected, it could have been a slaughter."

Piecing together Insabato's curriculum vitae as a terrorist
was fairly simple. He was an adherent of NAR, the far-right
Nuclei Armati Rivoluzionari, and of Terza Posizione in the
1970s. He was arrested in 1976 when, at the age of seventeen, he
fired a pistol against one of the offices of the Communist Party
in Rome. More recently, in 1992, during a football match be-
tween Lazio and Torino, he ostentatiously burnt the Israeli flag,
shouting, "Ebrei ai forni," "Jews to the ovens." Just days before
the bomb against Il Manifesto he had attended, on the occasion
of Jörg Haider's invitation to the Vatican, a rally in favour of
the Austrian politician, carrying a Palestinian flag.

On its defiant front page (titled "Siamo qui"—"We're here")
the day after the attack, Il Manifesto blamed the attack on the
"cultural humus which has allowed the neo-Fascists to be cleared
through customs and which has offered them political legiti-
macy." Inside, the editorial continued the attack, suggesting
that Insabato was the product of "the hypocritical right of Fini
and Berlusconi, which has never had the courage to deal with its
bloody history, as has—with difficulty and pain—a part of the
non-institutional left. This is the result. The sewer is still there,
with its great unpunished and its little soldiers." Italian terror-
ism, lamented the then Prime Minister, Giuliano Amato, is "a
volcano which is never spent." Another magistrate, investigating
the "new" Red Brigades, called Italy's terrorism "an under-
ground river . . . which suddenly re-emerges ever more violent."
Terrorism in Italy, he said, is "almost physiological." It's what
everyone seemed to say; as Alberto Arbasino once wrote, terror-
ism "has rapidly become an ethnic thing, a typical Italian spe-
ciality, part of the conventional countryside along with La
Mamma, the siesta, and pizza."[15]

A couple of years later, a similar sense of déjà vu. Marco Bi-
agi, a university professor who had written the White Paper of

proposed changes to employment law, was shot and killed at point-blank range as he returned on a bike to his house in Bologna. The scene under the arches outside his house presented a familiar picture: puddles of blood, the Red Brigade's five-pointed star etched onto the wall, numbered cards propped up on the asphalt where the bullets had been found. Responsibility for the killing was claimed in a twenty-six-page manifesto sent to an Internet news agency by the BR-PCC, the Red Brigades–Combatant Communist Party. Again the tragedy was almost unsurprising: Roberto Maroni, Biagi's boss in the government, said wistfully, "I can't say I'm surprised." Romano Prodi summed up the situation: "It's an endless chain of blood. It's a long, obscure line which has been with us for many years." The same pistol, it emerged, had probably killed Massimo D'Antona (another exponent of Labour Law reforms) three years before. To add to the sense of intrigue, one person investigating both murders was found hanged in his flat a few months later.

Bemused by it all, I began to read the decades of historians and sociologists who have analysed Italy's "terrorist phenomenon." Many have echoed the line that "terrorism does not invent, but rediscovers, recycles, and readapts that which is already in the womb of the nation," suggesting that there's something uniquely Italian about the country's terrorism.[16] *Many of the early studies of the* anni di piombo *thus suggested that the country had a "psychosis of the bomb." Ever since the Risorgimento, the argument went, the country had had a culture of violence which was "living and important." According to that theory, the historical roots of the* anni di piombo *were clear: In 1894 the French President had been killed by Italian anarchists, as were, later, the Spanish Prime Minister and the Empress of the Austro-Hungarian Empire. In 1900 Umberto I was assassinated; in 1921, in a theatre in Milan, another bomb claimed the lives of more than twenty people. In 1928, eighteen were killed during an attempt to assassinate another Italian monarch. Violence,*

*from the Risorgimento to the Resistenza, had been the catalyst
for every important turning point in Italian history. "No other
industrialised society," wrote one academic in the Rivista Storica Italiana in 1980, "has seen a terrorist phenomenon which, for
duration . . . diffusion and rootedness, can compare with that of
Italy."*

*More subtly, many have suggested that politicians have been
responsible for the terrorism. Some observers—like Sergio
Flamigni—hold certain politicians directly responsible as puppets of terrorists, as if terrorism were an extension of politics by
other means. But one doesn't have to go that far to understand
that there's something in political discourse here which, albeit indirectly and unwittingly, ushers in terrorism. The role of Parliament during the 1970s was decisive. Parliament was described
as a "conventio ad excludendum," an imperfect two-party system in which one party was permanently in power and the other
permanently excluded. Either that, or the opposition was fatally
accommodated, becoming part of the "constitutional arch," the
political "marriage" of opposing parties. There was the "opening
to the left" (involving the Socialists) or the "historic compromise"
(involving the Communists). The Christian Democrats were
thus described by Leonardo Sciascia as "invertebrate, available, conceding, and at the same time tenacious, patient, grasp-
ing; a type of octopus which knows how gently to embrace dissent
to return it, minced, into consensus."[17] Opposition was, effectively, impossible thanks to a unique aspect of Italian politics:
trasformismo. It's what Angelo Panebianco, in his essay
"Democrazia sommersa" (Submerged democracy), called "an
unhealthy relationship between government and opposition."[18]
In the words of Giulio Bollati, it was the "ability to take over the
themes and words of the opposition in order to empty them of any
meaning"; it was "a readiness to let oneself be captured," epitomised by "arguments in public and agreements in the corridors."
Trasformismo is appearance, spectacle, indifference to the items*

under discussion. Its aim is power."[19] Trasformismo, *according to critics of the Italian Parliament, meant that it didn't matter whom one voted for; despite differences at the hustings, all politicians were playing the same secretive game at the expense of the public. There was, for decades, no effective parliamentary opposition, and thus the solution for many radicals was extra-parliamentary and all that that implied. Terrorism was—in fact, is—the natural flip side of* trasformismo. *One was always compromise, the other its complete, and violent, contradiction.*

Thus some commentators on the "armed struggle" used the birth of British parliamentarianism as an example of what exactly was wrong with Italy: quoting Thomas Hobbes, writers such as Giorgio Galli saw the birth of the British Parliament as a means to contain the English Civil War. Verbal exchanges and the alternation of parties replaced cruder confrontations as representative democracy became "the game which impeded a civil war."[20] *That such exchanges were conspicuously absent in Italy meant that, in some sense, the latent civil war never found itself absorbed, reflected, or pacified by Parliament, and so raged on outside it. It's what Alberto Arbasino, in one of his meditations on the 1970s, called the "iron fist" of terrorism counterpointing the "quicksand" of Italian politics:*[21] *Since Parliament seemed, to an extra-parliamentary minority, unable to address certain issues, the only response was either "fists" or, worse, pistols.*

Even with the advent of a more confrontational, bipolar politics, politicians have been held indirectly responsible for terrorism. With all the finger-pointing, the hysterical "Fascist!" and "Communist!" jeers of the feverish politics, politicians unwittingly give rogue terrorists a sense of purpose and a rhetoric they understand. Such was the analysis, albeit more muted, offered by Gerardo D'Ambrosio in Milan in 2000 shortly after the bomb there. "We had hoped," he said, "that the resort to bombs for political purposes was finished . . . unfortunately it's not so . . . Every time the political exchanges get more bitter, one can al-

ways expect that someone will try to exploit the situation."[22] *Not only politicians, with their hyperbolic criticisms of opponents, but also intellectuals have been under accusation: Alberto Arbasino has written about "the responsibility and irresponsibility of the intellectuals," mentioning "the grey areas and ambiguities." It's not that campuses are necessarily cradles for terrorists but that their incautious language (the real, linguistic accusation against Sofri) ferments and foments. Many perceived an ideological overlap between terrorists and intellectuals, a caste of society which, in Italy, is esteemed higher than any other. The real difference between many terrorists and many intellectuals was a debate not about the end aspired to but about the most appropriate means towards it.*

Others discerned what was called cattocomunismo, *the quasi-religious, millenarian zeal of the terrorists. These evangelicals, having lost their orthodox faith, were still attempting to "realise the other world in this world," to pass "from an exigency of Christian totality to Marxist totality." One left-wing guru had, for example, spoken of Communists as a race born of a "virgin mother," and of his political group as a "combatant religious order." "The need," wrote one journalist, "for total and definitive answers, the rejection of doubt, are at the same time Catholic and Communist."*[23] *"The Red Brigades," wrote Indro Montanelli, "are, at least in origin, a cross between two different creeds: the Catholic and the Communist."*[24]

The end of the Cold War, and the not-unrelated eclipse of the Christian Democratic party, have given studies a new dimension, contextualising the anni di piombo *within an international framework. Against the backdrop of the Warsaw Pact and the North Atlantic Treaty Organisation, Italy has been seen as a border territory, on a knife-edge between the two sides. The reasons for what has been called a "tragic frontier experience" were both geographical (Italy being seen as literally on the front line) and political (the country had the largest Commu-*

*nist Party in the Western world, winning 19 per cent of the vote
in 1946 and thereafter increasing its polling at every election
until its peak in 1976 with 34.4 per cent). Thus historians have
written of postwar Italy as being "on the nerve front between the
West and Communism, for the entire Cold War under constant
observation, and its democracy ever under surveillance."[25] If
the terrorism of the 1960s and 1970s was chilling, it was because
that violence was a reflection of the Cold War, isolated examples
of a greater global conflict. As such, the acts of terrorism were
"signs of war, fragments of a planetary war fought underground which every now and again surfaced with its horror, its
devastating potential . . . to destroy all that it touched: peace, the
democratic confrontation, the truth . . . surfaced and moved on,
leaving behind blood and darkness . . ."[26]*

*In that respect, Italy has been compared to Germany, another
country torn in two by the "spaccatura dell'Europa," the rift of
an entire continent. The difference is that Italy witnessed "an
invisible iron curtain, crossing populations, classes, and con-
sciences," which "shattered" the unity of the country into "two
political, civil, and moral realities . . . almost two countries."[27]
Whereas in Germany a wall had become a very literal, concrete
example of a divided nation, in Italy the cleavage was ever more
subtle and submerged: Italy's "iron curtain" remained largely
invisible. The clandestine nature of the "armed struggle" was, in
fact, revealed to the Italian Parliament in 1990, when Giulio
Andreotti announced that ever since 1945 there had been a military presence on the peninsula called Gladio (the so-called stay
behind of Allied troops); subsequent investigations revealed that
weaponry and personnel from much of the* anni di piombo *overlapped with those of Gladio.*

*An equally serious problem was that Italy's postwar foreign
policy zigzagged unpredictably, swerving from philo-Arabic
policies (Colonel Gaddafi had even become one of Fiat's major
shareholders) to support for Israel. The timing of Italian*

"slaughters" was often uncannily close to similar events on what the president of the Slaughter Commission called the "chessboard" of the Mediterranean, especially in the Middle East. Thus, according to some, Italy's anni di piombo were a result not only of the Cold War but also of the Arab-Israeli conflict.

But there was something else about the terrorism which interested me. It wasn't really about terrorism, more about the so-called *cronache nere*, the "black chronicles" which dominated the media. By then I had been in the country for a couple of years and had become used to watching not only programmes specifically about mysteries with political undercurrents, like the murders of school-girl Wilma Montesi or of oil magnate Enrico Mattei, but also crimes and court cases played out in real time: Marta Russo, Novi Ligure, Cogne—all murder investigations which dragged on for months and then years, apparently hypnotising the entire country. The point, I thought, isn't that there are more murders in Italy than elsewhere. It's not even, despite the stereotype abroad, that Italy is a naturally violent country. The point is what happens after the murders: they become dramatised, televised, filmed, caught up in a media circus of flash bulbs, interviews, analyses on TV talk shows. Sometimes, as with the film *I cento passi*, the retelling is educational and noble. But often it's something baser. It reminded me of something an academic wrote in the 1970s. "Violence has mesmerised us," he wrote; it has been "aestheticised . . . rendered photogenic, if not exactly accepted, conferred with that fascination which is at the root of its hypnotic power."[28]

Crime, especially murder, is sensationalised, an opportunity for a macabre spectacle, like slowing down the car when you pass a gruesome traffic accident. It's the same the world over, of course, but certain aspects in Italy are very different: first of all, the blurring of fact and fiction. Everyone here can have an opinion on Marta Russo or Adriano Sofri or Cogne or Francesca Vacca Agusta because, in the end, we understand almost nothing about the crimes. There are no hard facts to go on. Witnesses, motives, magistrates—all are blurred until in the end the crime is just another topic for bar-room controversy and prey to televisual voracity. There's no sense of *sub judice*, so everyone is interviewed and analysed for years before the case even comes to court. In the end, it's obvious that, for example, certain TV studios become more important courtrooms than the real things. That ability to dramatise murders, to turn a grim crime into a gripping five-minute spectacular on the evening news, and then to spin it out for an entire evening of chat-show entertainment—with row upon row of leggy models offering their opinions about the murder weapon—is wholly Italian. And, of course, the more you talk about certain subjects, the less clarity there is. It becomes increasingly hard to see the wood for the trees.

I remember thinking vaguely about those topics one December as I was packing a bag to go back to Britain for Christmas. The beautiful, lilting voice of Fabrizio De André, the country's most famous and much-mourned singer-songwriter, came on the radio. The song, from 1973, is called "Il bombarolo" (The bomber) and is, like its subject-matter, an integral part of the nation's fibre. "Intellectuals of today," go the lyrics, "idiots of tomorrow, give me back my brain, which I only need between my hands. Acrobatic prophets of the revolution, today I'll do it by myself, without lessons . . . I've chosen another school. I'm a bomber."

The funny thing was that I didn't really want to go home. I wanted to see friends and family, but it was somehow an incredible wrench to leave Italy, even only for a few days. I had become as *campanilista*, as attached to my bell-tower, as everyone else. The thought of leaving Parma—nicknamed the *isola felice*, Italy's "happy island"—was worrying. I looked out the window and saw that it was snowing, the large flakes jittering like molecules under a microscope. I could see the rooftop tiles turning from pink to white. On the street below, people were putting skis on their roof-racks. Then, just as I was about to leave for the airport, my next-door neighbour Lucia dropped by to give me a sackful of her handmade *cappelletti* (the little pasta wraps of Parmesan cheese which come served in a watery broth at Christmas), as if to remind me of all the good food I would be missing in northern Europe.

There was another thing I would inevitably miss over Christmas. The sheer beauty of the country. The stunning style, the visual panache, the obsession with *spettacolo*. That, I knew as I sat on the plane, was what I would have to write about next: the Italian aesthetic. That, I thought, was the epicentre of what had troubled me about the *cronache nere*: it wasn't only the murders themselves but their televisual treatment. I knew I was living in the most beautiful country, a place which has produced the best art in the Western world and the greatest cinema of the twentieth century. But that was precisely the enigma: How is it that the most creative, cultured country in the world has the worst, most abysmal television on the planet?

5

THE MEANS OF SEDUCTION

Remember that an education through images has been typical of every absolutist and paternalistic society, from ancient Egypt to the Middle Ages. An image is an indisputable visual summary of a series of conclusions reached through cultural elaboration . . . [T]here's something about communication through images which is radically limited, insuperably reactionary.

—UMBERTO ECO

I don't know whether it's because of the Reformation, which was iconoclastic and "written," or because Britain has had, on the whole, the better writers and Italy much superior artists, but Italy is a visual country, Britain a literary one. Perhaps it's because there's such a forest of legal and bureaucratic language, very few people read newspapers, even fewer buy or borrow books. Every year or so there are official figures about "book consumption" from ISTAT, the national statistical research unit, and the results are always the same: a massive percentage of Italian adults don't read one book a year. To survive, the *edicole*—the little pavilions on street corners which sell newspapers—have to double as fetish-shops, selling gadgets and videos and soft- to hard-porn magazines alongside the newsprint. There is, one quickly realises, no populist press, and there will be an Italian best seller (Andrea Camilleri is the most recent example) only once a decade.

Reading, when it's done at all, is done under duress. Few of my students, I get the impression, have ever read a book for pleasure. The more time you spend in the universities, the more you realise that they are part of what the Italian media call the "illiteracy problem." Teaching is based on dictation rather than discussion. I've seen dozens of lecture halls in which a professor reads out his own book to his students. If someone interrupts the dictation with a question about what has been read, the affronted professor will pause, then go back and read the sentence again without explanation. Reviewing for exams involves buying and rereading the professor's book and learning it by heart.

Visually, though, the country is more cultured than any other. Each church feels like a museum: go into the duomo in Parma and, with a five-hundred-lira coin, you can light up the entire cupola and admire the angels and Apostles who usher the Madonna into heaven. This *Assumption of the Virgin* is the work of the city's most famous artist, Correggio (Antonio Allegri). Titian commented on the work: "Reverse the cupola and fill it with gold, and even that will not be its money's worth." (Dickens, visiting centuries later when the frescos were crumbling, was more scathing: "Such a labyrinth of arms and legs: such heaps of foreshortened limbs, entangled and involved and jumbled together. No operative surgeon, gone mad, could imagine in his wildest delirium."[1]) Every week, even in the smallest towns around Parma, a new art exhibition will open. A lot of my friends seem to be budding sculptors or photographers, or are studying the popular degree course in *beni culturali* (the appreciation and restoration of "cultural goods"). Many happily talk to me for hours, without a trace of pretension, about why one architect or artist is worthy of note.

Even on a more lowbrow level, the visual finesse of the country is always obvious. When I look out my window, I can see exquisite geometric chaos. Ripples of pink tiles, each roof facing a different direction from the one next door. The city looks like something from a fairy tale, or at least from another century. The whole place is immaculately lit up with minimal white lights which, through the foggy air, look like candles. People ride bicycles which seem to have been in the family for generations. *Palazzi* are propped up by columns which look as delicate and thin as pencils. The house fronts are all brightly coloured, normally the mellow, vaguely regal yellow which is called "Parma yellow" (a colour popularised by Duchess Maria Luigia, Napoleon's widow, who reigned in Parma in the early nineteenth century). Perhaps it's just that the sun shines so often: as you—used to rainy evenings in ugly British cities—watch the warm glow of a sunset, the rays kissing the marble and glinting off sunglasses, you realise that there's an entire spectrum of colour which is lacking farther north.

The care put into buying shoes, tablecloths, handbags, and clothes is extraordinary and, for a foreigner, unfathomable. When you buy a bouquet of flowers, it will take twenty minutes for the florist to prepare its presentation: leaves and sprays are added and discussed, paper and ribbons turned and twisted, and then removed if the colours are thought to clash. Shops are like stylised grottoes: salami hanging like bats from the rafters, corridors of fresh basil and rosemary lining your path to the counter. Buying clothes involves a level of sophistication and visual nuance which I didn't even know existed. Before coming to Italy, I had only ever heard of "green," possibly "light green" and "dark green," but here I was asked in shops to choose between pea-green, olive-green, bottle-green, clear-green, acid-green, water-green, lemon-green, sage-green, and so on.

The consequences of that visual rather than literary culture are evident everywhere. It's often hard to find anything which is remotely ugly, be it a building or a painting or, especially, someone's clothing. Italy, of course, produces the world's most esteemed fashion retailers, be they for the high street or the catwalk: Versace, Armani, Valentino, Max Mara, Benetton, Diesel, Dolce & Gabbana. The care about clothing means that you can go into a shop and describe the colour, cut, stitching style, and buttons you want on a shirt, and the shopkeeper will invariably find it. As in the restaurants, the more specific and picky you are, the more you're esteemed: "I would like a black shirt of a silk-cotton mix, no pockets, horizontal buttonholes, French cuffs but with a Venetian collar. Oh, and preferably minimally tapered towards the waist." If you get that far, however bad your Italian, you will have the respect of everyone in earshot. (The sartorial vocabulary is, like that for food, enough to fill a separate dictionary.)

That preening might sound like vanity, but it's not. It's simply a precision about presentation. Even at two in the morning, groups of women gather outside shop-windows and discuss the width of sandal straps in the same amicably heated way that old men discuss Verdi. Fashion is followed slavishly. When the "season" changes, and it happens almost overnight, the *cognoscenti* all begin wearing the same colour: last year lilac, this year yellow. Personal grooming is taken very seriously, by both men and women. As you drive out of town, huge billboards advertise the transplant cure for baldness: "Hair for Anyone Who Has a Head." Often if you casually say to someone, "You're looking well," the reply is: "Thanks. Yep, I've just done a [UV] lamp." I, being British, would be embarrassed, but here there's no bashfulness about wanting to look good. Tanning techniques are minutely discussed and dissected. A mountain tan, I learnt, has a different "depth" and "tone" from a beach tan.

Linguistically, of course, beauty is ever present. I sometimes play football on a team on the outskirts of Parma, and whenever I arrive in the changing room—and it happens to everyone—I'm greeted with kisses: "Hello, beautiful," or *"Ciao carissimo"* (Hello, dearest).

"Listen," I said to Luigi, our speedy winger, as we were lacing up our boots one Saturday, "you've got a trial with an English team next week, right?"

"Yes, beautiful."

"In England?"

"Yes, beautiful."

"Well, Luigi," I wanted to say it tactfully, "just don't call the English players 'beautiful' or 'dearest,' and don't kiss them, OK?" It was as if I had told him that the English don't have friends. He couldn't understand how men could behave so coldly towards each other.

"But," he was clearly bewildered, "if I can't tell my new football friends they are beautiful and dear to me, what can I say?"

"I don't know. You have to remember, beautiful, that you Italians are just much more civilised than us."

By now I've become so used to the sheer style that I can recognise northern Europeans at a hundred metres. They have grey hair, or none at all. They look awkward with their sunglasses. Young male backpackers don't have the complicated facial hair which is another Italian art form. Each time I look in the mirror, I hear Italo Calvino's description of

goofy and anti-aesthetic groups of Germans, English, Swiss, Dutch, and Belgians . . . men and women with variegated ugliness, with certain trousers at the knees, with socks in sandals or with bare feet in shoes, some clothes printed with flowers, underwear which sticks out, some white and red meat, deaf to good taste and harmony even in the changing of its colour . . .[2]

Northern Europeans, Italians know, are simply less stylish. The British also, I'm often told, spend so much time reading they forget to wash. Either way, British personal presentation is like British football: inelegant.

That search for beauty and style has its logical extension: a simmering but unmistakable sense of erotica. Every Italian town has one street which becomes, at that idyllic sunset hour when everything slows down, a free-for-all catwalk. Couples and widows and children and the card-sharks from the square walk back and forth, greeting and gossiping with friends. In Parma people will almost always look you up and down to get an overall picture of your size and style. Women, often men, will hold your stare for a second longer than is subtle (which, I suppose, makes shades imperative). It often seems that flirting is the oil of all human interaction. Frustrated young men in Italy constantly complain that it's all *fumo niente arrosto* (smoke and no roast), that—crudely—all the flirtation is a road to nowhere. Whatever the destination, though, it's an amusing journey because there are so many siren voices, so many seductive distractions.

It was late spring when the sexual tension in my university class, latent throughout the long winter, came to the fore. Maria Immacolata (Mary Immaculate), my favourite student, began coming to class with little more than a chiffon sarong thrown over a minimalist bikini. She's the daughter of an ice-cream magnate from Bari and was always the first to arrive, the last to leave. "What I miss most from Bari," she said coquettishly, aware that we were alone and that I was admiring her iodine skin, "are the waves." To illustrate, she rocked her pelvis backwards and forwards as if making love to the chair.

Then, as casually as if she were asking the time, she said, "Are you betrothed?" A few days later I found a fantastically explicit love-letter rolled up and shoved inside the handlebars of my bicycle.

Eroticism is everywhere. Even going shopping, if you're of a mildly puritan bent, is unnerving. The underwear section of one national department store is called "cuddles and seduction." There are more *intimerie*, "intimate" lingerie shops, in Parma than any other kind. The shop with the highest turnover per square metre in the whole of Italy is a lingerie shop on the outskirts of the city. It is, you quickly realise, another art form, taken to giddy heights of detailed eroticism. I have even been asked by a sleek shop assistant, on one apparently simple mission to buy candles, what sort of girl I was entertaining: "If it's a first date, I would suggest either pine or opium as the appropriate scents."

"But it's just for myself. Can't I go with something simple like vanilla?"

"Ah, you're English!" she said sympathetically, as if suddenly understanding my ignorance about the nuances of buying wax.

I used to ask my students to give ten-minute lectures in English on whatever subject they wanted. In the course of the year three girls chose, independently of each other, to lecture on lingerie. Never was the classroom so alive. There was a heated debate about when exactly a *perizoma* (a G-string) should be worn, about whether showing knickers straps outside your skirt is now out of fashion, about which push-up (Wonderbra) suits which form of breast. The male students, too, were suddenly awoken from their slumber, asking earnest questions about the implications of suspenders as presents and the strength of transparent straps.

That refreshing candidness about erotica means that never is there a sex scandal in Italy. Politicians, despite their Catholic avowals, proudly partner the most pendulous, beautiful celebrities, doing their credibility only good. In Britain "sex and drugs" is the dream tabloid story; in Italy it's just not news. One of Bettino Craxi's Socialist ministers in the 1980s enjoyed such a swinging lifestyle that he even wrote a book about Italian discos and their "culture." Another book published on the golden years of Craxi was written by Sandra Milo, an "actress" and acolyte of Socialist circles. She described orgiastic parties, invariably placing herself and famous politicians centre stage. Being much more mature than the British about such things, most Italians, if told that their local politician is enjoying a sex-and-drugs lifestyle, would express envy rather than outrage. Thus Berlusconi's former under-secretary at the Culture Ministry, a learned art critic called Vittorio Sgarbi, is admired for his fine taste not only in Renaissance art but also in women taken from the "dubious actress" drawer. He has such an amorous reputation that he stars in advertisements for a coffee brand: he's married to an ugly woman until he takes a sip, and he's then surrounded once again by beautiful nymphs. Every week he's asked onto talk shows to give his opinions on the female form and on the etiquette of sexual encounters. Berlusconi himself fell in love with his second wife, Veronica Lario, as she stripped on-stage during a performance of Fernand Crommelynck's *The Magnificent Cuckold*.

Cuckoldry is, of course, the flip side of the flirting. There is a knife-edge between flirting and infidelity, and given the ubiquity of the former, there's also a widespread paranoia about becoming a cuckold (which, as Italian referees know, is the worst insult you can level at a man). Long television chat shows are dedicated to either how to cheat successfully on your partner or how to avoid it happening to you. Another billboard frequently seen in Italy features a giant magnifying glass, advertising the services of a private detective: "Are You

Sure You Can Trust Her?" Graffiti on street walls often pub-
licises an enemy's shame: "Rinaldi Is a Cuckold!" There's a
whole niche humour about cuckoldry, and understanding the
various nuances about "being horned" takes years. Listen to
the endless conversations on the subject, and it becomes
obvious that, as well as the seething jealousy, there is a more
mature attitude towards the improbability of monogamy:
"Horns are like teeth," goes a Roman proverb, "it hurts
when they grow, but they give flavour to life."

In a culture which is so "visual," and which eschews anything
written, television has become the crucial source of infotainment. The minutes spent in front of TVs in Italy is on average, according to ISTAT, around 240 minutes per day (the
figure creeps up each year). This naturally means that, as an
instrument of political propaganda, it is unrivalled. It reminds
me of something Sofri had said, about how Italians outside
prison live the same life as he does, as if they were actually
locked up and stuck in front of the television. It is also om-
nipresent: in most bars and even restaurants the noise of a
football match or a garish quiz show will accompany conversation. When you walk down any street, you hear the drone
of a dozen television sets.

I had expected television to be another example of Italian
visual brilliance, a continuation of the enjoyable beauty and
erotica. Instead, switching on the television was like introducing an insistent shopkeeper into the living-room. Almost
all the time, the TV was trying to sell me something. Programmes are interrupted by promotional messages, which are
also euphemistically called "consumer advice" by presenters
who walk to another part of the studio to chat about a new
product. Then, a few minutes later, there will be an advertising break proper: the volume of the TV, at least on the three

Mediaset channels, actually increases during the ad breaks. Football matches, if there's a pause for an injury or a free kick, are interrupted, and "the line returns to Rome" for more "consumer suggestions." Programmes, after a while, come to seem like sing-along fill-ins between the adverts rather than vice versa. (Fifty-seven per cent of all Italian advertising budgets are sunk into television; in Britain the figure is 33.5 per cent, in Germany only 23 per cent).

The reason for the wall-to-wall advertising is that Italy has the lowest and most widely evaded licence fee in Europe. Television is, effectively, free, which means that the normal economic criteria of the market-place are completely reversed. There is no quality-cost confrontation, because the viewers are either not paying or paying minimal amounts for television. In reality, in Italy spectators are not buying; they're being bought. We are what the TV channels sell to advertisers, we as a "share," as an "audience." We, in reaching for the remote, determine the price. Or rather, a secret 5,075 Italian families determine the price. Auditel is the incredibly powerful entity which, using the viewing habits of those selected families, influences budgets worth billions of lire. The televisual advertising turnover is, at a conservative estimate, $3 billion, so every utterance from Auditel can move financial mountains. It means that television has become all about quantity and nothing about quality. Programmes must bring in the audience, *lo share*, which brings in the cash. Giovanni Sartori, as early as 1998, was writing in *Corriere della Sera* about the terrifying, deleterious effect of the most important non-governmental body in Italy: "Having Auditel figures published every morning," he wrote,

> imposes on the television producer a temporal horizon of twelve or twenty-four hours. Something which would kill any business (since businesses have to plan for the long term) and

installs a perverse competition. We will never obtain better television programmes if every morning they announce that RAI
1's news programmes "lost" and Canale 5's "won," or that a
cultural programme has been beaten 5-1 by the gossip-
mongering of "Harem." Because the next day RAI 1's news
programme will feel obliged to get back on top with stories
about a cow with five legs or the bedroom antics of someone
"rich and famous."[3]

The acuity of the criticism is the observation of the effect
not on normal television but on its most important service:
the news. And Italy's TV news programmes are, by a very
long way, the most important news providers of all the Italian
media. But they have been reduced to gossip and celebrity
banter. Reports are accompanied by pop music and proverbs.
Whatever's happening in the world, lead stories will usually
be about *maltempo* or *cronache nere* (bad weather or some
provincial murder). You will see two or three "news items"
which show topless women: a controversy about some motor-
cyclist's ex-girlfriend doing a topless calendar (they have to
show you the pictures to contextualise the report). Then
there will be something about some chorus girl getting back
together with the Inter Milan striker. This leads to a deeper
question, posed by the newscaster: "How does sex help the
performances of our favourite sportsmen?" Another clip
about footballers kissing topless girls. When the news isn't tit-
illating, it's caught up between infotainment and adforma-
tion: what new films and new pop songs are out. During the
summer, each edition of the "news" is accompanied by the
"deck-chair interview," a slot in which beach bums can talk
about the latest tanning techniques. Or else an investigative
reporter is dispatched, microphone in hand, to interview
holiday-makers about the latest trend in sand sports: beach
volleyball or Frisbee-throwing techniques. And (almost with-

out exception) during the "news" the whole system goes into meltdown, and the newscaster reaches for the phone on his desk. "Apologies, we're having technical difficulties." The whole thing is then rounded off by the newscaster announcing yesterday's viewing figures as if they contained vital cultural significance: "Last night," a newscaster will announce, "8 million Italians watched your favourite channel's new TV drama," and we watch a report about us watching what they broadcast last night. The disciplines of "hard news" are almost entirely absent.

The use of the female body in the mass hypnosis is central. Programmes now all have a middle-aged male presenter surrounded by anonymous adolescent girls, all enticingly grinning and revelling in their diminutive titles: the *letterine* (the "little letters" on a quiz show based on the alphabet) or the *schiedine* (the "little statistics" on a football show) and so on. Breasts are ubiquitous, even boringly so. It's unthinkable to have a glitzy studio show without a troupe of dancing girls dressed up in bikinis, and often even less. During a recent election, one local television debate was hosted by a woman who, other than serving the men coffee, took off an item of clothing each time the political debate became tedious. A friend and I remained glued to the boring discussion until she was stripped to the waist. A typical stunt from another show will have a woman in a bikini slipping into a glass bath tub filled with milk. To great yelps of delight from the studio, she will then strip whilst hidden by the milk and pass the bikini to the excited presenter. Each channel has its own little starlet who introduces the evening's entertainment, addressing the viewers as *cari amici*, "dear friends," and smiling at the camera as it zooms in on her shapely form (perfectly displayed as, hands behind her back, she swings her shoulders backwards and forwards, her top perforated by a "tear-drop" at the intersection of her bosom).

The best programme on Italian television is called *Blob* (on RAI 3, the "Communist" channel). It broadcasts out-takes from the cheapest TV of the previous twenty-four hours. It has a section called *protette*, a play on words which implies both "protection" and "pro-tits." It works, of course, because it pretends to be taking an ironic view of soft-porn TV whilst rerunning all the best bits: bosoms falling out of skimpy dresses, female presenters pole-dancing to pop music, or a famous politician enjoying a coy lap-dance. Another lead news item, towards the end of the year, is who is doing which calendar and with which "artistic interpretation." Actresses are interviewed in soft focus, with their twelve semi-naked photographs superimposed. A few weeks later, when you go to the newstands, there are row upon row of these mildly sexy calendars, hanging up next to the "Communist daily" and various soft-porn videos.

All of this is nothing compared with the hype surrounding "Miss Italia." Every year in Salsomaggiore, a small spa town near Parma, the most beautiful girls from throughout Italy gather to compete for the prize of becoming the country's "Miss." For an entire week the contest obsesses the nation: friends bet on likely winners and debate their various attributes. At the time of the gala final on Saturday, there's nothing else on the peep-show television. Sofia Loren was a competitor in the 1950s, winning the runner-up award of "Miss Elegance." Since the advent of the Northern League, there's also a competition called "Miss Padania" (the northern part of Italy, in the basin of the Po River and above).

It quickly becomes clear that Italy is the land that feminism forgot. It's not that there aren't many successful women in Italy; it's that they're never in the hungry public eye (unless they come with heaving cleavages). It's hard to think of any female role models in Italy other than those confined to the role of television confectionery. With a few notable exceptions, the Italian Parliament is a famously male domain. One recent survey analysed how much television time was dedicated to male and female government ministers: for every four hours of masculine chat, seven minutes were spent interviewing woman ministers. On Berlusconi's Mediaset channels, woman ministers were granted fifty-seven seconds of air time for the entire month of June (one-half of 1 per cent of the overall coverage). If they're not tinselled starlets on television, laywomen are simply famous for being mothers or relatives: women are rarely famous in their own right, but instead by virtue of their (virtuous) relationship to their men. Berlusconi often quotes his mother ("as my mother once said about me—I'm a kind of wizard"); Cecchi Gori, former president of the Fiorentina football club, always sat next to his during Fiorentina football matches. To be close to a mother gives off an aura of goodness.

I went to the newsstand to buy the Prime Minister's listings magazine, *Sorrisi e Canzoni* (Smiles and Songs). Even the title of the magazine hinted at the most important aspect of TV: karaoke and cabaret. Almost every programme, whatever its subject, is interrupted by someone reaching for the microphone and urging the audience to clap along. Today's sing-alongs are the dismal descendants of *Canzonissima*, a popular show whose title translates, literally, as "very, very song." I tried to distinguish one programme from the next, but in the end they all seemed exactly the same. The personalities were the same; the songs were the same ("My Way" and "Volare" are the usual favourites). The variety shows offered no variety on the tired theme. It was like watching *Sesame Street* without the clever bits. Hardly surprising, I thought, watching the syrupy nonsense, that Italy's greatest singers, Fabrizio De André, Francesco De Gregori, and Mina, have usually been very circumspect about appearing on television. Fellini, for years, objected to his films being broadcast on television, knowing they would be endlessly interrupted by "consumer advice."

In the end I decided to study the lifeblood of the whole enterprise: the advertising. The amazing thing is the way in which an image-based medium promotes images, not ideas. I had never before seen so many adverts for grooming products, so many adverts and "promotional messages" for cellulite removal, for electrodes which remove fat, for slimming devices, and for expensive cosmetics. "Let's remove those unpleasant cushions of fat," says a lady—this on national TV—"because it's so very important to feel beautiful and healthy." There will be a close-up of someone's buttocks as little pads send electric shocks into the flesh. Other money-spinners for the TV channels have a sexy middle-aged lady talking on the phone to a viewer as she displays her tarot cards on the carpeted table and narrates how much money you can win if you put the following numbers down for this week's lottery; other slots are dedicated solely to reading horoscopes or dispelling an "amorous curse" cast by a rival in love (there will be a mage, complete with aluminium-foil mitre). Or else there will be a man pretending to be outraged that he's selling so much jewellery for so little money, placing plastic necklaces on busty girls.

The problem of Italian TV has become so acute that in one of her very rare outbursts, Franca Ciampi, wife of the President of the Republic, recently said that Italian TV is now *deficiente*, "half-witted." When I talk with friends about it, especially older ones, they are dismayed and bemused about the "dumb and dumber" broadcasting. Italy's noble visual culture, they say, has been reduced to endless erotica, and the small screen is now a cheaper, bittersweet version of *La dolce vita*: a world obsessed with celebrity and sexuality, to the exclusion of all moral values. That, in fact, is the tragedy of Italian TV: it's not, actually, very Italian. To me the adjective implies intelligence, eloquence, and generosity; television offers the polar opposite. Part of the problem, and perhaps part of the reason it seems so un-Italian, is that so much of their television is imported: all the quiz formats, the *Big Brother* bonanza, the "reality" and "get-famous" shows are all programmes from abroad. Many of Italy's most famous actors are simply dubbers, never out of work thanks to the mass importation of foreign, largely American, films. And most of the films imported aren't quality ones but the cheapest ones available: "oil and muscle" B movies or something very close to soft porn. As a result, the country has all the vices of commercial television without any of the virtues; it's based on American shows and films and formats but without American meritocracy, without America's investigative journalism.

Certainly, much is admirable about Italian television. *Blob* parodies the viewer's incessant zapping, creating a collage of what we watch and splicing the footage to brilliant comic effect. *Le iene* (The hyenas) features aggressive, gatecrashing journalists, and their interviews—in which opposing politicians or personalities each occupy one-half of the screen—will one day be amusing historical sources. The quick-fire questions and (a rarity this) the rapid replies they receive are compulsive viewing. Many of the programmes and films broadcast on RAI 3 and La 7 (the small seventh channel) are of an exceptionally high quality. So, too, are many of the programmes broadcast in the middle of the night. The dignity of many of the local channels is also breathtaking. There are so many local channels that the country boasts a quarter of the world's total terrestrial channels: 640 of a total of 2,500. It's the local channels which broadcast the opera. They seem, in a way the national channels don't, to be part of our reality. Where national channels are provincial in the worst sense of the word, local channels, whenever I've seen them, are often provincial in the best sense.

Another reason not to be alarmist is that Italians, as viewers, are very unusual. The television may often be on, but it is watched in an active, rather than passive, way. In Britain, many people watch TV in the same way they might read a book, in silence and concentration. Here, the viewers are less supine; whenever I watch TV with friends, they invariably shout *"cretin"* at the television. It's like an irritating member of the family whom you have to invite but you choose to ignore. Also, the info-penetration of newspapers and radio might be minimal compared with television, but the level of intelligence they offer goes a long way towards making up the cultural deficit.

As usual, I went to Filippo for an explanation. "What you don't realise," he said, "what none of you foreigners realise, is that Italy's at a cultural cul-de-sac. You come here to gawp at buildings and chipped statues from five hundred years ago, and imagine that we're still at that level of cultural production. If I were you I would go back to the fifties and sixties. Switch off the television and watch some old films instead."

"Italia! Oh Italia!" wrote Byron, "thou who hast / The fatal gift of beauty." It's a line that could serve as the leitmotif for much of Italian cinema. During their golden era in the 1950s and 1960s, Italian auteurs maintained a very ambiguous attitude towards the country's pathological need for beauty and eroticism. A series of self-reflective films appreciated both the magnificence and the dangers of Italy's visual culture. They were examples of meta-cinema in which the visual culture was admired, scrutinised, and often scorned.

Visconti's Bellissima *is the prime example because it cuts both ways: it is, as the title suggests, lush and stylish cinema, but the plot is about the threat to society posed by the cinematic need for shallow beauty. A film crew are holding auditions to find a child actress, and one mother bankrupts her family and almost her morals in the desire to see her child on the screen: "You don't get if you don't give," says one member of the film crew to her, seductively asking for either money or sex. She does eventually see her child onscreen, but only by spying on the screen tests, where the film crew are ridiculing her daughter.*

It's the same with Antonioni, another of cinema's "realist" directors. "Beauty really is discomforting," says one of his characters in La notte *as he pours himself a deathbed glass of champagne whilst admiring the nurse. "Life would be so much easier if there weren't pleasure," says another character, the writer Giovanni Pontano, as he watches an erotic dancer whilst seated next to his wife. The settings of Antonioni's films could hardly be more luxurious: the Aeolian Islands and Sicily in* L'avventura *(a title which is also a euphemism for a fling), or the opulent party outside Milan in* La notte. *In both, the erotic temptations, the frisson of sexual infidelity, cause excitement and agony. In both, the shadow of disappearance and death falls across the frivolity, evoking the idea of Eros and Thanatos, where eroticism goes hand in hand with death, the dissolution of the self. The very thing which makes his films so beautiful to watch (languorous, moody women and their modern, worldly men) is the same thing which makes them tragic and emotionally depressing: human relationships don't last, all pleasures are ultimately hollow.*

Fellini's cinema shared the same themes and often the same actors. La dolce vita *was, like* Bellissima, *a self-referential film: both a celebration and a critique of the new, glamorous world of the cinema. And, like* La notte, *it was a film about the thwarting of literary ambition (even about the way in which the visual had superseded the verbal). The film was denounced as "obscene" by the Catholic hierarchy when it came out. The Vatican's mouthpiece publication,* L'Osservatore Romano, *called it "disgusting." The intention of Fellini, though, was a moral one: "There is," he wrote, "a vertical line of spirituality that goes from the beast to the angel, and on which we oscillate. Every day, every minute, carries the possibility of losing ground, of falling down again toward the beast."*[4] *La dolce vita was an attempt to distinguish angelic humanity from the bestial, and it duly became more than merely a cheap take on loose living. Thus the sexuality of the film is invariably derided: the diva Sylvia is simply a "kitten" (she even places a cat upon her head before the famous Trevi fountain scene). The result is a film which is erotic and numbing at the same time. Its scenes are, like Antonioni's, a modernist mixture of titillation and ennui. Everything, especially the media circles Marcello moves in, seems exciting and yet soulless.*

Pier Paolo Pasolini's most famous film, certainly the most brutal, is an attempt to identify those fetishes of the flesh with Fascism. Salò *(based on the Marquis de Sade's* 120 Days of Sodom*) is the story of young boys and girls selected for an orgiastic sojourn in the dying days of Fascist Italy. It's eroticism at its most obscene and animalistic. Characters don't have names, only rank (the masochistic Fascist is only ever referred to as Il Presidente). One boy is derided as a "weak, chained creature." The process of selecting the sexual slaves is presented like a cattle market as officers from the regime compliment and criticise. "Little tits to give life to a dying man" is the observation on one girl; the lips of another are pulled back to reveal imperfect teeth, and she's rejected. The film is a litany of vices, sexual and otherwise. Acts of religion are punishable by death; the eroticism is legalistic, so that the sex represents obedience rather than transgression. Against the soundtrack of lounge jazz, there's also pomposity. One Fascist reveller proclaims languidly: "I'm provoked into making a certain number of interesting reflections." The only possible conclusion from the film is that the path of pure hedonism leads to a new kind of Fascism.*

The connections between Fascism and erotica were also made by Bernardo Bertolucci. The Conformist *(adapted from Alberto Moravia's novel) is, like all great Italian cinema, a work of breathtaking style. It influenced a generation of American film-makers. Various scenes seem as immaculately posed as a painting: the long white benches of the mental asylum, the enormous, empty rooms of the ministry where one of the regime's officials is seducing the woman sitting on his desk, hitching up her skirt and stroking her thighs. Against the backdrop of a murder plot there are the latent lesbianism in Paris and the brothel in Viareggio, such that Fascism, at least cinematically, appears highly aestheticised and eroticised. Like Pasolini (with whom Bertolucci had worked on* Accattone *and* La comare secca*), Bertolucci was deconstructing fetishism and Fascism, and tracing the links between the two. Fascism, in fact, was a subject-matter which produced probably his greatest film:* The Spider's Stratagem. *It's told in flashback: a young man has returned to his father's village to unveil a statue to his memory. He is set on unmasking the murderer of his father, a famous "anti-Fascist," and returns to the village (in the flat Emilian plain) to visit his father's mistress and former friends. Only at the end does it become obvious that the whole narration has been a lie and that the hero of the story isn't quite what everyone thinks.*

The irony is that the two humanists who have most often been the scourge of the Catholic Church, Dario Fo and Pier Paolo Pasolini, have often used religious material—or at least moral criteria—to criticise the dehumanisation of modernity. They were endlessly accused of degrading Italy with their plays or films (even today there are usually great derisive noises when the name Dario Fo, Nobel Prize winner, is whispered in Catholic circles), but they recognised what was happening long before anyone else: cinema and then television had unleashed the genies of eroticism and consumerism. "Consumerism," wrote Pasolini, "has cynically destroyed the real world, transforming it into total unreality where there's no longer possible a choice between good and evil."[5] He called it "cultural genocide." Dario Fo, in his play Big Pantomime with Flags and Puppets, *foresaw a world in* which "viewers" are hypnotised by a televisual diet of football and advertisements.

In those early years of television and the economic boom, many analysts hinted that the country's new-found wealth was a false dawn. Italo Calvino wrote of "the suspicion that all our ostentation of prosperity is nothing more than a shallow varnish on the Italy of mountain and suburban hovels, of trains of emigrants, of town squares pulsating with Blackshirts."[6] With strikingly similar diction, Pasolini asked: "Do you know what Italy appears to me to be? A hovel in which the proprietors have managed to buy themselves a television."[7] The possession of, first, the television set and, then, the objects it advertised had become the height of economic aspiration. The consequences were, according to Pasolini, devastating:

> It was television which practically ended the era of piety and began the era of hedonism. It was the era in which young people were frustrated by the stupidity and the unattainability of the models proposed to them by school and by television. They tend unstoppably to become aggressive to the point of delinquency or else passive to the point of unhappiness.[8]

Television created dissatisfaction because it gave viewers a hunger which could never be sated, because, in the final analysis, it wasn't part of the real world.

None of this is, perhaps, unique to Italy. But for various reasons, Italian television is unlike any other on earth. Partly—and simply—because it is watched so much. Partly because there is an attachment to the television that makes it, metaphorically, part of the family (RAI, the national broadcasting corporation, is called la mamma). Partly because, in many cases years ago, the TV actually taught Italians Italian with educational programmes like Non è mai troppo tardi (It's never too late), which battled against illiteracy. The TV set is called the focolare domestico, *the "domestic hearth," in memory of the family fire-place it has replaced. The greatest reason for the Italian televi-sual anomaly, however, is simply that the Prime Minister owns three national channels.*

To understand how it happened, one has to understand the story of the "new wave" of Italian broadcasting which, coincid-ing with the end of the golden era of Italian cinema, began in July 1976. The Constitutional Court decreed that the state RAI channels would retain the monopoly on national broadcasting whilst at the same time allowing unlicensed, private channels to broadcast as long as it was on a "local" scale. In 1978 a new lo-cal channel sprang up: Telemilano. It served the residents of a suburb of Milan called Milano 2, a complex of some thirty-five hundred flats which had been built and sold during the previous decade by Berlusconi and his anonymous investors. In 1980 there were thirteen hundred private television channels; three years later, despite buy-outs and mergers, there were still more than seven hundred. In 1980 Telemilano became known as Canale 5. In 1983 Berlusconi bought Italia Uno, and a year later he bought Rete 4. Those three channels eventually bought out al-most all their rivals, such that the entire private-sector broad-casting was unified under the Mediaset umbrella of Silvio Berlusconi.

The smaller the enterprise, of course, the more important the advertising revenue. Thus Berlusconi's nascent television chan-nels were the early models for today's television. Programming was seamlessly integrated with advertising in the same way that now a programme is interrupted for a "promotional message" and news items are there to plug a product. Rather than being "alternative," the new private television channels and their low-budget programmes survived by becoming advertising vehicles. Often the advertising arm was barely distinguishable from the broadcasting business. The advertising revenue of the Mediaset channels was looked after by Publitalia, Berlusconi's advertising company, which, by 1990, had become responsible for 24.5 per cent of the entire television advertising market (the figure is now nearer 60 per cent). It was an arrangement which was to become a leitmotif for Berlusconian business: the buyer and the seller incarnate in the same person, the left hand closing a deal with the right. In one of his many master-strokes, Berlusconi bought the Italian rights to hundreds of American films and soap operas. He also owned Blockbuster in Italy, whereby anyone bored with Berlusconi's television scheduling would—in popping out to rent a video—still remain within his financial orbit.

A few of the Mediaset studios are still based at Milano 2. When you go there, the whole place feels like something from The Truman Show: *it's a kind of unreal, bourgeois bubble. No one need ever leave the million square metres of the estate: there's a chemist, a school, a police station. There's a strange combination of concrete and greenery: all the blocks are a rusty red colour and are linked by bridges and paths which weave over lakes and roads. It all feels slightly 1970s, not least the names of the blocks: Palazzo Aquarius and so on. The manhole covers have a simple "M2" imprinted, along with "Edilnord," the name of Berlusconi's construction company. At the centre of the complex you can see a tower of satellite dishes and the symbol of the Mediaset empire: a snake.*

The law maintaining RAI's national broadcasting monopoly was still in force in the early 1980s. Eventually, though, the law was changed because it had already been blatantly broken. Berlusconi wasn't broadcasting nationally; he was simply broadcasting the same programmes at the same times across the country, albeit on "local" channels. It was national broadcasting in all but name. Someone could watch the same imported film at the same time in Palermo or Parma, where different stations would coincidentally have a coordinated programme schedule. At one point, since such broadcasting was illegal, the pro-

*grammes were taken off the air; the ensuing outrage from view-
ers who wanted the next episode of* Dallas *or* Dynasty *enabled
Berlusconi to present himself, as he would often do in later years,
as the man representing "freedom" against "oppression." His
channels—at least according to the rhetoric—weren't subject,
like RAI, to* lottizzazione, *the habit of "parcelling out" television jobs to the families and friends of powerful politicians.
(Traditionally, RAI 1 had been the channel of the Christian
Democrats, RAI 2 of the Socialists, and RAI 3 of the Communists. One of the country's most famous television personalities,
Bruno Vespa, once spoke of the Christian Democrats as his "majority shareholders.") Berlusconi, then, appeared to represent the
future, the flamboyant entrepreneur who was liberating Italians
from years of boring, grey state television.*

*The legislative sleight of hand by which Berlusconi's broad-
casting scam became legal was known as Law 223, or "the
Mammì law" (named after the Minister of Telecommunications). It was proposed in 1984 and passed, eventually, in 1990.
It sanctioned de facto national broadcasting by Berlusconi, end-
ing for all time the monopoly of RAI and creating the RAI-
Mediaset duopoly. Five government ministers resigned in protest
at the legislation, already wary of Berlusconi's omnipotence. The
Prime Minister at the time was Bettino Craxi, who had been
best man at Berlusconi's second marriage and was to become
godfather to Berlusconi's daughter. (One of the many accusations against Berlusconi is that Craxi's offshore accounts received a 23-billion-lira injection as gratitude from an obscure
part of Berlusconi's Fininvest empire called All Iberian. Berlusconi was sentenced to two years and four months in prison for the
bribe. By the time of the appeal, however, the crime had fallen
under the statute of limitations, it had passed its crime-by date.)
Thus Berlusconi had become "His Emittenza," an ironic play on
words which evoked both his "eminence" and his broadcasting*

"emittance." Not only did "the Great Seducer" (another nick-name) own the means of production; he owned something much more important: the means of seduction.

The tactic is blissfully simple. It requires a small box in the corner of every room, plugged into the wall. It requires an aerial to receive the right broadcasts. (Eventually the notion of "the right broadcasts" might become irrelevant; if the owner of the "right" channels should also head the government, the rival RAI channels—rivals politically and economically—will also be his.) That benevolent media tycoon pays himself for advertising space on his own channels in order to promote his own products. As he becomes inexorably richer, he also becomes the consumers' most trusted entrepreneur. They recognise and agree with his Orwellian mantra "old is bad, new is good." Eventually the mores of millions of viewers will be so familiar to him that the viewers can be turned into faithful voters, guaranteed to be receptive to any slick promotion by a new political party.

Anyone who thinks that Berlusconi's ownership of Mediaset has played no role in his politics, or that his political position has no effect on Mediaset, is simply burying his or her head in the cathode tube. The more cynical will accept that there exists a porous membrane between his political and television interests but will defend it by claiming that RAI has always been a refuge for henchmen and political appointments. Berlusconi, they claim, is only continuing what has gone on for decades. Indeed, he's actually being more honest, because he's doing it openly. There is, though, a very important difference. In the past, the political parties colonised the television; Berlusconi is doing the opposite: he's a television entrepreneur who is colonising politics. For his supporters, however, the manner in which he created a televisual empire is precisely the reason he is fit to be our political

leader: he has, they say, *una marcia in più*, "an extra gear."
He created commercial television from nothing. It's a virtue,
not a vice.

The most convincing explanation, albeit the most mundane, for Berlusconi's political appeal is the simple fact that he
controls three television channels. Having a politician who
owns three television channels turns any election into the
equivalent of a football match in which one team kicks off
with a three-goal advantage. Victory for the other side, even a
draw, is extremely unlikely. Certain programmes, like the parliamentary programme on Sunday, *Parlamento in*, are like
long party political broadcasts. Some Mediaset channels are
worse than others. Rete 4 has an anchorman—Emilio Fede—
nicknamed "Fido" because he's so sycophantic to his boss.
He'll introduce news items on the opposition by shaking his
head and saying, in a stage whisper, "These stupid Com-
mies." He's painful to watch not because he's politicised but
because of the complete lack of professionalism. In a meritocracy he would be in the dole queue tomorrow. He stutters,
giggles, flirts, loses his thread. And yet he has become one of
the most important "journalists" in the country. Rete 4 is the
channel which, anytime Berlusconi is making an important
speech, will beam it live, without comment or criticism, into
millions of homes across Italy. The other two channels, Italia
Uno and Canale 5, are only minimally more balanced. Even
there journalists, like some referees, appear overawed. Asking
hard questions of Berlusconi is akin to criticising not only the
politician but everyone in the television studio who is employed by him, and so it's simply not done. Thus Berlusconi
has been compared, not unfairly, to Mussolini: both had a
balcony from which they could harangue, cajole, and persuade adoring viewers. Berlusconi, being the head of Italy's
"videocracy," is only different because he owns an electronic,
rather than a literal, balcony.

I remember watching another of my favourite programmes one winter, *Quelli che il calcio*. It was an ordinary Sunday afternoon when suddenly the Minister of Communications was allowed to interrupt the programme with an irate phone call. He was speaking live to the nation, aggressively berating a simple satiric item. In that moment, the notion of non-interference was highlighted as complete pretence. In a few minutes of arrogance, the entire vertical structure of power was laid bare: power drips imperiously from above. Since then, we've become almost immune to political directives about RAI broadcasts. Last year, from Bulgaria, Berlusconi denounced three journalists who, he said, "had made a criminal use of public television" in criticising him. The argument had its own perverse logic: since the RAI channels were public, paid for by everyone through the licence fee, they should be impartial, which is to say uncritical. The three journalists were promptly removed from our screens. One of them, Enzo Biagi, an owlish man well respected for his balanced, gentle journalism, wrote a front-page article for *Corriere della Sera* a few days later comparing Berlusconi to the German Chancellor of 1933–45. Aldous Huxley wrote in his famous preface to *Brave New World*: "The greatest triumphs of propaganda have been accomplished, not by doing something, but by refraining from doing. Great is the truth, but still greater, from a practical point of view, is silence about truth."[9] The real scandal about television isn't what's on; it's what's not.

Another example occurred on the eve of the sentence against Cesare Previti. Previti was, for decades, Berlusconi's lawyer and would, the next day, be sentenced to eleven years in prison for bribing judges. On the eve of that judicial decision, a history documentary was hastily cancelled, and Berlusconi's ally was allowed uninterrupted access to the sitting-rooms of the entire country. Rete 4, the outrider for the Berlusconi bandwagon, broadcast the press conference without embarrassment. The same channel reran the entire fifty-one minutes of Berlusconi's court appearance a week later (in an ongoing court case in which Berlusconi is accused of the same crime). In that week, it was hinted (by the Forza Italia politicians who were on the verge of introducing parliamentary immunity) that journalistic defamation would now come with a three-year prison sentence.

But more than just painfully partial towards its boss, Mediaset television has achieved something even more disguised. In many ways, the real problem with Mediaset isn't that it's political in the purest sense; it's that it's not political at all. The only thing on offer are bosoms, football, and money. Even someone who enjoys all three eventually finds it boring. It has created a cultural and intellectual implosion. In the words of Andrea Camilleri:

> If I were a believer—not one of those who only goes to Mass, but a believer who is perfectly convinced of his faith—I would say that Berlusconi is bad with a capital B . . . he has invested all that money in television in the worst way . . . he has lowered the cultural level of television and therefore of Italy . . . I blame him for that, because that cultural downturn is the cause of so many things.[10]

"Panem et circenses," says Filippo, "that's what the ancient Romans called it: 'bread and a bit of a show.' Give that to the masses and they'll be happy." An American friend, quoting Pynchon on paranoia, is even more dismissive: "If they can get you asking the wrong questions, they don't have to worry about the answers!"

"A really efficient totalitarian state," Huxley continued in his preface, "would be one in which the all-powerful executive of political bosses and their army of managers control a population of slaves who do not have to be coerced, because they love their servitude."[11] That, sadly, is the feeling one gets watching certain Italians watching their television. Mediaset has managed to create the conditions for a one-party state without coercion, without resort to the truncheon and the castor oil. The powerful opiate of television has been sufficient to create an almost invincible political hegemony— invincible precisely because the viewers, and voters, are complicit in its creation.

I was sitting in the pub one night. It was the Dubh Linn just by the duomo. Giovanni was opposite me, lighting another Diana cigarette. He stared at the packet on the table and asked me if it was true that the British secret service had bumped off Princess Diana. He, like hundreds of my students, was convinced of it.

"No, no," I said, suddenly offended that someone was slandering my country. Thinking about it, though, I realised that perhaps that's exactly what I was doing to his country: believing all the conspiracy theories and understanding absolutely nothing, writing scurrilous essays which only showed Italy in the worst possible light. Maybe, I suddenly thought, all these tragic stories aren't real at all. Maybe they never actually happened, and I've simply fallen victim to Italy's most pervasive ailment: paranoia. Perhaps I'm being unfair to the country, I thought. Then again, I reasoned, to ignore that pessimism and paranoia would have been to edit out the emotional atmosphere of Italian life; and I justified my sometimes-bilious dismay about Italian TV by telling myself that a vast majority of Italians shared my scorn.

Giovanni, probably seeing that I was rather too deep in thought, decided I needed to get out of Parma for a while. He invited me to his house, hundreds of miles to the south, in Puglia. "That's where Padre Pio lived," he said, explaining that it was Padre Pio's face I kept seeing framed in shops, resting on mantelpieces, adorning key-rings or Zippo lighters. His was the only face in Italy with more exposure than Berlusconi's. "You need a pilgrimage," Giovanni said, stubbing out his cigarette.

6

PIETRA AND *PAROLA*

*Italy is a land full of ancient cults, rich in natural and supernatu-
ral powers. And so everyone feels its influence. After all, whoever
seeks God finds him . . . wherever he wants.*

—FEDERICO FELLINI

At the beginning of the twentieth century, San Giovanni
Rotondo was a tiny village in the rugged Gargano mountains
of Puglia, the region which forms the heel and spur of the
Italian boot. Even forty years ago it was linked to Manfredonia (the nearby port) only by a mule track which zigzagged
down through olive trees to the Adriatic. Now, though, San
Giovanni Rotondo is Italy's most-visited tourist spot, welcoming more than 6 million visitors a year. It has overtaken
Lourdes as Europe's most popular destination for Catholic
pilgrims. It has more than a hundred hostels and hotels, and
will soon have a new church designed by Renzo Piano. There

is also an imposing new hospital, one of Italy's largest and most modern.

The cause of all this is San Giovanni's most revered son, and one of the best-known Italians of the twentieth century: Padre Pio. When he was beatified on 2 May 1999, most of the country became immersed in preparation for the big event (even the Serie A game between Roma and Inter was postponed to the following day). Pope John Paul II celebrated a televised Mass in St Peter's, and then travelled down to San Giovanni Rotondo to celebrate Mass there. The million pilgrims in attendance were transported by more than five thousand coaches (one hundred from Poland alone) and nineteen special trains. One thousand chemical toilets were set up in the village, and huge TV screens surrounded its two main squares.

Long before San Giovanni Rotondo became famous, another nearby village, Monte Sant' Angelo, was a place of pilgrimage: it formed the end of the medieval pilgrim's "Route of the Angel," which wound its way from Normandy to Rome and beyond. Its fame derives from a mixture of local lore and millennial angst. The story goes that in AD 490, a local man went up into the mountains, searching for his prize bull. He found it at the entrance to a cave, way up on the most precarious promontory. The bull was reluctant to move, so the man shot an arrow at it: the arrow turned in the wind and embedded itself in the man's forehead. The Bishop of Siponto was called on for advice, and when he arrived at the grotto, he received a visitation from the archangel Michael, who ordered him to consecrate a Christian altar on the site. It's not known what happened to the man with the arrow in his forehead, but the result of his misadventure was the famous Santuario di San Michele. In AD 999, the Holy Roman Emperor Otto III made a pilgrimage to the sanctuary and prayed that the apocalypse prophesied for the end of the first millennium wouldn't happen. A thousand years later and the same worries, together with the beatification of Padre Pio, prompted a sudden reawakening of religious piety and pilgrimage.

I'm met off the train at Manfredonia by my friend Giovanni, whose family lives in the town. It's almost midnight and he drives me to my hotel. By the reception desk there's a cabinet of Padre Pio mementoes—letter-racks, mirrors, diaries, plates—each one bearing his by-now familiar image: a high forehead, grey beard and bushy eyebrows, deep-set eyes above a slightly bulbous nose. The set of his mouth makes him look like he's wincing. He seems kindly but austere. A sleeve, or more usually a fingerless glove, covers up the reason for his fame—his stigmata. Giovanni says it's a farce: "This used to be one of the poorest parts of Italy, but it has suddenly become very wealthy, simply because of Padre Pio."

Padre Pio was born Francesco Forgione in 1887 in Pietrelcina, a small town halfway between Naples and Manfredonia. He was ordained into the order of Capuchin monks in 1910 and moved to San Giovanni Rotondo in 1916. He stayed there, almost always within the Chiesa di Santa Maria delle Grazie, until his death, at eighty-one, in September 1968. Almost exactly fifty years before, on 20 September 1918, he became the only Catholic priest to have received the stigmata. A month after the wounds appeared, he wrote to his spiritual adviser, Padre Benedetto, describing what had happened:

> After I had celebrated Mass, I yielded to a drowsiness similar to a sweet sleep. All the internal and external senses and even the very faculties of my soul were immersed in indescribable stillness. Absolute silence surrounded and invaded me. I was

suddenly filled with great peace and abandonment, which effaced everything else and caused a lull in the turmoil. All this happened in a flash . . . I became aware that my hands, feet, and side were dripping blood. Imagine the agony I experienced and continue to experience almost every day. The heart wound bleeds continually, especially from Thursday evening until Saturday. Dear Father, I am dying of pain because of the wounds and the resulting embarrassment I feel in my soul. I am afraid I shall bleed to death if the Lord doesn't hear my heartfelt supplication to relieve me of this condition. Will Jesus, who is so good, grant me this grace? Will he at least free me from the embarrassment caused by these outward signs?[1]

Between the wars, Padre Pio's fame grew, thanks to the stigmata and the countless stories about his miracles: there were tales of bilocation (being in two places at the same time), inexplicable cures, celestial perfumes, instant conversions, and prophetic visions. Every Italian seems to have a favourite anecdote: he blessed a pile of envelopes brought to him but refused to bless one (when it was opened, it was found to contain coupons for the football pools); he knelt to pray for George VI before his death had been announced; he appeared in the cockpit of an American aircraft during bombing missions in the Second World War. His most celebrated feat was to have picked out a letter from Poland which pleaded for his intercession on behalf of a mortally ill woman. "We cannot say no to this one," Padre Pio is supposed to have declared. The woman recovered, and the Polish priest who had written on her behalf, Bishop Wojtyla, subsequently became better known as Pope John Paul II.

Padre Pio's relations with the higher echelons of the Catholic Church were strained. Doctors were repeatedly sent to inspect his wounds, and there was an attempt to have him transferred to Spain (averted only by the intervention of the

Ministry of the Interior). But Padre Pio's admirers have included Gabriele D'Annunzio, who was one of his correspondents; the TV presenter Luciano Rispoli, at whose marriage he officiated; and the showgirl Lorella Cuccarini, who likes to drop his name in interviews. The magazine *Gente*—a cross between *Hello!* and *The Catholic Herald*—regularly runs new anecdotes about him and offers readers cassettes of "his actual voice." Abroad he's just as popular: the Padre Pio Foundation of America has a doting Web site, and there's a bookshop entirely devoted to him in Vauxhall Bridge Road in London.

In November 1969 it was decreed by the Vatican that he had died in the *odore di santità* (scent of saintliness), and the case for his beatification was formally put by the Bishop of Manfredonia. The process is a tortuous one: first the Tribunale Diocesano gives its verdict, then the matter is passed on to the Congregazione per le Cause dei Santi in Rome. The theologians and cardinals on this committee re-examine all the relevant writings and testimonies, and, if they are satisfied that someone deserves to be recognised as a *beato*, medical evidence is called on to demonstrate that miracles occurred as a result of his or her intercession. (Following the beatification, Padre Pio was proclaimed a saint in May 2002.)

The day Giovanni and I arrive in San Giovanni Rotondo it is raining heavily, and the town—with its roads and woodlands disappearing into the low clouds—resembles a new ski resort. Cranes are everywhere, constantly gyrating as they lift lumps of concrete into place for the next huge hotel. Opposite the façade of Santa Maria delle Grazie are a series of staircases that rise high into the hills, flanked by statues of the Padre and the Madonna. Nearby, a Portakabin serves as the studio of the official radio station, La Voce di Padre Pio.

There is normally a three-hour wait to get into the church,

though we enter quite quickly thanks to the rain. The hushed queue snakes round the monastery, past strategic notices and collection boxes. You can get objects blessed every fifteen minutes, and a line of people has already formed with wedding rings or car keys at the ready. The Padre's tomb is a massive marble edifice, surrounded by wrought-iron railings and boxes into which photographs and letters can be posted. Some two hundred people are gathered round it, lighting candles, falling to their knees, and whispering prayers.

There's a spontaneous outburst of Hail Marys as we approach Padre Pio's sealed-off cell, above which are written Thomas à Kempis's words from *The Imitation of Christ*: "Worldly honours have always sorrow for company." Through the glass you can see every book, painting, and photograph, as well as his comb, perfectly preserved. The bed is made, and by it are his size-nine shoes, purple-black and almost as wide as they are long because of the bleeding and swelling. In the nearby chapel a plaque marks Pio's seat and the exact location in which he first received the stigmata. Facing the piazza outside, still teeming with pilgrims, is a narrow window. It was here that, like the Pope, Padre Pio used to bless his visitors, raising his hands so that everyone could get a look at his bandages.

Back outside in the rain, every shop is offering *articoli religiosi*, from paintings and postcards of the man to statues costing as much as four million lire. With an embarrassed smile, Giovanni tells me that his father built a house here for an old lady—it had a large garden, three storeys, and a lift—whose income derived entirely from the sale of these trinkets. I come from a Methodist background, and I'm uneasy with icons and relics, but my objections here are mainly aesthetic: too many semi-naked women releasing a dove to the heavens, where, of course, the famous Capuchin priest is sitting.

We walk towards the hospital, the Casa Sollievo della Sofferenza, or House for the Alleviation of Suffering, which dominates the town with its massive white façade topped by a statue of Saint Francis. In 1940 Pio decided that a hospital should be built. Legend has it that he single-handedly sought funding for the building from his visitors, placing donations in his handkerchief every day and emptying out the coins onto his bed every evening (in fact, the hospital also received 250 million lire from UNRRA—the United Nations Relief and Rehabilitation Administration—in 1947). A protein used to treat diabetes was discovered in the hospital's laboratory, adding to its renown, and—peculiarly—visitors are offered guided tours round its theatres and wards. On the anniversary of Pio's death, tens of thousands of pilgrims gather to walk round the hospital through the night, keeping a candlelit vigil.

We return to Giovanni's house in Manfredonia. His father shakes his head when we begin talking about the town: he knew Padre Pio and describes him as *scontroso*, "surly." (Similarly, Rispoli, the TV presenter, says that Padre Pio was *"burbero, ai limiti della scortesia"*—"gruff, on the verge of discourtesy.") Everyone seems sure that he would not be pleased with what now goes on in his name. Certainly the town bears very little resemblance to a description of it by another priest in 1915, the year before Padre Pio's arrival. "Only a deep silence is around me," he wrote, "sometimes interrupted by the sound of a bell hung on the neck of some sheep or goat which shepherds take to graze on the mountain behind the convent." Now the Frati Cappuccini have a Web site, urging exorbitant contributions to the new church and quoting by way of encouragement the implausible last words of Padre Pio: "Make it big." There's the constant noise of cranes and cement mixers, and I think of the words of the priest in *La dolce vita*: "Miracles are born out of solitude and silence, and not in chaos like this."

The following day is warm, the sky entirely clear. We are going to visit the sanctuary at Monte Sant'Angelo, the place of the man with the arrow in his forehead. Giovanni, though, refuses to drive there: the village is very dangerous because of a feud between two families which started fifty years ago when some livestock were stolen and the two sons of the offending family were killed and dumped in the town. It's not a place Giovanni wants to leave a smart car, so we take the coach. The scenery, as we rise away from the sea, is spectacular: hairpin bends take us towards whitewashed houses where linen, hung from every balcony, billows in the wind. The town seems older than San Giovanni: the streets are narrow and steep, with labyrinthine flights of steps leading to the medieval quarter. The red-tiled roofs you can see from the top of the mountain are huddled together at odd angles. From here you can see clean across the Adriatic to the coasts of Albania and Montenegro. Even the local delicacy reflects the influence of the Catholic Church: *ostie ripiene*, literally "stuffed hosts," are two large, obviously unconsecrated Communion wafers around a filling of almonds and honey. Lining many of the pavements are religious stalls: next to the tiny bottles claiming to contain the *profumo di Padre Pio* are ashtrays inscribed with some words of advice to users: *"Stronzo, smetti di fumare"* (Idiot, give up smoking).

The Santuario di San Michele is carved into the mountain. "This," it says in Latin above the entrance, "is the house of God and the gate of heaven." Legend has it that the archangel Michael left a footprint here, which has prompted thousands of pilgrims to scratch the outlines of their own hands and feet into the stone slabs. Some, those in the prime positions, have become templates into which other people have placed their own hands. And I do have some sense of a gateway, even if it's not a strictly religious sense—more the feeling that centuries of pilgrims, millions of them, have put their hands in the same spot mine is now, and that their touch has gradually eroded and smoothed and humanised the hard stone. It's like cathedral steps hollowed in the middle after centuries of use.

As we look at the initials and dates, I realise there's something very reassuring about antiquarian graffiti, about the fact that people over a thousand years ago were making this journey with miracles and the millennium in mind. Two centuries after Otto III, Saint Francis of Assisi visited the *santuario* but—feeling himself unworthy—didn't enter it. We, of course, do, and admire the Byzantine Madonna of Constantinople and the filigree crystal cross (a gift from Frederick II), which is said, like so many others, to contain wood from the true cross.

We emerge from the cold *santuario* and sit on a wall overlooking the sea. Gulls are soaring in the breeze, and way below we can just see a fleet of fishing boats setting out from Manfredonia. Eating my *ostie ripiene*, I feel, if not the piety of the pilgrim, at least the serenity of the pilgrimage.

Being Italian implies being Catholic. Even for a non-believer, being Italian implies absorbing the mores and morality of Roman Catholicism. It doesn't offer a set of beliefs or liturgies to which a rational adult can choose to adhere; it offers a way of life, and of death. It's a cradle-to-grave religion which is not only devotional but also political and social and aesthetic. It seeps into every corner of the country, into every stage of every life. "I know," Federico Fellini once said, "that I am a prisoner of two thousand years of the Catholic Church. All Italians are." Or, as Hippolyte Taine, visiting Italy in the years immediately after unification, put it: "Italians are entirely accustomed to Catholicism. It is a part of their eyes, their ears, their imagination, and their taste."

The connections between the country and its Catholicism are most obvious in the language. One hardly ever hears the words "Christian" or "Christianity" in Italian. The words, even the concepts, have been almost entirely replaced by "Catholic" and "Catholicism." People talk about not the Christian (let alone Jewish) commandments but the "Catholic commandments." Even Catholicism sometimes goes unmentioned and is replaced by "the Church," as if it's already understood that we're talking about an indivisible concept: Roman Catholicism.

I used to get irritated by that dogged belief in *extra ecclesiam nulla salus*: that no one outside the (Roman Catholic) Church can possibly be saved. Bishops still talk of the Catholic Church as the only true church of Jesus Christ, dismissing all other strands of Christianity as heretical. Many cardinals mention millennia of Judaism or centuries of Protestantism with an acid sentence, and you begin to see why the country is so amazingly homogeneous: nothing other than the Church will be tolerated. "Only the truth has rights," I read in cardinals' sermons, or—echoing Cardinal Newman— "Liberalism is a halfway house to atheism." The absolutism, the absence of religious debate or individual theological interpretation, is incredible. There is, a priori, a reluctance to accept an interlocutor. In bookshops, I would find Protestant texts shelved under the dismissive heading "Sects."

There is, I realised, a dogged insistence that only Rome holds any legitimate claim to the guidance of Christianity. Only from Rome can there be any certainty. Whereas many Protestant communities might encourage theological or spiritual debate, here, once *"Roma locuta est,"* "Rome has spoken," debate is closed. What irritated me was the ignorance of, often intolerance towards, anything outside the Catholic Church. "You're Protestant?" people would ask me nervously. "Does that mean you can't eat pork?" The intolerance not just of other religions but of other types of Christianity is unfortunately fostered by the upper echelons of the Church. Protestantism is dismissed even before it's understood. In August 2000 a Church declaration (called *Dominus Jesus* and endorsed by the Pope) announced that the Catholic Church represented the only "valid" and "genuine" Christian episcopate. Any other type of ordination—either Anglican or Nonconformist—was simple heresy. Even to many Catholic onlookers it appeared like something from the Middle Ages. The inspiration for such announcements is invariably Joseph Cardinal Ratzinger, a man who heads what is called the Congregation for the Doctrine of the Faith (an organisation which acts as the guard dog against pluralism and tolerance; the congregation is a direct descendant of the Inquisition).

It doesn't take long to realise that Roman Catholicism is excruciatingly conservative and—like Italy itself—acutely hierarchical. Its spiritual nourishment is provided by a monarch and his minions. The role of the priesthood is, for a Protestant, astonishing, and the notion that the apostolic succession is incarnate in one infallible human being left me a little incredulous. The knock-on effect is a priesthood which is an intermediary, which intercedes on your behalf. Your personal faith is delegated and entrusted to, interpreted by, another person. Modes of behaviour which find no justification in the Bible become habitual, ritualistic. If I hadn't felt so strongly about Christianity and what it means to me, I wouldn't have cared; but Catholicism was the one thing I longed to understand, and at the same time the thing that most disconcerted me. It seemed as if there were a type of spiritual safe, guarded

only by initiates. They, not the Bible, held all the keys. It began to appear that Italian Catholicism is based more on the
pietra, the papal stone, than on the *parola*, the biblical word.

An obvious consequence is a visceral anticlericalism. In
Emilia-Romagna there's even a shape of pasta called the *stroz-
zapreti*, "priest stranglers." I'm frequently asked by the army
of anticlericals what my most creative British blasphemy is.
The disappointment, not to say disbelief, when I'm unable to
produce a decent blasphemy is tangible. "Our priests," I always have to explain, "simply aren't powerful enough to
make us want to blaspheme. You would have to go to Ireland
for that." The one thing that really got me thinking was the
fact that a Catholic church is the only place in Italy I'm guaranteed not to hear singing. Or I might hear singing, but not
the joyful, uplifting arias I can hear just walking along the
street. It's more timid, doleful. Since the congregation is re-
cipient rather than participant, sacred music is sung largely by
the priest, not the people.

The Vatican, in fact, is viewed by even the most devout
Catholics as a country of purple finery, of power and prestige,
which often seem the antithesis of Christianity. In 1563, the
Venetian ambassador to Rome described the atmosphere of
the Vatican: "Here adulation is dressed up as honesty, a con as
courtesy. Every vice appears masked. Simulation is the soul of
the court." It's a judgement which has been repeatedly
echoed. According to anonymous priests who recently published an insider's critique of the Vatican, "Pretense in the
Vatican becomes second nature, which has the end of domi-
nating the first [nature]. The hypocrites are flatterers and tu-
tors of all the faked virtues, whilst they defame and persecute
the truth."[2]

Slowly, however, as I went to services, I began to enjoy
precisely what, for centuries, had been the butt of jokes by
northern Europeans and Americans: the ritual. From Henry

James to Charles Dickens, Catholicism was criticised as nothing more than laughable foppery. One word always seems on the tip of their Protestant tongues: "paganism." James described one Pope as "that flaccid old woman waving his ridiculous fingers over the prostrate multitude"; he eventually "turned away sickened by its absolute obscenity."[3] Dickens was no less scathing. Churches, he said, looked like a "Goldsmith's shop" or a "lavish pantomime"; "I have been infinitely more affected in many English cathedrals when the organ has been playing." For their tastes, Catholicism was all too visual, tactile, the air too thick with incense. Dickens couldn't stand the "perfect army of cardinals and priests, in red, gold, purple, violet, white, and fine linen."[4] But that folkloric side, the blood-and-earth atmosphere, the glint of gold, and the clicking on and off of electric candles, is exactly what I began to enjoy. It's a religion which is felt rather than thought. Seeing and touching and smelling have become integral to believing, which is why churches are museums, houses of both high art and the desperately kitsch. Their centrepieces are often relics which can be glimpsed through narrow grates: a fist of earth from Calvary containing Christ's blood (in Mantova); San Gennaro's blood, which occasionally liquefies (in Naples); the remains of Saint Nicholas (at Bari). Relics, if you're imaginative, are just morbid meditational prompts in the Church's sensuous assault on its believers.

I found myself having to think very deeply about what I actually believe. I wanted to explain why it's possible to believe in a Christianity profoundly different from Catholicism. For me a "state of grace" is not something that someone else can give me. If I have sinned, forgiveness is proceeded by my repentance. I couldn't understand where the external confessional came in the equation. It seemed, historically, a good fund-raiser or, more recently, a means to keep sheep in the Catholic fold after apostasy. It was also probably, I thought, in some ways responsible for the habitual impunity of Italian society. As for the iconography of the Madonna, it initially left me bemused. Outside Catholicism, there is no comparable figure. Protestants admire the Virgin as the mother of Jesus Christ, but there is not devotion to or a cult or veneration of her. Since Mary was human, she is not prayed to, her intervention isn't invoked. There are saints in Protestantism, but their role is symbolic, an imitation to be followed rather than venerated and iconised. They are entirely separate from the deity.

In long discussions with Catholic friends—those who believe profoundly in their faith—my initial irritation began to subside, and I started to appreciate how wrong I had been about certain things. Catholicism came to appear—like all religions—beautiful and bizarre, contradictory and yet coherent. Despite my aversion for Mariolatry, I did appreciate its importance: it's completely unquantifiable, of course, but the Madonna is probably the reason that some notion of the family as a "sacred unit," having evaporated elsewhere, still exists in Italy. It's certainly the reason that maternity has such an exalted status. The confessional, it slowly dawned on me, contains an admirable sincerity. It recognises transgression but transcends it. I began to recognise the amazing work of hundreds of thousands of volunteers who, through Catholic organisations, dedicate entire weekends, or entire summer holidays, to helping immigrants or the ill or the aged. Whenever I spoke with those volunteers, they would always urge me to read not encyclicals from the Vatican but the gentler words from the Second Vatican Council (1962–65). That theology, they said, talked about a social rather than an authoritarian religion and represented the true Church. The Second Vatican Council was an attempt at a modern Magna Carta, an attempt to involve bishops, even the laity, in the decisions of the Church. Many would say that its objectives have by now been entirely defeated by the Church's extraordinary conservatism, but the documents from Vatican II stand out for their lyricism and tolerance. In the encyclical *Nostra aetate*, for example, the Church announced its "sincere respect for those ways of acting and living, those moral and doctrinal teachings which may differ in many respects from what she holds and teaches, but which none the less often reflect the brightness of that Truth, which is the light of all men."

One day, I was getting bored with my work, bored of sitting at home with the computer whirring insistently. I shut it down and decided to read the King James Version of the Bible. It opened on that verse urging hospitality to strangers. At that exact moment, the doorbell rang. The timing was uncanny, and I walked towards the door, curious to see who had been "sent." There in front of me was a priest, politely asking if he might bless the flat since it was Easter. I invited him in. I was supposed to read a prayer (which mentioned loyalty to the local bishop, of course, before God even entered the equation), and then he started blessing the flat. I even found myself ushering him towards certain objects—computer, football boots—which need all the holy water they can get. Then we sat down and gently argued about theology for an hour.

The lack of patriotism in Italy is presumably connected to the fact that the Vatican and its papacy were once the enemies of the Italian state. The lack of pride or goodwill towards Italy is in large part thanks to the hostility of that other country called the Vatican. After the Risorgimento, the attitude of the Vatican towards the new nation was one of suspicion. The Vatican demanded from its devotees a veto of the newly born Italian state. Catholics were urged not to participate in elections (on pain of excommunication) and were warned in apocalyptic terms of the dangers of the lay state which was besieging the Holy See. Until 1920, the papacy forbade foreign (Catholic) heads of state to visit Rome, fearing that it would give the Italian state undue recognition.

Only with Mussolini's Lateran Pacts of 1929 were diplomatic relations established between the two states, allowing the two to begin their loving, sometimes suffocating, embrace. Not for the last time, it appeared that the Catholic Church was more at ease with right-wing dictators than with parliamentary democracy. In Italy, a whole range of cardinals (Ildefonso Schuster, Archbishop of Milan; Giuseppe Siri, Archbishop of Genoa; Giuseppe Pizzardo; Nicola Canali; Alfredo Ottaviani) were proud advocates of Fascism. The Church's collusion, however, barely seemed to affect its postwar prestige (apart from the agreement with Mussolini, there had been a concordat with the Nazi regime, and Pope Pius XII remained eerily silent on the Holocaust). A former Vatican librarian, Alcide De Gasperi, became the leader of the newly formed Christian Democratic party, which duly won the vital 1948 election. (De Gasperi's wily young secretary was Giulio Andreotti; an old joke went that when De Gasperi went into church and closed his eyes to pray to God, Andreotti got up to sort things out with the priest.) Catholic organisations like Azione Cattolica (which by 1954 had attracted 3 million members) were to provide other historic leaders of the Christian Democrats like Aldo Moro.

The intricate system of spiritual blackmail and bribery (excommunication of Communist voters, for example, was announced in 1943) meant that the Catholic Church was always able to nudge and knead Italian political life. Traditionally, for example, Madonnas started weeping around election time, especially if it looked like the left was on the brink of victory. In 1948 in Naples, when the Communist Party looked likely to assume power, no fewer than thirty-six Madonnas began to shed tears. It's a good example of the strange clandestine control the Catholic Church has over Italian politics, of its uncanny ability to let the interior, spiritual side of life well up and overflow into the purely political. Although abortion and divorce were tortuously legalised in the 1970s, there are still strange laws which hint at the reach of the Catholic Church. All religious teachers within schools, for example, have to receive a stamp of approval from the local Catholic bishop.

Pope John Paul II is, few doubt it, a deeply spiritual man. He fights for what he believes in. He teaches Christianity to millions of people. He has always urged peaceful resolutions. He has acknowledged Judaism as Christianity's "older brother." Under his command, the Catholic Church has also partially apologised for its own intolerance during the Counter-Reformation. Now a bowed figure shaking with Parkinson's, he still relentlessly travels the world, angrily admonishing those who fail to heed his slurred words. He has sometimes tried to promote the unity of Christianity and urge ecumenicalism. Against the wishes of both the Catholic hierarchy and the Greek Orthodox Church, he visited Greece in 2001 and pleaded that the Western Church and the Eastern Church become the left and right lungs of a united Christianity. He also apologised for the sins committed by Catholics against the Orthodox Church during the Fourth Crusade. That brave decision to apologise was seen as a wooing of not only the Greek Orthodox Church but also the Russian one. Wojtyla is a Pole who suffered under Soviet rule, and the political implications of his pontificate were, during the Cold War, very obvious. In 1984 he dedicated the Soviet Union to the Immaculate Heart of Mary (as was commanded by the Virgin in the revelations at Fátima). He has made it his dying ambition to be admitted to Russia.

For a number of reasons, though, John Paul II has taken his Church in the opposite direction from Protestantism. There has been not a convergence between the two faiths but an ever-widening gap. The Pope has beatified more people (1,310) and made more saints (280) than were given the honour during the previous five centuries of Catholicism. To mark the twenty-fourth anniversary of his succession, he added another five "miracles of light" to the Catholic rosary. Depending on how you look at it, it's an example of either a proliferation of faith or a proliferation of ephemera. The figure of the Pope, too, has radically altered. John Paul II has become an expert media magnet; even Catholics complain that the incessant travelling and press releases and political stances somehow detract from what's actually written in the Bible.

His pontificate will also be remembered for the centrality of the Fátima Madonna. The bullet which, on 13 May 1981, was fired at Pope John Paul II is now lodged in the crown of the Madonna of Fátima in Portugal. The Pope's desire to place the bullet there was the denouement of the story of Italian Catholicism in the twentieth century. Fátima, like Lourdes or San Giovanni Rotondo, is a vital place of pilgrimage for modern Catholics. On 13 May 1917 (exactly sixty-four years before the shooting of John Paul II) three young peasants in Fátima received visions from the Madonna. The revelations were in three parts. The first warned of the condition of hell for transgressors against God. The second revelation, a few months later, was more temporal: "If my requests are not granted," the godhead revealed to the children, "Russia will spread its errors throughout the world, raising up wars and persecutions against the Church." The political message, on the eve of the Bolshevik revolution, was understood and widely publicised. Strange, specific observances were apparently required of true believers: the necessity of the rosary, the wearing of the brown scapular. On 13 October, just days before Lenin took power in Russia, seventy thousand believers gathered in the small Portuguese village, where the children had promised a miracle to testify to the truth of the message. Observers described a moment in which the sun seemed to "dance" and change colour in the sky (an event now classified by the Church as "a veritable miracle").

The third "secret" was written down in the 1940s but remained unrevealed for the rest of the twentieth century. Only in 2000, at the ceremony in which two of the Portuguese peasant children—Francisco Marto and his sister Jacinta—were beatified, did John Paul II make the third secret public: speaking of the killing of a "white bishop" by enemies of the faith, it was interpreted as a prediction of the assassination attempt against the Pope himself. The shooting had occurred in 1981, on the day the Church calls the Feast of Our Lady of Fátima. Karol Wojtyla, with his grey hair and white cassock, was slowly being driven through the crowds outside St Peter's. A Turk, Mehmet Ali Agca, stepped forwards and fired. The Pope (the first non-Italian pontiff since 1523) collapsed, apparently whispering, "Mary, mother of mine," as his entourage rushed towards him. The Pope, though, has never shown any interest in who, apart from Agca, was responsible for the shooting. Rather, he's constantly emphasised who it was who saved him: "One hand shot, another hand guided the bullet," he once said. On the first anniversary of the shooting he went to Fátima to give thanks to the Virgin and place the bullet in her crown.

The other important event of late-twentieth-century Vatican history was, of course, its connection to murky finance. During the 1970s, a suave American bishop from Chicago, Paul Marcinkus, had risen to the top of the Vatican's "bank," the so-called Institute for Religious Works (the Istituto per le Opere di Religione, or IOR). Roberto Calvi, another ambitious banker, had meanwhile risen through the ranks of the Banco Ambrosiano in Milan. It was traditionally a bank for Catholic investors; even the name was taken from Milan's patron saint. When the two were introduced by a Sicilian tax expert, Michele Sindona, they worked out an intricate banking scam in which the Vatican would be the conduit for the exportation of huge

*sums of capital. The IOR's secrecy, as well as the respectable front
it offered Ambrosiano, made it the ideal accomplice.*

*Throughout the 1970s, Calvi shifted billions of lire into offshore
accounts in Luxembourg, Nicaragua, Peru, and Nassau. The
transactions were so complicated that when the lire returned to
Italy, propping up shares in the Banco Ambrosiano or falsely inflating other investments, the provenance was never certain and
no one could prove that the IOR and Calvi were engaged in a
very profitable paper-chase. By the late 1970s, the bank had accu-
mulated debts of $1.3 billion to businesses which were little more
than addresses in the Caribbean. As the sums loaned became ever
larger, the Bank of Italy—which oversaw the 1,060 banks on the
peninsula—began to investigate. Sindona's businesses were already creaking, as many began to suspect that his "golden touch"
was nothing more than false accounting and spurious share issues.
The man sent in to study Sindona's accounts, Giorgio Ambrosoli,
was first threatened, then murdered in July 1979. The man sent to
investigate Calvi's own bank, Emilio Alessandrini, was also murdered by a terrorist outfit (Alessandrini was also linked to the investigations into Piazza Fontana, having been one of the first to
incriminate Pino Rauti and his Ordine Nuovo). There was also
an attempt to frame managers at the Bank of Italy, and a new
governor, Carlo Azeglio Ciampi, was chosen to head the difficult,
and dangerous, investigative operation.*

*Magistrates investigating the murder of Ambrosoli and the
strange, faked kidnapping of Michele Sindona kept coming
across references to one Licio Gelli. Gelli was a former Fascist,
having fought in Mussolini's volunteers in his teens, and was to
become—alongside Andreotti—the most mysterious figure of
postwar Italy. One journalist described him with the following
evocative words:*

> *[Gelli] understands more than he lets on; he's courteous, meta-
> phorical, allusive, slippery. He weighs his words, doesn't raise his*

voice; he measures his gestures. Nothing seems to upset him . . .
[N]ever have we been caught up in an enigma more enigmatic,
in a sibyl more sibylline.[5]

The investigating magistrates decided to raid Gelli's various
addresses: his suite at the Excelsior Hotel in Rome, his villa in
Arezzo, an old business address in Frosinone, and the Giole tex-
tile factory in Castiglion Fibocchi. At the factory, a safe was
found containing a mass of documents and a list of 950 names:
members of what emerged as the "register" of Propaganda Due
(P2), a Masonic lodge which included fifty-two officials of the
Carabinieri, fifty army officers, thirty-seven members of the
Treasury Police, five government ministers, thirty-eight members
of Parliament, fourteen judges, ten bank presidents, and vari-
ous journalists and editors. In short, the most powerful men in
Italy appeared tied to a secretive, occasionally murderous or-
ganisation whose manifesto was called "A Plan for the Rebirth
of Democracy." That manifesto, discovered in the briefcase of
Gelli's daughter at Rome airport, included a rewriting of the
Italian constitution, control of mass media, the removal of par-
liamentary immunity, and the suspension of union activity.
Gelli was the "venerable maestro" of a Masonic lodge which
seemed to link, albeit without explanation, coups and bombings
and murders throughout the 1970s.

The startling revelations about P2 seemed to explain much
about the underbelly of Italian life. The discovery of the Mani-
festo was an event which, in the words of one historian, "touched
one of the deepest constants in postwar Italy, and one that it is
most difficult to write about with any degree of historical cer-
tainty. Behind the surface of Italian democracy lay a secret
history, made up of hidden associations, contacts, and even con-
spiracies, some farcical and others more serious."[6] *The discovery*
of P2 was a moment which, as it was poetically described to me
by one politician, was like the effect of approaching and grasp-

ing the aerial of a cheap television: suddenly the interference and blurred picture come into focus, and you can finally see, hear, and understand what has been going on. Retrospectively, it was possible to see connections between cases, and understand various mysteries. It began to look as if the paranoia about a parallel state, a shadow government which controlled banking, business, and the media, might not have been misplaced after all. Not for the first time, the Italian media were caught up in, rather than just reporting, the news: the Rizzoli family, owner of Corriere della Sera *and at the time a quarter of all other Italian newspapers, was heavily compromised by its proximity, and that of its journalists, to P2.*

Recent revisionism of P2 in Italy has suggested that the aspirations of the lodge were purely financial and that very few of those involved knew of its more sinister operations. Others suggest that the whole lodge, looking so sinister from the outside, was, from the inside, a chimera which many P2ers didn't even realise they had joined. Whatever the truth, the traces of Gelli and his P2 are evident in every iconic crime from Borghese's "coup" of 1970 until the Bologna bombing of 1980, which claimed eighty-five lives. The subsequent parliamentary inquiry wrote: "This committee has reached the reasoned conclusion, shared by several courts, that the lodge . . . established ongoing links with subversive groups and organisations, instigating and countenancing their criminal purposes."[7] Terrorist groups had been prompted and nudged, the report said, by P2.

As for the Banco Ambrosiano, as the investigative net closed in on Calvi, the rogue banker, he escaped to London. There he was found hanged under Blackfriars' Bridge in June 1982. Calvi's secretary, Graziella Corrocher, had also fallen to her death in what, by contrast, appeared a genuine suicide. When Sindona was arrested and imprisoned, he was passed a poisoned coffee by ignoti, *or "unknowns," an act which fulfilled his prediction that he would be murdered in prison. The Banco Am-*

brosiano, saddled with epic debts and no returns, duly collapsed. The most obvious beneficiaries of the whole affair were the Vatican and the political parties. No major political party wasn't on Calvi's payroll: they had collectively received as much as 88 billion lire from him throughout the 1970s. Bettino Craxi's name, and the number of his Swiss bank account credited with $7 million by Calvi, were amongst Gelli's documents. The Vatican, for its part, displayed a reluctance to excuse or even explain itself. The creditors asked Paul Marcinkus, the American bishop, for a return on their investment but were met with only silence. The IOR, responsible for creaming off millions in mysterious deals, washed its hands of the dirty affair.

I mention the whole story not because it's in any way representative of Italy or Catholicism but because three of the subplots from the Calvi case and P2 re-emerged onto the scene exactly twenty years to the day after the shooting of John Paul II: it was 13 May 2001, the day of the Feast of Our Lady of Fátima. The noble banker from the Bank of Italy, a man who had fought against the Fascists in the 1940s before becoming Prime Minister in the 1990s, was then President of the Republic. Carlo Azeglio Ciampi was, on this election day, expected to oversee the smooth, constitutional handover of power. The man who was to become Prime Minister was once on the roll-call of P2 members and is the epitome of the lodge's avowed intention to "rebaptise Italian democracy" through control of the mass media and the rewriting of the constitution: Silvio Berlusconi. Meanwhile, the Pope, twenty years after the shooting, is celebrating Mass in St Peter's.

In the morning's newspapers I see that the son of Roberto Calvi is now claiming that his father had confided in the Pope. Calvi, before his "suicide" in London, had told his son that he had spoken with John Paul II and that the shooting of the Pope was organised by the same people who were hounding and threatening Calvi himself. The Vatican was so intimately involved with Calvi, went the son's theory, that the Pope himself almost

*became another victim of the banking fiasco and its masonic
connections. As ever, I wasn't sure what to believe: there seemed
so much paranoia and* complottismo—*conspiracy theorising—
but at the same time there seemed so many reasons to justify the
paranoia.*

February 2003. It's snowing heavily, and as we enter the
village, Filippo slips the car into first gear. All around us
are imposing mountains, their peaks like whipped cream.
Rainbow-coloured peace flags hang from the balcony of almost every house; a few tricolours also billow in the wind.
But something about this village feels very unusual. You can
sense it looking at the architecture: it's plainer, simpler,
"straighter." There's no baroque here, no extravagant *centro
storico*. It looks, to a Welsh eye, like home.

An hour or two later it's pitch-black and we're outside the
church. There are about two hundred people huddling in the
snow, lighting torches. The flames twist in the wind, wax
drops onto the fresh snow. People greet relatives they haven't
seen for months, maybe years. The procession eventually sets
off, and we walk uphill for half an hour. Occasionally we pass
farmhouses, the walls of their outhouses punctured by diago-
nal gun-openings facing back down the valley.

We reach a clearing, and a huge bonfire is spitting sparks
high into the night sky. Everyone plants his or her burning
torch in the snow. Within minutes, from way up on the
mountain tops, other bonfires are lit by unseen hands: first
one, on the distant peak a mile away, then another, then another. The adults start singing four-part harmonies as their
children roll snowmen. It's a stunningly beautiful scene. It's
serene and—in a way that only a mountain winter can be—
very warm.

I had been meaning to come here for years. I'm drawn to
these places, these Italian villages with odd British connec-

tions: Mozia and Joseph Whitaker, Marsala and John Wood-house. But Torre Pellice, this Piedmont village, is different. This is, for me, a pilgrimage. This is the centre of Italian Protestantism, a place with a noble history of religious and military resistance. Tonight, this bonfire is lit to commemorate liberation from Catholicism: on 17 February 1848, the famous edict of Carlo Alberto (King of Piedmont and Sardinia) finally recognised the political and social existence of the Waldensian and Jewish communities. Tomorrow, Monday the seventeenth, is a local holiday. It sounds rather insignificant until you realise that this is a people whose ancestors were burnt, throughout centuries, for their Christian beliefs. No one says it tonight as we chat with *vin brûlé* in our hands. But that's the importance of these pyres: they're lit to recall the sacrifice of thousands of Waldensians who lost their lives "protesting" for Protestantism.

It all started with Valdo, who, in around 1170, began preaching the gospel to anyone who would listen. He refused to accept the bishop's ban on his preaching and was excommunicated and persecuted, as were his followers. Centuries later, Martin Luther initiated the Reformation as he "protested" against the Diet of Spires in 1529. It wasn't protesting in the sense of disobedience; it was conceived as a positive action: *un'attestazione pro*, bearing witness in favour of something. In the eyes of Protestants, reading the Bible was the most important Christian activity. The most daring smugglers in Italian history became the *colportori*, the itinerant preachers whose only ambition was to give people copies of the Bible in the vernacular. Many were killed for no sin greater than distributing the Bible. The tiny community of the Waldensian valleys became a pawn in the wars of religion between Catholic countries largely in southern Europe and Protestant ones largely in the north. It was that atmosphere which inspired one of Milton's most moving sonnets, "On the Late Massacre in Piedmont":

Avenge, O Lord, thy slaughtered saints, whose bones
Lie scattered on the Alpine mountains cold,
Even them who kept thy truth so pure of old,
When all our fathers worshipped stocks and stones.[8]

The more you scratch the surface, the more you realise how the tiny Protestant community in Italy has often had a hand in history. Switzerland would never have become one of the banking capitals of the world if it hadn't benefited from Protestant immigrants from Tuscany, especially Lucca. It's hard to imagine the Risorgimento without reference to Protestantism's influence: Garibaldi, author of ferocious anti-Catholic literature, was appreciated in Britain precisely because he was seen as a counterweight to Europe's Catholic powers, a man who could usher in a latter-day Reformation. The British, self-interested as always, saw the invasion of the Papal States with much satisfaction, be it political or religious. One of the most original and interesting Italian prime ministers of the twentieth century, Baron Giorgio Sidney Sonnino, was blessed with both Tuscan and Welsh parents, and his Protestantism informed much of his attempt to introduce universal suffrage as early as 1882. At the same time, his blind belief—typically British—in monarchy prompted his *Torniamo allo Statuto* monograph, urging a return to the Statuto Albertino, in which the monarch would enjoy executive powers.

In fact, although there are endless attempts to airbrush religious minorities out of the national narrative, Italy has always been surprisingly pluralistic. The oldest Jewish community in Europe (established in 161 BC) is in Rome. The relationship hasn't, of course, always been harmonious: centuries before the Inquisition and the Race Laws of 1938, Emperor Domitian built an arch in the centre of Rome to commemorate the victory of Titus over the Jews of Jerusalem in AD 70 (the Talmud forbids Jews to walk under the arch). But the contribution of the Jewish community to Italian life—not least during the literary renaissance in Turin in the postwar years—is immense. So, too, is that of Islam: Palermo was, from 831, called al-Madinah, and the island remained under Arabic rule for over two hundred years, during which time a host of new crops—cotton, sugar cane, lemons—were introduced. Walking around Sicily, one can still see the remnants of that Moorish culture in the aquatic Saracen blue which decorates ancient doorways and walls. Today Islam is, by a very long way, the fastest-growing religion in Italy, thanks to a combination of converts and immigrants.

The next day, Filippo and I go to the service. We sing "Il giuro di Sibaud," commemorating the repatriation of 1689, when members of the Waldensian community fought their way from Switzerland, across mountain passes, to reclaim their stolen territories in Italy, in these valleys. The pastor keeps repeating one question: "Waldensian, what are you doing here?" The delivery is both gentle and stern. Outside the church the feeling is very international. Women are in the traditional bonnets and frocks, but all nationalities are here: Germans, Swiss, British, Americans, South Americans. And that, in fact, is the feeling in this valley. There's a tolerance about all sorts of differences. It's quiet and contemplative. People speak different languages and sit in the cafés reading *The New York Review of Books* or *La Riforma*. Perhaps I feel so comfortable here because, quite apart from the hospitality, I feel in a religious minority. You sense you're far from state religion here. You're far from government. Probably as far as you can get on Italian soil.

I don't write all this to proselytise Protestantism. I only write it because I'm trying to understand better a corner of Piedmont and what it means to hundreds of thousands of Italians who feel alienated by the papal version of Christianity. And also, I suppose, I've come to Torre Pellice because I'm still drawn to those Italian villages where there are memories of eccentric Englishmen—not because I'm patriotic, but because it makes me feel a little more at home, a little less like a foreigner. Torre Pellice's Englishman (actually born in Canada) was a one-legged veteran of Waterloo. General Charles Beckwith arrived in the early nineteenth century and built 170 tiny schools across the mountainside. It was Beckwith who built the Waldensian temple in Turin in 1853, the first outside the valleys.

What really interests me, I suppose, is the influence all this has on Italy. Or rather, doesn't have. How does the mind-set of a country change when it is steeped in Protestantism or Catholicism? What are the consequences for a country like Britain, moulded by the Reformation, or for a country like Italy, moulded by its antithesis, the Counter-Reformation? Quite apart from the theological debates, politically Britain was radically altered. An entire state of the realm was disposed of in a few breathless years: into the vacuum stepped, first, ambitious monarchs, then parliamentary dictatorship, and eventually parliamentary democracy. The main consequence, though, was the "word." Protestantism went hand in hand with printing. John Foxe's famous comments about printing epitomise the sense that it was the divine weapon against the Pope:

> God has gone to work for his Church, combatting his powerful adversary not with the sword but with the art of printing,

with Scripture and the letter . . . [T]hus the Pope will have to abolish knowledge and printing or else the latter will have victory over him.[9]

Protestantism and printing ushered in a flowering of literary culture, deeply prompted sometimes by Protestantism (Milton) and sometimes by the rediscovery of the profane or the classical (Shakespeare). Certain genres of literature died out; others were invented. Anticlericalism—like blasphemy—exists as a literary genre only in Catholic countries: Boccaccio, Guicciardini, Masuccio, Sacchetti—all are inconceivable against a Protestant backdrop. In Britain, the genre, having peaked with Chaucer, died out, only occasionally surfacing with Gothic novels like Ann Radcliffe's *The Italian*. Meanwhile, the novel became—after the initial impetus of *Don Quixote*—a largely northern European phenomenon. The novel form was the literary consequence of the Reformation. It represented the discovery of an individual consciousness and internal thought processes. One only need count the number of novels in Britain whose titles are names and surnames (*Pamela*, *Clarissa*, *Tom Jones*, *Daniel Deronda*, *Robinson Crusoe*, and so on) to understand the centrality of conscience and consciousness.

In terms of the visual arts, though, Britain committed cultural suicide. The iconoclasm was ferocious, razing some of the most important spiritual centres of the country. Anyone who, for example, goes to the ruins of Rievaulx Abbey in Yorkshire can't help but be moved by the rapacity of the English anti-Catholicism. Now Britain's most famous abbeys and cathedrals are visited by art historians who admire the masonry, the fan vaulting, the woodcarving, and the sound of the organ. Occasionally there will be stained glass, but normally pictoral, representative art is entirely absent. The emphasis is on simplicity and austerity. In fact, for over a century, from the mid-sixteenth to the mid-seventeenth century, British painting was almost non-existent. The visual arts in Britain, paralysed by the iconoclasm of the Reformation, only recovered in the second half of the seventeenth century, when French Huguenots and Dutch Protestants arrived from mainland Europe, having fled their respective countries because of the revocation of the Edict of Nantes in 1685. In the visual arts, Britain was, as it's always been, an importer of ideas. Compare the paucity of artistic achievement with the blossoming of literary culture, and the visual-verbal watershed of the Reformation is obvious. Architectural inspiration continued to be wholly based upon Italian examples: Inigo Jones (who many academics argue was a covert Catholic) and Sir Christopher Wren imitated Italy. St. Paul's in London, following the 1666 fire, was redesigned by Wren both as an imitation of and as a counterpoint to St. Peter's.

The consequence for Italy was the reverse. The country's architects built ever more grandiose exteriors and lavishly decorated the interiors. The tradition of the *Biblia pauperum*— the "poor man's Bible" of images rather than texts—was extended and exaggerated: Christianity was to be taught through the visual arts. In terms of literacy and illiteracy, though, the country suffered. The *Indice*, listing banned books, crippled nascent printing industries across the peninsula, especially in Tuscany and Venice. Books required an imprimatur from the Church. Learning was being limited to the learned, the initiated, the clerical classes. Only abolished by Paul VI in 1966, the *Indice* represented four centuries of censorship. It represented the ambition to control knowledge, ignore it, rather than reach for it.

The more abstract implications of the watershed are difficult to pin down. Some have suggested that Catholicism is, for better or worse, about obedience; Protestantism, for better or worse, is about responsibility. In one, the highest achievement is submission to a Christian leader; in the other, the submission is to one's individual Christian conscience. The implication for Italy is an innate delegation: we form part of a hierarchy and look up to our superiors. It's a vertical food-chain. Italy is a country reliant upon intervention, on go-betweens, on intermediaries. We absolve ourselves of the need to make a decision because someone higher up has made it for us. As Giorgio Tourn has written:

> In the medieval world, delegation meant submission to a feudal power, the removal of one's own responsibilities into the hands of the nobles, patrons of art and the founts of production. In fact, the notion of individual consciousness didn't even exist. Today, in [Italy's] modern society, this behaviour translates into a resigned submission and into a self-interested dependence on the power of the state. The accusation which Italians level at their state—that it's dysfunctional, that it fails to intervene, that it's bureaucratic—finds analogies in all modern states, but in ours it assumes pathological proportions because of this enduring sense of dependence and delegation.[10]

The other abstract consequence of Catholicism for Italy is the formal obedience to the law coupled with a daily breaking of it. We go through the motions of legality, but it's something we do grudgingly rather than because we believe in the law itself. (The fact that Italy has the lowest birth rate in Europe is, perhaps, the crudest example.) Because there are so many regulations and diktats from ecclesiastical authorities with which, for decades and centuries, we have been unable to agree, we feel justified in going against the teaching, even if we formally, officially, apparently adhere to it. According to many observers, Italian Catholicism causes the chasm between appearance and reality, between what is declared publicly and what is practised privately. Also, since there is a profound anticlericalism which extends far beyond disdain for religious orders, Italians are acutely suspicious of politicians and Parliament. The gap between the Italian government and its people, completely the reverse of the almost-reverential way the British regard their state, is symptomatic of a culture in which the clerical, learned classes are separate from the vulgar masses. Above all, the predominance of one strand of one religion means that Italy, for all its divisions, is remarkably homogeneous. It is mono-cultural. The research into different faiths is minimal. Invariably, they are simply ignored. No non-Catholic interlocutor is possible, permissible. It creates a cultural castle in which outsiders, those on the other side of the *limes* (the fortified boundary of the Roman Empire), are seen as heretics and barbarians.

There's something very reassuring about discovering that what you've been pondering for years has actually been written about for centuries (even if it means your observations are probably, therefore, not particularly original). When I read the famous criticisms of the Catholic Church written by the Swiss historian Jean-Charles-Léonard Simonde de Sismondi in 1818, I can empathise; and yet when I read Alessandro Manzoni's defence of Catholic morality, a written reply to Sismondi, I can recognise the phrases I've been trying to understand ever since I've lived here. In the end, debating the differences between two sides of the same faith is, as Sismondi wrote, like "trying to box in the dark."[11] You can't entirely see or understand what you're up against. Probably you don't even want to come to blows. You simply want, as in all religions, to see in the dark.

7

"FEWER TAXES FOR EVERYONE"

The Italian manager wakes up from his nightmare in a sweat, but is quickly reassured. No fear, this is Italy. The shareholder exerts power over 100 per cent of the business, even though he controls in reality only a minimal part . . . [W]hat could anyone ever criticise him for? Perhaps of having turned a blind eye to a contract which was disadvantageous to the company, but which causes enormous benefits to the aforesaid shareholder, possibly offshore? Perhaps of having carefully hidden from shareholders how many billions the "captain's" extravagant lifestyle costs the company every year? Our feathered manager calmly turns over and falls back to a beatific sleep.
—SALVATORE BRAGANTINI

Italy invented capitalism. Or at least in Pisa and Florence and various other city-states, Italians invented the modern banking system based upon the extension of credit. It's still a country of instinctive, creative entrepreneurs: like in football, there are brilliant *fantasisti*, and the economy appears, at first, close to utopia. Largely because of the obvious anomaly that the Italian economy is, with the exception of a handful of enormous companies like Fiat, based on small to medium-sized enterprises. The engine of the country's economy is often minute, local family-run businesses which produce textiles or foodstuffs or expert engineering. The percentage, for example, of the workforce employed in companies with fewer than ten employees is, in Britain, 7.2 per cent; in America it's only 3.0 per cent. In Italy, the figure is 23.3 per cent.[1] There's still—it's obvious when you walk around the narrow backstreets of any city—an artisan class which produces, in small outlets, the finest objects of the Italian economy: the furniture, the prosciutto, the suits, the shoes, incredible intricacies of micro-engineering, and so on. Quite apart from their deserved economic success, these small enterprises give the country an other-worldly atmosphere because they're still involved in the old-fashioned art of manufacturing. Unlike in Britain, with its "tertiary economy" of financial services and management consultants, in Italy people still "make" things. Go into any of the tiny artisan grottoes and before you even see the intricately blown glass or the marbled paper or decorative tiles, you're hit by the scent of oil, sawdust, the smell of a cooking kiln.

Shopping in Britain and the United States is fairly soulless, because every city has the same stores, the same products. The landscape is dominated by ugly out-of-town supermarkets which have replaced woodlands and agricultural land. They are accompanied by huge car parks, the asphalt stretching as far as the eye can see. At home, I went to one store for all my shopping: food, clothes, medicine, furniture, gardening gear, books and newspapers and videos. Here, there's a specialisation which, admittedly, I found initially bizarre. To make the same purchases, I would have to go to eighteen different outlets, each specialising in niche products. It's more time-consuming the Italian way but infinitely more refined. The standard of service in the shops is exquisite, the lack of speed is serene. Fast food has been replaced by "slow food." There is still "character" involved: shopping is, simply, a pleasurable experience.

There's another thing you notice about the economy at the lowest level. There's a kind of generosity, which means that people exchange presents in the way that the British shake hands. It's part of that *tessuto sociale*, the "social fabric," which invariably seems better knit in Italy than anywhere else. Every time you meet a friend, he will offer you something, regardless of whether you're at his house or yours, or just passing each other on the pavement: a new CD, a book he's just finished, some new piece of pottery he's found, a new crate of wine he wants to share. Such is the extravagant generosity amongst friends that there's an old-fashioned exchange of merchandise in which the whole notion of money is almost irrelevant. For years I have had to struggle to pay restaurant bills: normally whomever I'm with will surreptitiously pay whilst I'm still swigging the digestive. When you become a regular in various shops, the shopkeepers don't worry if you can't pay for a few weeks. The economy, unlike that in Britain, seems to improve rather than erode communities.

There was also a kind of wisdom about money which made me smile. Whilst I was in a queue at the butcher's once, an old lady from Milan saw me counting out my cash: "The reason," she whispered in my ear, stating both the obvious and the profound, "for the existence of the butcher is that to buy meat you need money." I looked at her, thinking her slightly mad, but she was already laughing and slapping me on the back. There seemed to be a whole range of proverbs about swift payments and bad debts, about saving but not being avaricious. It's hard to explain exactly, but there seemed to be a whole humour and intelligence around the matter of money. People would talk about it all openly (unlike in Britain) and explain their investment tactics or their business schemes. Whenever the subject of money came up, everyone seemed to have advice about how to earn more or spend less.

When I did start trying to earn money rather than spend it, I found life very strange. There were no recruitment agencies other than for blue-collar work, and even though I applied for work as a hod carrier, they took one look at my CV and decided, I assume, that I would be too fragile. There were no vacancies other than those subject to enormous competitions for public-sector work, which, inevitably, a foreigner wouldn't win. The marketplace for jobs seemed simply stagnant. And, in a strange way, I began thinking that workers are treated worse here than in post-Thatcherite Britain. The wages on offer are minimal, and even if there are endless guarantees negotiated by the unions, there's no sense of equality between employers and employees. If you got a job in Italy, I felt, you would be so thankful you would put up with anything. The hierarchy—that rigid, indestructible hierarchy I had so often discerned—seemed set in stone in the Italian workplace. A job was like a gift from above, and you would almost not object to snail-paced promotions as long as you had your knees under a desk. It seemed, occasionally, more important to have the job than to do it.

This is when I discovered the meaning of the word *conoscenze*, "acquaintances." Apply for a job where you don't know the employer and you're wasting your time; if you know someone, however, it runs like clockwork. Once I had asked a friend for a hand and he had made a couple of phone calls on his mobile from the bar, I found a job teaching within a matter of minutes. "Why didn't you ask earlier?" he said, bemused. It was as simple as that. It all came down to *conoscenze*.

I had to be registered for VAT, which was only possible if I was registered as an Italian "resident," which in turn was only possible if I had a *permesso di soggiorno*. Two weeks before the start of the academic year, then, I was outside Parma's Questura per Stranieri, the "police office for foreigners." Knowing the acute problem of queues in Italy, I arrived at seven-thirty, half an hour before the office opened. There were already about fifty people mingling on the pavement—Moroccan men holding hands, swapping cigarettes, a group of what I assumed were eastern European women huddled together, lots of men from Africa wearing faded football shirts, their wives in lime green robes. Eight o'clock arrived and the antique door of the *questura* was still shut.

Eventually the heavy door swung to, and a policeman—decked out in shades and epaulettes—ushered us in. When, towards ten o'clock, I arrived at the counter and shouted my request through the bulletproof glass, I was given the application form for a "sojourn permit." I went to the bar across the road and began filling in the form. More and more people came in, clutching their precious forms: Albanians, Ukranians, Tunisians, Somalis. We passed around Biros borrowed from the bar for the cost of a coffee. Jokes started flying around in pidgin Italian about how Albania, or Nigeria, was more efficient than this, and shouldn't we all just go back to where we came from. By the time I had explained the form to various people, and filled in my own, the *questura* had already shut.

Seven-thirty the following day. The same crowd on the pavement, waiting for the office to open. We greeted each other like old friends. The man in the West Ham top was there. He shook my hand, delighted that the English were subjected to the same routine as Africans. After queuing for only forty-five minutes, I proudly presented my application for sojourn in Italy. The application process, of course, would require months, but, equipped with the carbon copy, I could go to the town hall to apply for "residency." Then to the tax office, to apply for VAT status: another morning gone. I was beginning to understand why people talk about doing an "operation" in a bank or an office: it really does require military precision to navigate your way through the documentation. Worse was yet to come, though. The university presented me three contracts for the three courses I was supposed to teach. Since they are formal pieces of paper, it wasn't enough to sign them: each had to be *bollata*, given an official postage stamp sold at tobacconists. Then, I was told, I had to be insured in case of personal injury incurred whilst lecturing on English literature: another 300,000 lire. A few days before the beginning of the course, I went to the faculty library to see what books were available. The stern signora from the secretarial office ran up to me: *"Ma che fai?,"* "What are you doing?"

"Trying to find a few books for next week."

"These are for the exclusive use of permanent staff. You're hired as a freelance and must buy your own." She produced the business card of a friend who could help me out.

"But I'm allowed to use the blackboard, right?"

"Haven't you read your contract?"

I hadn't, of course. It slowly dawned on me as months went by that since I was working freelance, there was no date specified as to when payment would arrive. Assuming things were done monthly, I had only looked excitedly at *quanto*, "how much," not at the much more important information, *quando*, "when." Months went by; the deep blue sky of late summer gave way to the dense fog of autumn. The snow began to fall in December, and the local electricity monopoly, called AMPS, wanted its heating bills paid promptly at the post office. Any tentative payment enquiry at the university accounts office was brushed off with brilliant ventriloquism: "It is foreseen that the pre-agreed payment as stipulated in the contracts for freelance teachers will be honoured before the end of the academic year." Months later, that line had turned into "before the beginning of the next academic year." Late payments, I realised, were the norm. Anyone who works freelance in Italy automatically faces a liquidity crisis for the blunt reason that no one ever pays when the invoice arrives.

The biggest shock, however, came with the banks. I noticed that about nine thousand lire left my account at the end of every month. Not a massive sum but, to put it in my currency, it was the equivalent of a large pint of beer which I would have preferred to have in my fist. That, the bank replied innocently, is a government tax.

"You mean, I pay even when my account is in credit?" She slowly nodded her head. I looked down the rest of the statement, which I had had to pay to see. "What's this?"

"That is a surcharge because you withdrew money on a Sunday." It was all, according to this polite lady, very normal.

"And this?" I pointed out some other minor charge— probably only a shot's worth of beer, but I was curious now.

"That is the bank's monthly administration cost."

The list went on and on. Little trickles of beer vanishing out of my account. At home, I had only ever paid interest on an overdraft. That was the only payment my bank had ever had from me. On the rare occasions when I was in credit in the United Kingdom, they had the little luxury of being able to earn more interest on my money than they paid to me. But it was very, very simple compared to here. I suddenly found banks particularly interesting. Walk round any city—especially Milan—and there are banks on every single street corner. In Parma alone there are forty-two different banks, and that's before you start counting their various branches. Banks are like political parties and television channels: there's no end to the available choice (even if, in the end, they all look the same). In a large city, there will probably be a few hundred banks on offer. It's clearly a very profitable business.

Eventually, thirteen months after starting work at the university, I did get paid. But the net sum was, after taxes and deductions like IVA and IRPEF and INPS and everything else, only about half the gross sum. Once that was whittled down by my bank charges, I would be almost *al verde*, "penniless," once more. It was like being on a treadmill in a gym which goes far too fast. You never get one step ahead.

There exists, of course, another type of employee: the *dipendente* or the *statale*. The former is someone who, normally, has his job guaranteed *a tempo indeterminato*; he is a full-time, long-term employee of a company. The *statale* is a public-sector worker, which is the luscious promised land of the Italian employee. Typically, *statali* are envied by everyone else because they enjoy a short working week, an easy workload, and no responsibility. Many are career bureaucrats, skilled in shuffling mountains of paper; some have second jobs and private enterprises on the side. On the surface their lot looks wonderful: not only is their job comfortable; it is guaranteed for time immemorial. Legally, in Italy, it's almost impossible to lay off workers, so if someone has a contract *a tempo indeterminato*, he could, if he wishes, sit back and enjoy life. Better still, there are extraordinary practices like "the thirteenth" and, sometimes, "the fourteenth." These are bonuses paid out regardless of performance. At Christmas, one receives a double payment: the twelfth and phantom thirteenth months together. Sometimes, at Christmas or before the summer holidays, one receives a fourteenth month's paycheck. Even if you resign, you get paid according to the number of years you've been an employee. It's called the TFR, the *trattamento fine rapporto*, the "end-of-relationship treatment." I've often tried and frequently failed to explain the TFR to British economists: "It's a one-off payment you get when you resign."

"You mean," they reply, "when you're sacked?"

"No, also when you resign."

"But that makes companies the bankers of their employees' wages?"

"Now you're getting there. Everything is a bank in Italy."

Slowly I realised that for all the blissful working conditions of a *statale*, wages are minimal. They're paid extra at the end of the year, or the end of the term of employment, only because they're normally paid miserably. Often a highly qualified university professor will be on about eight hundred euros per annum. Specialising medical students will be on much less. This is why Italian employees continually complain that they are *presi per i fondelli*, "taken for a ride." Job opportunities are scarce, and those that do come up are accompanied by risible wages. Taxation sees to the rest. It all creates an atmosphere in which everyone has an acute sense of injustice. I haven't seen him for years, but there used to be a man on stilts whom I would pass every day in Piazza Garibaldi. He would be shouting at the passers-by, many of whom stopped to listen to him, nodding in sympathy as his spittle fell on the pavement. There, by the base of his two-metre stilts, were long letters and documents which announced the injustice to which he had fallen victim. He was, apparently, quite famous, performing daring stunts across the country to publicise his plight. Listening to him reminded me of those forays into the post office when I first arrived here. Everyone seemed to have her own story of a scam or rip-off she had suffered. When one person started talking about his or her mishap, half a dozen others would chip in and start recounting their own swindles, which were similar or possibly even worse. We pay to have a bank account, pay to see our balance, pay to drive on the roads we paid to build . . . "*Oneri impropri!*," people shouted. Two magical words which I had heard day after day in chats with friends. "*Oneri impropri!* Unfair burdens! Do you realise," they would say, "how incredibly unfair the Italian tax burden is?" Everyone nodded, me most vigourously. I was beginning to see that there might be another way of doing things.

I started to notice that a whole load of transactions were

simply conducted in cash. Perhaps because of the confusing number of banks and documents, there's clearly a feeling that traceable transactions—receipts, Visa slips, or cheque-book stubs—are inconvenient. Paying with plastic is impossible in many places. If you are buying a table or an overcoat, even paying the bill in a restaurant, you'll often be asked whether you're paying in cash. If so, the prices are almost always *trattabili*. That, of course, is the case in any country, but in Italy even adverts for houses worth hundreds of millions of lire announce through various euphemisms that they're ready to reduce the cost if payment is in *contanti*, "countables." If you negotiate a job contract, a percentage of the sum will often be offered under the counter.

Rather self-righteously, I initially thought all the economy *in nero* was rather naughty. I expressed mild disdain to a couple of friends in the pub, and they insisted it's like that in all the world. "No," I replied, convinced by at least a few international referents, "Italy is almost unique in Europe. Of course people avoid taxes all over the world, but here it seems almost systematic. It's more unusual to pay your taxes than to dodge them."

"But that's because we have the highest tax threshold in Europe," they replied. And they were half-right. The vicious circle is that tax evasion ushers in tax increases, which only encourage tax evasion and continue the cycle. Most people calculate that there's bound to be a pardon sooner or later, so there's always the opportunity for retrospective fiscal honesty down the line. The sense that the state isn't on our side, the notion that all taxes slip into private pockets, means that there's something almost admired about avoiding contributions. I had even seen political leaders urging a *sciopero fiscale*, a "tax strike," or suggesting that the RAI licence fee shouldn't be paid, because the network was in the "wrong hands." Fiscal resistance isn't a serious offence, because, people say, the state is a thief. It's almost more honest to become part of the black economy. It's a line one politician, Silvio Berlusconi, has eloquently spoken about: taxpayers, he has said, feel "morally at loggerheads with the state," observing that the state's laws go against "our natural sense of justice."[2] It was Berlusconi who, in the fierce election of 2001, used the simplest slogan, the line which most chimed with Italians' desires: *"Meno tasse per tutti,"* "Fewer taxes for everyone."

So when it comes to transactions, even long-term contractual commitments like tenancy, a large percentage is always outside the official loop. Renting property "in the black" is very common because it suits both sides: the landlord pays no tax, so the rent is lower. You're welcome to do it legally and above-board, but then you're likely to end up in a bedsit somewhere under the ring road. If you can compromise on your morals a bit, the opportunities increase exponentially.

And if you want to buy a house, the scams are even more labyrinthine. Buying property involves so many middlemen (not only estate agents but "notaries," the richest of all Italian "professional orders") that it's not surprising that Italians are bemused by the ease and speed with which foreigners buy houses. Here, the costs and complications are so high it's clearly best to keep house buying a once-in-a-lifetime experience. The only way to save yourself 30 or 40 million lire is to take a few short cuts. Many estate agents suggested to me that if I were to pay them in cash, they would accept a 1.5-per-cent instead of 3-per-cent cut. With the "notaries" you can even pretend that you've bought the house for half the price, thus halving his cut (although you will be left with property which is worth, on the vital stamped paper, only half of what you actually paid). Alternatively, there's something called a *scrittura privata*, a "private document," a sort of "for our eyes only" agreement. Thus you can buy property for two different prices: the official one (cutting your costs, future taxes, and so on) and the "private" one (which is the real price you agree to pay the seller). Not for the first time, it became difficult for me to distinguish what was going on. There seemed, at all levels, to be parallel paths—the official one written on paper, and the hidden one going on in verbal agreements between "gentlemen."

The other problem was that frequently I was offered a flat which, given the official/reality divide, wasn't actually "in existence." The widespread practice of illegal building means that you can find something which—given your modest budget—appears a bargain: a two-bedroom attic flat on split levels in a part of the city that feels crumbling but lively. The estate agent notices your enthusiasm and whispers in your ear about how negotiable he is when it comes to cash payments. The problem is that if the flat or a part of it, say the second level, is "abusive," it simply doesn't exist in the annals of bureaucracy. The notary has been bypassed to save money, and in buying the property, you make the gamble that the "unpardoned" building doesn't get discovered, because you would have inherited the "abuse." You would, to officialise the "abuse," have to pay for the "pardon," or else keep it secret and risk the fine. It would be very unlikely anyone would ever discover your inherited "abuse," but if you had snapped up the bargain, you would already be on the well-trodden road to collusion with "illegality." Anyone who had a grudge against you could simply do the ultimate in betrayal: "denounce" you.

Since all the efficiency and speed and creativity of the market are "in the black," one is, ultimately, tempted there. Everything else is so grindingly slow, so incredibly costly, that quick cash is king. Once I had grown out of my petulant scorn for the hidden economy, I began to understand why it existed. The daily trials of conducting business are absurd. There are so many documents. It's natural, only human, that a submerged alternative exists. "Don't worry, we'll work it out between ourselves," people kept saying to me kindly, dropping their prices if I paid in cash. Stay in the country long enough and you simply have to become "cunning" in order to survive. With a shrug of honest admission, everyone in Italy confers to having broken the law at some point (it's hard not to when "being an accessory to tax evasion" involves leaving a shop without the till receipt). Catholics mention original sin and our fallen nature; politicians talk about being realistic rather than ideological about the law. Everyone has a bit of "black." It's only a matter of degree. *Così fan tutti*: everyone's guilty of something, so if you go looking for dirt, you'll find it anywhere.

The other side of the economy is the complete opposite of those small enterprises: huge para-statal companies employing hundreds of thousands of people. As in politics, in economics there was a marked continuum between Mussolini's regime and the First Republic. The many acronyms from Fascism such as IRI (the Institute for Industrial Reconstruction), IMI (the Italian Property Institute), and AGIP (the Italian General Agency for Petroleum) survived untouched. To those state enterprises, founded in 1933, 1931, and 1926, respectively, was added another in 1953, ENI (the National Petroleum Company). Thus the public-sector workforce remained much as it was under Mussolini: in 1942 IRI had employed 210,000 people; in 1955 it was still employing 187,000 people and would, seven years later, become Europe's biggest industrial group after Royal Dutch/Shell.

The other catalyst for Italy's postwar reconstruction was Mediobanca, founded as an offshoot of the Banca Commerciale Italiana in 1946 and nestled just behind La Scala in Milan. It was, until his death in 2000, for over fifty years the private domain of a banker called Enrico Cuccia. Here, too, the continuities with the Fascist period are marked: Cuccia had married the daughter of Alberto Beneduce, the man who, under Mussolini, had been president of both IMI and IRI. Mediobanca provided credit to the country's commercial ventures, receiving in exchange large shares itself or positions on the board. (It now has a market capitalisation of almost £7 billion and owns, amongst other assets, Assicurazioni Generali, Europe's third-largest insurer. Mediolanum, a bank in which Berlusconi has a 36-per-cent stake, is now part of the controlling shareholder group of Mediobanca.)

For all the subsequent criticisms aimed at the Christian Democrats, their rebuilding of the Italian economy was a brilliant piece of strategic management. Mediobanca, with its secretive system of overlapping interests, provided capital investment. Those semi-public corporations (often blamed for the later distortions of the Italian economy) for decades laid the foundations for Italy's industrial revolution. Thanks to their partnerships with private enterprises, those para-statal companies offered Italy the best of both worlds: the guiding hand of the public state combined with the acute capitalist judgements of private enterprise. As a result, the raw materials and the physical infrastructure required for the country's economic miracle were quickly put in place. To give just one example: steel production, controlled by IRI through the Finsider company, had reached 3 million tons by 1955; the obvious beneficiary was Fiat, which in turn increased production by some 400 per cent during the 1950s.

Thanks to the low value of the lira, and the low labour costs of the immediate postwar years, the "miracle" was export-led. For much of the postwar years, the percentage growth of exports—cars, chemicals, clothes, and so on—was in double figures. The crisis only arrived in the 1970s. Since Italy was more dependent upon oil than many of the other industrialised countries, it was particularly susceptible to the hike in oil prices at the beginning of the 1970s. The end of the Bretton Woods Agreement on fixed exchange rates and the devaluation of the dollar (in both 1971 and 1973) meant that Italian exports (ever the success story of the economy) were hard hit. Industrial unrest was also causing a wage spiral. The hourly rates of workers between 1964 and 1968 increased by 22.8 per cent; during the four years after that period, they rose by over 95 per cent. Inflation was perceived as a way out of the Italian crisis, not least because the continuing fall in the value of the lira meant that the engine of the Italian economy—exports—could be kept competitive. (Meanwhile, imports, of course, and especially oil, became as a consequence ever more expensive, which itself fuelled the inflationary spiral.) It was in this period that the most surreal effect of Italy's economy took place: everyone became a millionaire, and calculators started to come equipped with that unique button of three zeros in order to save time when adding up.

The more serious problem was that the economy was being subordinated to the survival of various political parties. Since they depended so heavily on patronage, on the ability to place their supporters within the bureaucracy through "recommendations," any attempt to cut down on the mushrooming public-sector workforce would have been tantamount to political hara-kiri. Thus organisations like the Cassa per il Mezzogiorno (the Fund for the South) and the Ministry of State Participation were just the most famous examples of the bureaucracy providing jobs rather than services. Despite its important role in postwar reconstruction, the huge public sector had "become the centre of party power, paving the way to the general tendency of the so-called spoils system."³ It served politicians to do exactly what was worst for the Italian economy: exponentially expand the size of the bureaucracy, thereby increasing the size of their grateful clientele. At the beginning of the 1970s, just over 30 per cent of all salaries and wages in the south of Italy was due to public-administration jobs. The circumstances were exaggerated in the south, but even nationwide the percentage of employment in the public sector had doubled from just over 9 per cent in 1951 over 18 per cent in 1990.

There was nothing particularly new about the size and inefficiency of Italy's bureaucracy, which had, for centuries, been the brunt of bitter criticism. "In Italy," wrote Stendhal, "and especially in the neighbourhood of the Po, everyone's conversation turns on passports." He describes in The Charterhouse of Parma *one clerk who "waved his hand several times in the air, signed his name, and dipped his pen in the ink to make his flourish, which he executed slowly and with infinite pains . . . The clerk gazed at his flourish with satisfaction, added five or six dots to it, and finally handed the passport back."[4] Luigi Barzini was even more scathing. Bureaucrats, he said, "are as a rule impatient, overbearing, hurried, ignorant, indifferent to other people's problems, insolent, and sometimes corrupt . . . Italians of all classes (unless they are important people with powerful friends) spend a substantial part of their time standing in angry queues, in front of office windows, or waiting endlessly merely to have some simple right recognised. What their rights are, nobody knows for sure. Uncertainty is used, in Italy, as* instrumentum regni.*"[5]*

There were other problems. Mediobanca was the epitome of the salotto buono, *an exclusive club of a few high financiers whose interests overlapped wherever possible. In fact, there had been "a massive rush towards the concentration of capital. Between 1966 and 1967, twenty-nine companies possessed over 34 per cent of the entire equity capital."[6] That trend would continue during the following decades, witness to both the financial muscle of a few very large corporations and the small size of Italy's stock exchange. Given the size of the Milan Borsa, it had traditionally been simple artificially to inflate or deflate stock prices. Shareholder rights were minimal, consolidated accounts were until recently unheard of, public information was nearly impossible to obtain. Business empires were split into the usual Chinese boxes;*

if you opened the lid on one company, you didn't see the contents but just another box. Meanwhile, many of the largest and most influential companies remained unquoted and in private family hands.

The simplicity of market economics was somehow being side-stepped. As a consequence of the predominance of family-run firms, company bosses tended to double as both major shareholder and managing director of the company. The habit of rank outsiders casting their economic judgements on the company by buying or selling shares was nigh-on impossible. The defence was based, as ever, on complication and esotericism: share-ownership which was indecipherable and a habit of Chinese boxes. Take, for example, the 2001 takeover of Olivetti (and therefore of Telecom Italia) by Pirelli. It was masterminded by Marco Tronchetti Provera (former husband of Cecilia Pirelli) and his Benetton allies (Benetton Edizione Holding, responsible for not just the clothing empire but also a Formula One team and almost all of Italy's motorway service stations). In the deal, about 7 billion euros were paid for a 23-per-cent stake in Olivetti (in a move which would have been illegal elsewhere, a premium was paid only to certain shareholders). The resulting Chinese boxes should give some idea of the Byzantine, secretive world of the stock market: Tronchetti Provera now owns 53 per cent of GPI, which owns 55.1 per cent of Camfin, which owns 29.6 per cent of Pirelli and Company, which owns 100 per cent of Pirelli and Company Luxembourg, which owns 27.7 per cent of Pirelli SpA, which owns 60 per cent of Newco, which owns 27 per cent of Olivetti, which owns 54.9 per cent of Telecom Italia, which in turn controls 56 per cent of Telecom Italia Mobile and 54.6 per cent of SEAT Pagine Gialle, which is responsible for the seventh national television channel, now renamed "La 7." Looking at that empire, and it's by far the simplest example of the genre, one sees the usual pattern emerge. In a few family hands all the aces are held: telecommunications, publishing, mass media, offshore stopovers, and so on. None of this is, of course, illegal. It's simply that high finance is like so much else: not exactly transparent. It enables minority shareholders to become controlling shareholders with more interest in the control than the company. The companies themselves become like pulleys, increasing the power obtainable with minimum effort.

All of this produces a crisis of credit in the ancient and the modern sense of the word. Credit in the sense of "credence," because no one believes that the system is fully functional and as fair to outside traders as it is to inside traders. There's a crisis of confidence. And credit in the financial sense, because historically the weakest link in the Italian economy is its investment sector. Italian banks are notoriously the most cautious investors imaginable. Venture capital is a notion entirely foreign to them. Meanwhile, individual Italian investors, at least those outside the cosy salotto buono, have for years been disinclined to invest money in someone else's Chinese boxes. There was for years an enormous export of capital abroad (an estimated $3 billion in 1969, before the crisis had even begun). Foreign investment, too, was minimal (even in 1999 it was only one-ninth of Britain's), largely due to the opaque quality of Italian finance.

The Parmalat scandal, nicknamed "Europe's Enron," unfortunately underlines the point. It has become one of the biggest corporate frauds in European history. Since the 1960s, Calisto Tanzi had built up his dairy company into the eighth-largest enterprise in Italy. It employed 35,000 people around the globe. The success was based upon brilliant business decisions. Tanzi had turned his product into a global brand first through technological innovation—supplying long-life milk in cardboard cartons—and then through high-visibility sponsorship in Formula One and football. Tanzi's public image was that of a humble, devout philanthropist: he would go to church daily and donate huge sums to restoration works. Like everything in Italy, on the surface it all looked glorious. The familiar seeds of financial *fraud, however, were all there. Tanzi, like many Italian entrepreneurs, ran his company as if it were his own personal fiefdom. His relatives came before shareholders. One of many dubious transactions which caused the implosion of the company allegedly involved siphoning funds, almost $500 million, from Parmalat to his daughter's travel company.*

The irony of the Parmalat story is that the company was actually hugely successful. It wasn't, like Enron, a failing company but instead a buoyant business. Had Tanzi stuck to selling dairy products, he would never have made the news. The crisis arose because—as with dozens of Italian companies in the past, including Berlusconi's—Parmalat began to use hundreds of offshore subsidiaries from Lichtenstein to the Cayman Islands. So far investigators have unearthed 260 subsidiaries linked to the Parmalat mother company. It was, needless to say, a strange way to run a dairy concern.

Over a period of twenty years, Tanzi seems to have relied on debt to swell his company. He reportedly created fake billings which allowed him to inflate revenues and thereby gain access to huge loans. Exaggerated contracts could be collaterised, or sold as assets, to raise even more money which was then moved into a number of offshore accounts. The money was often used to overpay for acquisitions across the globe, especially in South America. The suspicion (investigations are still at the preliminary stages) is that the overpayment for those acquisitions allowed even more money to be slipped into other offshore accounts. Moreover, overpriced assets appeared to justify the endless issuing of more bonds. Through this back-to-back credit and nonexistent cash accounts, Parmalat managed to manipulate its precarious balance sheet.

After years of what now appears to be illicit business behaviour, company executives were so brazen that they reportedly faked an account with the Bank of America, in which they claimed to have deposited just under $5 billion. When, on 19 December 2003, the Bank denied any knowledge of the account *(apparently set up by the Parmalat subsidiary, Bonlat, in the Cayman Islands), the entire Parmalat deceit unravelled. At least eighteen executives, including Tanzi, are either in jail or under house arrest pending trial. Since then, one worker has committed suicide and thousands of others are facing unemployment. It's now estimated that as much as $17 billion could be unaccounted for. As usual, the main victims are Italy's bewildered investors and savers who feel, not for the first time, that it would be safer and more profitable simply to keep their money under the mattress.*

Transparency International, a company which analyses the "corruption" factor across the globe on behalf of potential investors, now ranks Italy at the bottom of all western European countries. On the world stage, it rates worse than Estonia and Botswana because its free market is perceived as being besieged by complicated "holdings." Investors simply aren't attracted, which means that the big companies get bigger and the little ones struggle to stay afloat. It's economics at its most excruciatingly conservative. "The anomaly," as Salvatore Bragantini has written, "of a capitalism which thinks it can do without a real market of capital, in the fifth or sixth industrial power in the world, is too absurd to be able to last."[7]

The years 1992–94 saw, in some ways, the rectification by market forces as much as by judicial ones. The advent of the Exchange Rate Mechanism, and the monetary orthodoxy demanded by Europe in preparation for the euro, meant that Italy, like Britain, was forced to reduce budget deficits. The rules of the game were international, and Italy's record of inflation and budget deficits was being sternly criticised from both inside and outside the country. (At the time of the signing of the Maastricht Treaty, Italy's inflation still stood at almost 7 per cent, and 20 per cent of all state revenue was going simply on interest payments for the public debt, which was itself over 100 per cent of GNP.) What was new at the beginning of the 1990s was not that the bureaucracy was inefficient and discretionary (only use-ful to those with the right contacts) but that it was a luxury the country could no longer afford. The situation was exacerbated by the tradition of tax evasion, which meant that in order to re-coup a percentage of the earnings of the country's citizens, vari-ous governments almost had to "bribe" them to buy into Bots (government bonds) by offering absurdly high interest rates, which the state, again, couldn't afford. "The Cake Is Finished," read one headline in Corriere della Sera at the time of the crisis, as if to suggest that the system of corruption had collapsed not so much because of an outburst of righteousness but simply because there was nothing left to go round.[8]

Mani Pulite, "Clean Hands," was the name given to the "pool" of investigative magistrates who, in that brief period from 1992 to 1994, caused a political and economic revolution. It was a period which marked the end of the First and the begin-ning of the Second Republic. After fifty years, the music seemed to stop: the rules of that game of musical chairs (in which no seat had ever been removed but politicians simply changed position according to the political music of the time) were suddenly rewritten. In their indignation, the magistrates, overwhelm-ingly supported by the Italian public, removed all the chairs in one fell swoop. Entire political parties which had, for decades, been taking hefty kickbacks on the contracts they dispensed were brusquely rejected; the city of Tangentopoli, "Bribesville," was razed by zealous "revolutionaries" who fought to apply the letter of the law.

What's strange reading the story with a foreigner's eyes is that everyone had always known that corruption was rife in Italy, many even had the evidence, but until the early 1990s nothing was done. It was politically or legally impossible. For years com-mentators had derisively talked about politicians' secret accounts and offshore holdings. Elio Veltri and Gianni Barbacetto had already published Milano degli scandali; Giampaolo Pansa had written Il malloppo (*The Swag*). *The scandal of 1992–94, then, wasn't shocking because of the discovery of corruption; the real shock came in the fact that it was finally possible for the millions of long-suffering, law-abiding Italians to do something about it. As Pietro Scoppola wrote on the tenth anniversary:*

> *The majority of Italians, although they had never extorted from, or corrupted, anybody, had always tried to interpret in the most limited way their obligations towards the state. They used "recommendations" as a daily means of survival. The country plunged into the enthusiasm prompted by Clean Hands as into a rite of collective liberation. With widespread indignation against the corrupt and the corrupters, largely fed by the press, an entire population deluded itself that it could in some way redeem itself of its own vices in the arena of civil ethics.[9]*

The sudden crumbling of the First Republic looks, in retrospect, very much like the velvet revolution of 1989. A system which had, since the end of the Second World War, been monolithic and menacing self-imploded within the space of a few breathless months. There's more than imagery to link the two events. The collapse of the Soviet Union, and the end of the Cold War, had much sharper consequences in Italy than in other European countries. The credibility of the Italian Communist Party obviously collapsed, but so did that of the Christian Democrats. Their winning card (and that of their junior coalition partners) had always been that they represented a dam against "red terror." Once that threat was gone, the dam looked rather unnecessary and—many finally dared to say it out loud—rather corrupt.

Many accused politicians would later argue the bribes were simply "election funds." The number of personal accounts held offshore, however, awash with billions of lire, began to shock the public. The circumstances of the arrest of Duilio Poggiolini, head of the pharmaceutical department of the Ministry of

Health, became emblematic of the corruption of an entire era. Billions of lire were found stuffed into a cushion. Some $120 million were found in three of his homes. He had fourteen Swiss bank accounts, sixty expensive paintings, diamonds, krugerrands, gold ingots stacked in shoeboxes.

That, though, was to come later. In April 1992, after the general election, the country's politicians had to choose a new President of the Republic. They were on the eighteenth ballot of the tortuous process, with the usual names in the hat, when one of the anti-Mafia judges in Palermo was killed. Giovanni Falcone, his wife, and his bodyguards had been assassinated as they drove from Palermo airport to the city centre in an explosion which tore apart hundreds of metres of the motorway. The indignation against Italy's injustices reached new levels. Scenes from the funeral, in one of which the young widow of a bodyguard accused the Church of containing Mafiosi who would have to get on their knees if they wanted her forgiveness, were shown on live television. Bedsheets were hung out from balconies across Sicily, mourning Falcone and his escort. (Within months, Paolo Borsellino, another of the investigating magistrates, was killed as he visited his mother.) By then, it had become obvious that the revolution was being fought on more than one front, and Parliament was finally awoken to the acute danger of civilian disorder facing the country. Seven thousand troops were sent to Sicily, and a new President of the Republic, Oscar Luigi Scalfaro, was finally chosen. "The abuse of public money," he said,

is a very serious thing, which defrauds and robs the faithful, taxpaying citizen and shatters completely his trust: there's no greater evil, no greater danger for democracy, than the turbid link between politics and business.[10]

His indignation seemed shared by the rest of the country. The bitterness of ordinary Italians was prompted by the fact that the *only tax in Italy which had been imposed with anything like systematic efficiency, the* tangente, *had been the one which vanished into private hands. The response was that the Clean Hands pool enjoyed an enormous ground swell of support: people began wearing T-shirts that read,* "Milano ladrona, Di Pietro non perdona" *(Thieving Milan, Di Pietro [one of the investigators] is unforgiving). Finally it seemed as if those words written in every Italian courtroom,* "La legge è uguale per tutti," *"The law's equal for all," were coming true. Endless graffiti appeared across Italy:* "Grazie Di Pietro," *or* "Forza Colombo." *Over the ensuing months, Gianni de Michelis, a former Foreign Minister, was pelted with eggs and tomatoes in Venice. Bettino Craxi was showered with coins outside the Hotel Raphael:* "Do you want these as well?" *chanted the mob.*

The human toll of the revolution wasn't only counted amongst Italy's magistrates. Throughout the next eighteen months, and as a 27-billion-lira bribe, the biggest of all, was unearthed, a long list of suicides added to the list of illustrious corpses. Those deaths would change the symbolism of the revolution, turning it from a morality play into a national tragedy. As always, "slaughters" accompanied the upheaval. In May 1993, five people died when a bomb exploded in the Uffizi museum in Florence. In July five people were killed by a bomb in Milan.

By then, Carlo Azeglio Ciampi had replaced Giuliano Amato as the Italian Prime Minister. The lira had, like the pound sterling, become the object of currency speculation, had duly lost 15 per cent of its value, and had been forced out of the Exchange Rate Mechanism. Parliament, which had traditionally benefited from legal immunity, had been handed more than six hundred requests to lift parliamentary privilege; Craxi himself was the subject of seventeen different investigations and would later flee to exile in Tunisia.

Thus the most obvious consequences of Clean Hands was that there was a political abyss into which almost anyone could step.

The Christian Democrats ironically renamed themselves the People's Party. The Communists had already changed their name to the Democrats of the Left. The Northern League, one of whose number had brandished a noose in Parliament to publicise his revolutionary credentials, was gaining ground in the area of Italy above the Po River. The MSI, the neo-Fascists led by Pino Rauti until 1993, had reverted to the more presentable Gianfranco Fini for leadership. The progress of these two fringe parties—the Northern League and the MSI—was shown in various elections in 1993. In June, Milan, traditionally the power base of Bettino Craxi and his Socialists, elected a mayor from the Northern League. In the autumn, Gianfranco Fini was narrowly defeated in his bid to become mayor of Rome (taking 46.9 per cent of the vote); later, he would decide to rename the MSI the National Alliance.

There was still, however (as one notorious businessman put it with the usual football metaphor), a "midfield" which was "desolately empty." In January 1994, that businessman sent a video to Reuters, RAI, and his own television networks, announcing the formation of a new political party, Forza Italia:

> *As never before, Italy . . . needs people with heads on shoulders and a consolidated experience, capable of giving a hand, making the state work. In order to make the system work, it's indispensable that opposed to the cartel of the left there be a "pole of liberty" capable of attracting to itself the best of a clean, reasonable, modern country. Around this pole there must gather all those forces which refer to the fundamental principles of Western democracies: in the first place the Catholic world, which has contributed generously to the last fifty years of our history as a united nation.[11]*

As rhetoric, that announcement was of unrivalled brilliance. The combination of moderation, modernity, cleanliness, and

statal good sense instead of a left-wing "cartel" is stunning.
Berlusconi's popularity rested, not least of all, on his Midas touch
in business and on his wholehearted endorsement of Antonio Di
Pietro (whom he would ask to be his Minister of Justice): "His
[Di Pietro's] moralising anxiety belongs to everyone. My news-
papers, my television channels, my group, have always been in
the front line in supporting the Clean Hands judges." Another
Clean Hands magistrate, Tiziana Parenti, would later take her
place on the Forza Italia benches in Parliament. Italian poli-
tics, above all its economics, seemed to be entering a bright, new
dawn.

Memory, though, is short. Only a few years after the Clean
Hands earthquake, the whole episode is already being assidu-
ously rewritten.

Every few weeks during the summer, my girlfriend and I
make the spectacular journey across the mountains which takes
us from the humid basin of Parma towards the warm, windy
air of the Tuscan coast. At one point in the Cisa pass, as the
road winds through the pine forests, the mountains loom into
view. They appear snow-peaked because of the white quarries
where huge blocks of marble are dynamited and lined up by
the sides of the roads. It's this white marble which, interlaced
with black or green, makes Tuscan cathedrals—in Pisa or
Siena—look like something squeezed from a toothpaste tube.
Last summer, we decided to stop in a little mountain town,
Aulla, and eat a sandwich in the main square. Opposite us
were two rhetorical monuments. One was to the fallen from
the war, and described in one long-winded sentence, the "ar-
dent hearth of vivid fire which at the beginning of Nazi-Fascist
oppression released a spark which inflamed the children of the
Resistance, who won fame with the legendary sacrifice of their
women and their bloodied men who on an impassable path
underwent atrocious slaughters, devastations, and reprisals."

Next to it was a small needle of white marble, which was dedicated to the victims of the Clean Hands revolutionaries. "Intolerance, like bombs, kills precious liberty," it says. "When the word is feeble," read the words of one parliamentarian who committed suicide, "there's nothing left but the gesture." "Let us remember in the dark of every injustice the victims and their executioners" are the words of the Aulla mayor engraved into the marble. Billboards announce that the town is a "Di Pietro–free zone," and there's a cunning quotation in Latin: *"Summum ius, summa iniuria"* ("The greater the law, the greater the injustice," which implies, I suppose, that the rule of law is not a particularly good thing). As ever, the roles of criminal and victim are so blurred and confused that no one can ever be sure whether Italy's "Jacobin justice" is worse than the "criminals" it prosecutes.

Having been (in his own words) in the "front line" of support for Clean Hands in 1994, Berlusconi has also completely changed tack. Although he won that election in 1994, his government was dogged by accusations of corruption against his entourage. His brother, Paolo, and Marcello Dell'Utri, cofounder of Forza Italia, were both accused of directing "black funds" in various hidden parts of Berlusconi's Fininvest holding company. Berlusconi himself, whilst ironically hosting a G7 summit at Naples about organised crime, was served an *avviso di garanzia* (notice of investigation) in December 1994. His troubled government fell weeks later as the indignant Northern League withdrew its support from the coalition. Since then Berlusconi had been in opposition (an experience he describes, with his usual biblical sense of destiny, as the "crossing of the desert"), fulminating against the judges whom he once claimed as allies.

Other investigations have begun, not least into the means by which, during the privatisation of IRI overseen by Romano Prodi, Berlusconi managed to block the acquisition of

Sme (IRI's food entity) by a business rival. The accusations centre on Cesare Previti, Berlusconi's Roman lawyer. The accusation goes that Previti had bribed the Roman judge who "refereed" the deal, thus allowing Berlusconi to block his rival's acquisition. For reasons unknown, the bid of Berlusconi's consortium was accepted, whilst that of Carlo De Benedetti was (despite agreement having been reached on the 497-billion-lira purchase price) rejected. The means by which Berlusconi acquired Mondadori, Italy's largest publishing house, is equally mired in controversy. It is, of course, impossible to know what to believe, especially since the man gazumped by Berlusconi in the Mondadori deal, Carlo De Benedetti, himself owns *La Repubblica* and *L'Espresso*, which means that parts of the "left-wing" media have no pretence of impartiality in reporting such "scandals."

Thus Clean Hands is being rewritten, and the "revolution" has almost come full circle. Those who once seemed to promise a cleaner future have been suspected of dirty pasts; they have shifted their support from the revolution to the restoration. The defence line of those "new" politicians is incredibly clever. The Second Republic, they say, is really very different from the First, and you can't judge one according to the rules of the other. Before 1992, corruption was so rife in the upper echelons of politics and finance that it was impossible not to collude in some way. Now that Clean Hands has taught us all a lesson, we should wipe the slate clean and start over again. Berlusconi's best defence, one which can be deployed only through hint rather than admission, is that he was only ever doing what everyone else was doing during the old days of the *salotto buono*. It's exactly the same line that Bettino Craxi used in 1992, when he deployed the classic Italian defence not that he was innocent, but that everyone else was just as guilty. Craxi admitted to "an irregular system of financing" but underlined that "all the parties took part in it." According to that defence, the only difference between Berlusconi or Craxi and their electorates is the scale, rather than the character, of the crime; and if that's true, it's obvious that any punishment meted out appears excruciatingly selective.

Maybe Craxi wasn't any worse than the rest of us; maybe, the Forza Italia rhetoric goes, Berlusconi is no worse than we are, and we're hypocrites if we pretend he is. Some Italian commentators, like Pietro Scoppola, have said precisely that: the lynching of high-ranking politicians was supported by the public since it represented some kind of vicarious absolution; we're all guilty, and we needed "illustrious" names to redeem us of our sins. When the "revolution" began to reach lesser names and impose "cleanliness" instead of "cunning," the bedrock of support for the magistrates collapsed. Thus the fact that Berlusconi is under accusation only means that the magistrates are biased against him. He has, in fact, become a master of the art of *vittimismo*, complaining that every accusation against him is simply the work of "Jacobin judges." Seven years after he offered Antonio Di Pietro a job, Berlusconi now says: "*Tangentopoli* never existed. Clean Hands was only a colossal conquest commissioned by the Communists and Democrats of the Left." Thus, according to the man who most benefited from the whole affair, Clean Hands wasn't cleaning up Italian democracy at all but strangling it. There was, say his supporters, an excess of *protagonismo*, in which a handful of judges suddenly appeared to enjoy centre stage; the leaks to the press about imminent arrests turned the judicial process into spectacular, televisual witch-hunts; the "cautionary custody," which locked up politicians for months on end, was an abuse of judicial power, especially since white-collar criminals pose no threat to society. Instead of trying to root out Italy's perennial problem of corruption, Berlusconi shifted his political position 180 degrees. He became a *garantista*: a guarantor of civil rights against judicial witch-hunts, against a "judicial *coup d'état*."

I decided to go to Sicily to see how much had really changed in the decade since Clean Hands. The scene looked like something from a war. Women were wailing. Some occasionally collapsed with grief, and an ambulance was called. It arrived dramatically with sirens blaring, in full view of camera crews. There was an indignant priest, shaking his head at what was going on. On the other side were armed police and military, huddled around heavily defended Jeeps and holding large weapons. The *terapia delle ruspe*, the "therapy of the bulldozers," was a new front in the very strange Italian civilian war. It was a shock therapy, and one which few Sicilians ever expected to see: the military were bulldozing their houses.

This was in the spring of 2001. The "therapy of the bulldozers" was the sting in the tail of the outgoing left-wing government (Berlusconi won the 2001 election by a landslide), an attempt to raze the various houses and hotels which had been built illegally around one of the country's beauty spots. The war on *abusivismo*—"illegal building"—was a side-issue during the bitter election campaign. And yet left-wing politicians, Legambiente and Italia Nostra (Italy's environmental pressure groups), and northern Italians in general have constantly denounced *abusivismo*. The practice of erecting enormous hotels and houses without planning permission might sound innocuous until you realise the scale on which it happens. Four thousand seven hundred and eighty illegal houses sprang up in Sicily in 2000 alone, which represented another 717 thousand square metres of cement poured out around the island's besieged holiday resorts. Those figures simply represent the "illegal" building in one part of the country. Legal and illegal houses combined now mean that Italy has a higher per capita consumption of concrete than any other country in the world. In the last five years another 163,000 illegal houses have sprung up, invariably in Italy's south, and especially in Sicily. Now the country has a very unusual "housing problem": there are simply far too many houses for a declining population. Two and a half million houses aren't even lived in, whilst hundreds of thousands more are built every year. It's a particularly poignant problem for Italians because it's an affront not only to ethics but also to aesthetics. *Abusivismo* is more than just another example of the hazy attitude towards abiding the law and the authority of the state. Its importance lies in the fact that it's the one instance in which illegality is very clearly ugly. Critics of *abusivismo* consequently denounce not only the illegality but also the visual impact of the rampant building, suggesting that Italy, traditionally the *bel paese*, is at risk of extinction.

The most important front of the war against *abusivismo* is one of the country's elegiac beauty spots: Agrigento. It's an ancient town squeezed between the mountains and the sea on the southern coast of Sicily where the Greeks, in the fifth century BC, built temples out of ochre limestone. Most of them are still standing, and are referred to as Agrigento's Valley of the Temples. It's Agrigento that the Greek poet Pindar once described as "the finest city among those inhabited by mortals," a place where, Empedokles wrote with uncanny prophecy, people "lived their lives as if they were supposed to die the next day and built houses as if they were immortals."[12] Despite Sicily's reputation as an island which is secretive and impenetrable to outsiders, it's hard to disguise what's going on in Agrigento and the Valley of the Temples. It's a strange story, though, and one which could have been written by Agrigento's most famous inhabitant, Luigi Pirandello: nothing is quite what it seems, everyone contradicts each other, and you're never certain what to believe.

The town is only a couple of hours on the train from Palermo. The railway snakes across the island, past Corleone and onwards between rugged hills and golden wheat fields. Every now and again you can see, from the window, the concrete shell of some abandoned construction project. Agrigento is the end of the train line from Palermo, and it feels like it. Rubbish has been uncollected for weeks, the pavements smell of rotting fruit and fish. There are stray dogs and sun-bleached posters promoting parties for last May's general election. Electricity cables are slung casually from one house to another, barely above head height. When I walk down the main street, I'm almost knocked over by two men on two mopeds who are somehow carrying a double mattress between them. But the town is eerie and beautiful. It's on about the same latitude as Tunis and is set on a steep hillside. People sit on the pavements outside their houses, waiting and talking and shouting jokes to their neighbours. If you ask someone for directions to your hotel, he will either ignore you or walk you there himself.

When I finally arrive in my prisonlike hotel, the jovial, sedentary *maître d'hôtel* is watching television. As he shows me my cell, I ask him what he makes of *abusivismo*. He just laughs, and cryptically quotes Constantine: "With the sign of the cross we will win." When night falls, you can walk to the edge of the town and see the temples a mile away: rows of floodlit orange pillars. Beyond them is the sea. It's also a place of mournful and austere Catholicism. One of the town's tiny squares is called Piazza Purgatorio. When I go into a bar, an old woman, surprised to hear a foreign accent, offers me a glow-in-the-dark rosary and a picture of the Madonna (stamped with "ecclesiastical approval" from the Archbishop of Palermo). Her advice for my travels is a mixture of the medical and the Catholic, a sort of prescription-devotion: "Say two Ave Marias before breakfast, and a Gloria to this blessed Madonna before you go to bed."

The next day, Legambiente's Sicilian lawyer, Giuseppe Arnone, arrives in a large Jeep. He opens the passenger door for me before driving through the steep, narrow streets, saying nothing. We stop outside the courtroom, its two guards armed with sub-machine-guns and sunglasses, before driving towards the outskirts of the city. Eventually Arnone pulls up on a blind bend in the road and points at a building which looks like a large doll's house sawn in half: all the interior walls and floors are showing. To the left, on the outer and under side of the blind bend, is the rest of the building. "The law limiting the building craze came after this landslide in 1966," says Arnone, speaking for the first time. "It was caused, of course, by overbuilding on a fragile hillside. By now, that landslide and the reasons for the protective legislation have been forgotten, and the whole process has started again."

Within minutes we are at the temples. We walk onto the narrow ridge of the hill between the city and the sea. There's a forest of columns—the Temple of Hercules, the Temple of Concordia, the Temple of Juno, and the rest. Linking them is a wide path, lined on each side by cacti. Many of their large, flat leaves are engraved with declarations of love or of political opinions: "Pachu loves Sabri," or "Communists are the shit on your shoes." Like Agrigento, it's all both beautiful and depressing. The sun is so hot it blurs the near distance: you can just make out, within a few hundred metres of the proud, crumbling temples, a motorway on massive concrete supports. Huge *palazzi* hem in the area, and nearby cranes are heaving new (illegal) breeze-blocks into place. Agrigento itself, about a mile away on the hilltop inland, is a wall of white concrete.

"The 'therapy of the bulldozers,' " says Giuseppe Arnone, "is a physical as well as a political battle. It's the cranes against the bulldozers. And it's a race to save one of the most important archaeological areas in Europe." He explains how the economics of *abusivismo* works: despite being a stone's throw from the temples, agricultural land in the area is worth very little. Growing wheat or grapes has a very low and very long-term yield. A hotel built there, however, would be incredibly lucrative since tourists and academics arrive from all corners of the globe. So people build on their land, and the profits are so great that they can be shared out with the "local authorities," who thus give them the retrospective go-ahead for the building.

During the 2001 election, Italy's most popular novelist, the Sicilian Andrea Camilleri, tried to persuade the inhabitants of Agrigento to get out of their "tunnel of illegality and *abusivismo*." The trouble is that the people in Agrigento aren't used to thinking in terms of the Italian state. Many are so poor that they care little for archaeologists, novelists, lawyers, and highbrow politicians from northern Italy who wag their self-righteous fingers. But the strange thing about the Agrigento story is that it's not the poor who are building houses (the traditional defence of illegal building); it's the wealthy political classes. Precisely those people who are supposed to be most bound by the law are above it. "Here," says Arnone, "anyone with money can do what he wants. There's a seriously criminal administration and a class of politicians who are simply thieves." Giuseppe Arnone is a man so reticent that he's almost impossible to interview. He doesn't say much, only hints occasionally at what is really going on. What is clear, given those long silences, is that Agrigento is a very dangerous place for a law-abiding lawyer.

I have often read in newspapers that Agrigento is the *zoc-colo duro*, the "hard hoof," of the Mafia. That's why the more you understand it, the more *abusivismo* seems not chaotic lawlessness but precision profiteering. "Nothing," says Arnone, "ever gets done here without the correct 'clearance.' " There's clearly nothing in Agrigento that money and connections can't achieve: all the illegal houses have running water, telephone lines, and electricity, even though they don't, on paper, exist.

Meanwhile, the week that I'm there, the bulldozers are poised to go to work on new houses. In Licata, a few miles east along the coast, the order has just been given to raze another eighty houses. But in Agrigento and Licata nothing is happening. The troops are back in their barracks on stand-by. There seems to be a truce. Andrea Camilleri had already understood which way the wind was blowing: "The bulldozers aren't here anymore; they have retreated in orderly fashion. This is a good sign of the way things are going." The reason is that, since the spring offensive against *abusivismo*, Silvio Berlusconi has become Prime Minister. More than that, he was the first man in the history of Italian democracy to win sixty-one out of the sixty-one directly elected parliamentary seats in Sicily. The implications are obvious. The "therapy of the bulldozers" had given offence, and Berlusconi isn't going to repeat the error. He knows on which side his political bread is buttered, and it's widely predicted that he will now do everything he can to encourage the cranes instead of the bulldozers. *"Figuriamoci!"* says one person I speak with, which (given the tone) translates as "but of course!"

Few people really expect the bulldozers to win the war anymore. The new houses will be "sanitised" and therefore given the *condono*, the "official pardon." That *condono* only encourages more illegal housing. It's the magic wand of Italian illegality, repeatedly waved over criminals in return for a fine. Avowals are made about being tougher in the future, which never discourages others from attempting the same scam. "Every hypothesis about an official pardon," says Legambiente's president, Ermete Realacci, "will only serve to increase new abuses and further degrade the few corners of our coast which have remained uncontaminated." The practice of pardons, it's obvious, just encourages more of the same: if you're not supposed to build on a particular site, you build anyway, and then pay a paltry fine and sanitise the illegality. Every few years, the Italian government, strapped for cash, agrees to recognise thousands of new constructions in return for a little investment: 207,000 houses, originally illegal, were sanitised in that way between 1994 and 1997. It doesn't matter if you've broken the law: it will be changed to accommodate you and your accommodation.

La speculazione edilizia (Real-estate gambling) was the novella Italo Calvino considered his best work. It describes the "new social class of the postwar years," the "improvising entrepreneurs without scruples," and the way in which they caused the "squalid invasion of cement":

> It was the houses: all of these new buildings that were being put up, tenements from six to eight storeys high, their white mass like a barrier shoring up the crumbling slope of the coast, opening up as many windows and balconies as possible on to the sea. The concrete fever had got hold of the Riviera: over there was one building already lived in, with its geranium tubs, all looking similar, on the balconies; here was a recently finished development, its window-panes marked with snaky chalk squiggles, waiting for the little families from Lombardy eager to go to the seaside; farther on, a castle of scaffolding and, under it, the turning concrete mixer and the estate agent's sign advertising the new flats on sale.[13]

The book was written during 1956–57 but could equally be applied to the entire postwar period, in which money flowed as fast as the concrete. It's a trend captured in the opening shots of Francesco Rosi's film *Le mani sulla città* (Hands over the City): all you can see from the window of a helicopter are tons and tons of white concrete. In one long and uninterrupted take, the camera shows Naples and all its rampant redevelopments. The buildings look the same: tall white cubes with tiny windows, stretching for miles and miles over the hills and towards the port. When the camera looks directly down, you can see the grid of the city, the narrow streets between the new buildings and, as it zooms in, the lean-to shacks between the motorways.

The film, made in 1963, is similar to Rosi's other films: a plea to battle against the abuses and illegality of society. It is a nightmare vision of the new Italy: the collapse of a *palazzo* is used not to slow down development but to speed it up. The "Party" (the Christian Democrats) get rich by assigning building contracts to Mafiosi, who in return guarantee the politicians their votes. The city council's one honest politician, a Communist, is powerless to stop the speculation and is reduced to traipsing from office to office looking for proof of illegality which doesn't exist. As far as the law goes, *tutto è in regola*, "everything is according to the norms." The lawless has been legalised. The commission of inquiry can reach no conclusion. Politics is reduced to the buying and selling of votes, made possible by the vast amounts of money slushing around the construction business. Besieged by angry women, the mayor unfolds huge notes and passes them around. Looking over his shoulder, he smiles and says, "*Consigliere*, see how democracy works?"

The cost, unfortunately, isn't only financial. When I first arrived in Italy, in the spring of 1999, there was a short newsflash: a block of flats had collapsed in Foggia in Puglia.

Seventy-one people died. I was astonished, not just by what had happened (the flats, constructed at the cheapest costs conceivable, had just caved in to gravity), but by the fact that a few days later it wasn't even mentioned. It was, I was told, a not-uncommon occurrence. Thirty-five hundred people have been killed since the war in landslides alone. Part of the reason is that Italy has a uniquely sensitive ecosystem: sixty-four hundred miles of coastline, two mountain ranges, tectonic fault lines, volcanoes. Many reports from around the country, whatever the season, are about the physical battle for survival. Earthquakes flatten entire suburbs, landslides obliterate villages, fires rip through ancient forests, and volcanoes spit out molten lava. The elements, given the sheer number of human lives they claim, seem simply crueller than elsewhere. But the problem is compounded by the human desecration of the landscape, and the deaths often seem an almost biblical revenge for the violations of the land.

After a few days watching immobile bulldozers in Agrigento, I decided to make my way back to Palermo. Most of the other journalists had already left weeks before. Waiting for the train in Agrigento's railway station, I went into the small chapel. Under a little image of the Madonna were the words "Monsignor Montucci decrees that whosoever pronounces four Glorias in front of this shrine shall receive one hundred days of indulgence." It's that, I suppose, that lies at the heart of the moral conundrum of *abusivismo* in Sicily: transgressors are indulged rather than punished, and all sins are forgiven as long as one says the right prayer, or pays the fine to the politicians' coffers.

I left the railway station's chapel and decided to hitchhike back to Palermo along the coast. I had little optimism, given the rude grunts I had received in many bars and hostels. By then, though, I had learnt that each time I was exasperated by life in Italy, an act of breathtaking civility was just around the corner to restore my faith. Within five minutes a man stopped. The car, like most in Sicily, was so dented that it looked like aluminium foil folded over a leg of lamb. There were already seven in the car. The driver had just stopped to explain why he couldn't pick me up. *"Auguri,"* he said. "Best wishes." Another soon stopped to explain he had to turn off. It's inconceivable that something of the sort would ever happen in the north. Two rich kids predictably stopped slightly ahead of me. One step towards them and they sped off, laughing. Then a baker picked me up. "I'll take you to where there are a lot of girls. That's what you're interested in at your age, isn't it? You American, then?"

"British."

"Myself, I've never been to the Continent," he said, examining me as he overtook a lorry loaded with lemons. I wasn't sure if he meant "Continent" as in Italy or Europe.

"Britain's not really the Continent either. It's a collection of islands like Sicily . . ."

The baker then delivered a soaring, eloquent monologue explaining exactly what he had intended by the word "Continent": "For me," he said, "the Continent implies anything that creeps onto this island, that tells me what to do. I don't care whether that's Rome or London, if you come here and want to be my boss, you're the Continent." He went on for an hour, summarising his notion of autonomy from any authority. Each time his voice sounded stern about the "Continent," he would offer me another of his *arancini*, balls of fried orange rice. He left me at a beach full of adolescents, including the two now-sheepish rich kids who had driven by earlier. "My house is over there if you ever need anything," the baker said, extending his flour-dusted fingers.

This was in Marsala, a town whose name implies in Arabic

"the port of God." It's famous as the home of the sweet dessert wine and as the landing place of Garibaldi and his "thousand men" in Sicily as they exported the unification movement to the south. I sat on the beach watching the huge rollers crash against the coast, splashing the private deck-chairs which everyone has to hire. (Even in Sicily many of the beaches have been privatised.) Huge speakers blared out Europop. Stunningly beautiful girls, their fluorescent bikinis flattering their dark skin, were throwing Frisbees to each other, seemingly hoping that they would get taken by the wind to the deck-chairs where the single men were sitting.

I looked at the sea and beyond, trying to catch sight of the North African coast. Sicily, I suppose, has always been held up as the epitome of what's wrong with Italy. And yet, sitting there in the sunset, I thought it also seemed exactly what's right: despite poverty, the generosity is instinctive. Despite daily reports about murders and kidnappings, it also appears blissfully peaceful and serene. Things might be serious, but I had never heard so much laughter. In fact, behind the stereo-typical lawlessness is hidden what many consider the real, earthy intellectual caste of Italy. Sicily has been the cradle of the country's greatest modern writers: Giovanni Verga, Luigi Pirandello, Giuseppe Tomasi di Lampedusa, and Leonardo Sciascia. Reading them, you get an idea of the sheer aridity of the island. Always in the background there's a sense of mortality amidst the dust. Grandiose concepts like dignity and honour still dominate the moral—and immoral—spectra. And because everything is a hall of mirrors in which nothing is ever concrete, words are always carefully chosen, no utterance is ever idle.

Sicilians are admired because, as Sciascia wrote, they "little love to speak"; their lives are "made up more of silences than words."[14] A friend from Parma who now teaches at Palermo University talks admiringly of Sicilians' *flemma serafica*, their "seraphic phlegm," which enables them to put up with poverty whilst watching the profiteers. Another friend from Parma, a middle-aged man whose son spent a long time on the island recovering from heroin addiction, says that Sicilians are the most noble and intellectual of all Italians. "They have," he says, "the perfect combination of hardness and refinement. You see it in all that studied politeness, the dutiful examination of their own behaviour."

After a few idle days at Marsala, I went to Mozia, which is, along with Agrigento, one of the southern Mediterranean's richest archaeological sites. It was here that the Englishman Joseph Whitaker began painstakingly retrieving bits of boats and weapons and burial sites from the shallow waters around his offshore island, San Pantaleo. In his villa you can still see marine charts tracing the Carthaginian sailing routes between southern Sicily and Spain, North Africa, and Greece. Nearby improbable windmills sit in the shallows, sucking in the sea to produce hillsides of glistening salt.

When I got back to Palermo, it was 14 July, the day of La Santuzza, or Santa Rosalia, the patron saint of Palermo. The city centre is still largely as it was after the Allied bombing raids from the Second World War: abandoned houses have no front walls, so you can peer in and see abandoned cookers and a tree sprouting in the kitchen. Lone walls rise up and lean randomly without any purpose. There are still piles of mortar and horizontal Doric columns where the bombs fell more than fifty years ago. Against that backdrop, La Santuzza appeared beautifully, elegiacally pagan. Loudspeakers were hung from street corners to relay the voice of a husky French actress, which was alternated with the stern tones of the Archbishop of Palermo. "I am Santuzza," said the actress, "I am the city, I live between the mountains and the sea." Meanwhile, beautiful, busty girls mounted on huge iron horses were wearing twelve-foot dresses and lighting extravagant fires. Fat, topless men were looking bored as they pushed the oars of the float, occasionally stopping for a cigarette when the man in a suit at the front received an order from his walkie-talkie. The air smelt of lighter fuel and incense. Behind me a Vespa screeched to a halt inches from my calves. The guy took off his helmet, excused himself, and made the sign of the cross.

8

FORZISMO

In good faith, first of all and above all, Italian politicians look after their own interests and the interests of their relatives, of their allies, of their friends, of their protected ones. There have always been lefts and rights: they divided and still divide because of personal issues, because of divergences on particular opinions. But as for the general principle, one is much the same as the other.
—FATHER CURCI (1810–91), ITALIAN THEOLOGIAN

Silvio Berlusconi is, without doubt, the most controversial and unconventional leader on the world stage. Short and balding but permanently suntanned, always wearing a dark double-breasted suit and with a quick grin at the ready, Berlusconi is both fascinating and frightening. For many he is a Faustian figure, a politician whose ascent to power is viewed in apocalyptic terms. Forzismo, say his opponents, is a twenty-first-century televisual version of Fascism; worse, it's the latest example of the grey area between the Roman Parliament and the Sicilian underworld. He is, they say, incapable of separating his private interests (a $7 billion empire ranging from television and banking to football and publishing) from public policy. For others, he is a saviour, the man who has rescued Italy from descent into Communism and political chaos; he's a brilliant businessman, full of swash-buckling bravado. He has, say his supporters, re-established respect for Italy on the world stage. For them, the many corruption charges against Berlusconi are evidence not of corruption but of latent Communism.

Berlusconi has often spoken of Italy being in the throes of a civil war. It's an exaggeration, but it's certainly obvious that there's a visceral loathing between two halves of the country. This mutual hatred and disdain might not have spilt over into another civil war, but there is once again a very obvious civil stand-off in which one half of the country looks on the other with absolute contempt. This cleavage is as obvious to Italians as it is to a foreigner. As Angelo Panebianco, a journalist for *Corriere della Sera*, wrote in January 2002:

> [There is] a type of "battle between civilisations." On one side are those who retain that the current government is a sort of infection, a repository of wickedness and illegality, and on the other are those for whom that same infection can be seen in the relationship between the political left and the magistrature. The division between the two Italys is radical. It's a division about values and principles which cancels any possibility of communication and compromise.[1]

The polarisation between the two camps is underlined by two influential books. One, more a magazine, is *Una storia italiana* (An Italian story). It was distributed to about 12 million Italian homes by Berlusconi's publishing house, Mondadori, at an estimated cost of some 11 billion lire just before the 2001 election. The name of the author wasn't on the cover. Instead, there were, on the front and the back of the book, 114 photographs of the same man. Balding, smiling, shaking hands, cheering football teams, greeting world leaders, being blessed by the Pope: Silvio Berlusconi. A horoscope at the front of the book suggested that Berlusconi's destiny was written in the constellations: Silvio, I was told, was born a Libra and is thus "a communicative person, capable of strong passions and profound loves. Charismatic, thanks to great adaptability and innate talent, he stands out in the activities which he brings before the great public, has optimum ability to judge, analyse, and synthesise, constructs all reasoning with stringent logic, managing to confer clarity on every debate."

Reading *Una storia italiana* was gripping, like reading a rags-to-riches fairy tale, and just as enchanting. It was impossible to put the thing down. (I was so fascinated that, the first time I read it, I phoned the publishers to ask for permission to use one of the photographs for the cover of the English version of this book. It was a photograph of Berlusconi on a balcony in Milan. He was grinning as thousands of supporters waved flags. The photograph looked strangely doctored: flags were blowing in opposite directions, their lettering was suspiciously legible. The leader was holding roses which looked like they had been painted in.) After the horoscope comes the opening chapter, describing Silvio's family, his love for his mother, his "spiritual exercises" in Bermuda, where he retires with his friends to read the "great classics" of the Western canon. The text was easy to read, because between every paragraph was a photo: baby Silvio, Silvio at school, Silvio singing on a cruise ship accompanied on the piano by someone called Fedele Confalonieri. It was also almost impossible to read the book and not think, "I want to emulate this man; I want to become like him, or at least follow him, certainly vote for him": his life is a dream, a childhood fantasy. He's been a musician, a businessman, a TV impresario; he has a beautiful wife, good-looking children, houses and gardens and cruise ships and private planes. Most of all, he adores football; his team actually wins things; he wins things. He wins everything.

For many, however, *An Italian Story* was nothing more than that: a story. It was an incredibly vain, slick, seductive story, a glossy piece of propaganda. Many found it ridiculous and rather embarrassing. Friends of mine in Parma, during a rally of environmentalists, decided to put out a large bin, offering any of the passing 12 million Italians who had been sent the "story" the opportunity to throw it away for recycling. "For a Clean Recycling," read the banner. To anyone with a sense of irony, the allusion was obvious, and much repeated over the ensuing months: *riciclaggio*, "recycling," was to become the keyword of the 2001 election.

Recycling is an issue which has dogged Berlusconi for decades, and it came back to haunt him during the election. The allegations that his humble beginnings were aided by epic money laundering on behalf of the Mafia dominated the campaign, particularly when a rival "Italian story," *L'odore dei soldi*, was published two months before the electorate went to the polls. Its claims were equally fantastic and received ample publicity on those television channels (of the state RAI network) still outside Berlusconi's reach. The book was based on an interview with an anti-Mafia judge, Paolo Borsellino, shortly before he was killed in 1992. During the interview Borsellino had hinted that the Mafia, having at its disposal vast sums of money made from drug smuggling, laundered it through companies in the north, including (according to the authors) Berlusconi's Fininvest holding company. The title of the book was particularly apt. The crime of Mafia collusion in Italy is called, evocatively, *odore di Mafia* (literally "the whiff of Mafia"). The book was called *The Whiff of Money*.

The allegations went that Berlusconi was a prime example not of the peasant, murderous Mafia in Sicily but of something more sophisticated exported to the north. This was something much larger, more sinister, and more disguised: the "White Mafia" of financial scams, money laundering, and international investment rackets. The book quoted the old notion that you enter the arena of democratic politics by leaving "your wallet and your pistol at the door." The implication was not just that Berlusconi would bring "his wallet" into government if he won the election; the allegation also went that he had friends in Sicily with some very sizeable holsters.

Both stories, Berlusconi's own and that of his enemies, were gripping. *Una storia italiana* and *L'odore dei soldi* formed a perfect symmetry, one full of implausible, heroic achievements, the other full of improbable accusations. As with the country's press and television, there was no room for the middle ground: Berlusconi was either a saint or a sinner, and the ordinary voter was confronted by two versions of his career both so incredible that it was hard to know what was reality and what fantasy. If, as was probable, the truth lay somewhere between the two stories, no one was willing to say so.

I tried, not for the first time, to understand Berlusconi's origins. Complication and confusion, as should now be clear, are the smokescreens of Italian life, and Berlusconi is a master of the art. When he began building his thirty-five hundred flats on the outskirts of Milan in the 1970s, he created endless financial Chinese boxes which were entirely unfathomable to outsiders. Bizarre businesses were set up under *prestanomi* ("nicknamed" accounts with dummy holders) and furnished with money (some 140 billion lire) which washed up from anonymous banks in Switzerland. Or else money arrived through the Banca Rasini, where Berlusconi's father had worked and which has frequently been cited in Mafia trials in recent years. At the same time, Fininvest, the empire which is the driving force behind Forza Italia, was set up with twenty-two "holdings." It would take an accountant an eternity to understand what was going on. To many the Chinese boxes seemed a suspiciously complicated way of building a few blocks of flats.

The story of one of Berlusconi's gardeners on his Arcore estate is equally bizarre. Berlusconi had bought the estate after two murders, a crime of passion, prompted the owner to sell the property in the mid-1970s. Berlusconi, having moved in, employed someone called Vittorio Mangano, a man later handed down two life sentences for murder and heroin trafficking. Apart from being resident on Berlusconi's estate, Mangano was on close terms with Berlusconi's business partner and Forza Italia general, Marcello Dell'Utri. Maybe it's all just coincidental, maybe not. "For me," Mangano said during a prison interview in July 2000, "Berlusconi was like a relative. The trust he had in me was the same as that I had in him and his family. I like Berlusconi, still do. He's an honest person, write it!" Is a compliment of honesty from a convicted murderer an asset? Does that mean he really is honest? The extraordinarily complicated facts are all out in the open, hundreds of thousands of dubious transcripts and transactions (dubious because they cast doubt in both directions: towards both the investigators and the investigated). Only the interpretation differs. Berlusconi's response to the (hardly new) accusation of being a closet Mafioso was illuminating: as RAI ran long debates on the subject, Berlusconi was indignant, aggressive, threatening. "Contain yourself," he screamed to one RAI presenter in a live telephone call with which he had interrupted the programme.

The programme in question was Michele Santoro's *Il raggio verde* on RAI 2 (the channel which had originally publicised *L'odore dei soldi*). Forza Italia's general, Marcello Dell'Utri, the man at the centre of the scandal, was later given a chance to defend himself. For once an Italian studio was silent rather than noisy; instead of the usual revolving glitter ball, the lighting was low. The advertising breaks were announced by a string quartet. It takes courage for a journalist from Palermo to hint live on national TV that a man of Dell'Utri's power was possibly guilty of involvement with the Mafia. At the suggestion Dell'Utri whitened visibly, his skin tightening in disbelief at the arrogance of the suggestion. "I have never in my life seen evidence of the Mafia," he stuttered, caught off guard by the frankness of the frontal attack. "Then you must be a very distracted *palermitano*," the journalist replied. Thereafter, Berlusconi refused (temporarily) to appear on the RAI TV channels, as did those in his coalition. They retreated to the safety of Mediaset journalists. His allies spoke of cleaning up the ranks of RAI after the election. Others urged Italians to refuse to pay their license fees to RAI, since it was clearly Communist. Berlusconi's own Mediaset television channels resorted to impassioned pleas not to believe the allegations: on Rete 4, for example, the newscaster Emilio Fede couldn't contain his outrage, banging his fists on his desk as he denounced the dirty tricks of the left. Each time he tried to introduce another story, he couldn't do it; he started frowning, almost on the verge of tears, and returned to defend his boss, Berlusconi. Not for the first time, the nation's television channels became, like the country at large, polarised into shrill declarations of love or loathing for Berlusconi. The actual issue, of whether there was any truth in the allegations, of whether Berlusconi really was dangerously close to collusion with organised crime, was lost in the hysteria.

Some saw sufficient grounds to indict Il Cavaliere, suggesting that suspicion really is "the antechamber of truth" as far as the Mafia is concerned. Weeks before the election, the cover of Britain's *Economist* showed a photograph of Berlusconi, with the headline "Why Berlusconi Is Unfit to Govern

Italy." The article, which caused an even bigger storm than *L'odore dei soldi*, duly proceeded to list Il Cavaliere's legal difficulties. "The public's acquittal," the magazine warned, could become "a terrible condemnation of the electorate."[2] The reply from Forza Italia was the same as usual: a conspiracy of left-wing intellectuals had it in for the honest family man Silvio Berlusconi. *The Economist*, far from being a a sober organ of financial analysis, was a "Communist publication" edited by wannabe Stalinists.

Despite the ferocious criticisms of Berlusconi, it's easy to understand and empathise with those who voted, in their millions, for his Forza Italia movement. It's immediately obvious, watching him, that his leadership is extraordinary and magnetic. The aggressiveness with which people defend him bears witness to his charismatic appeal. His closest friends, lawyers from the 1970s or his pianist from the early cruiseship days, are still sworn allies and are now in Parliament or heading arms of the business empire. Loyalty in Italian politics is in short supply, but Berlusconi has it by the bucketful. There is, perhaps, something noble in the way he sticks doggedly by his friends and vice versa. There is clearly a strong motivational factor, eerily reminiscent of the football terraces: "us against them." Those friends, and subsequently his political supporters, seem to see in Berlusconi something like a Midas touch, the ability to turn everything he touches into gold: real-estate deals, TV empires, the Milan football team. The list, by anyone's reckoning, is breathtaking. The success of his financial empire is stunning. That sense of being a winner—like Milan, *costretto a vincere*, as the slogan goes, "obliged to win"—means that to his charismatic appeal is added a sense of destiny: it's his fate to see everything he touches succeed. Every whim of his turns out to be winning intuition. *Una storia italiana* explicitly says as much: the heavenly constellations decree that Silvio Berlusconi is, quite simply, a winner. And nothing breeds popularity like success.

Berlusconi therefore plays on his wealth. His electoral bandwagon was, in 1999, a cruise ship hired at his own expense. He has consistently argued—and one can understand the argument, if not necessarily believe it—that his wealth actually makes him a more honest politician than the others: he is so rich that he is above corruption. Poor politicians might be prey to the odd envelope passed under the desk, but a rich one would never need to be. (This is precisely what Thackeray suggested in *Vanity Fair*: "A comfortable career of prosperity, if it does not make people honest, at least keeps them so. An alderman coming from a turtle feast will not step out of his carriage to steal a leg of mutton; but put him to starve, and see if he will not purloin a loaf."[3]) I get the suspicion, talking to Forza Italia voters, that Berlusconi's wealth is the main reason they vote for him. He is envied and emulated. Voting for him is an endorsement of that lifestyle of cruise ships and villas and Sardinian retreats (and beautiful women and winning football teams): the leader's lifestyle has become his substance. He flaunts his wealth because, sadly, he knows how admired and envied he is. It's an asset rather than a hindrance.

Thus, set against the backdrop of Italian politics—traditionally inhabited by mildly boring, indistinguishable characters who all wear the same suits and pronounce the same long-winded sentences—the leader is actually quite exciting. Certainly, when you find yourself at the ballot-box and are confronted by dozens of splinter parties, Forza Italia has a ring to it. You at least know whom you're voting for. It is simply, to put it in marketing terms that Forzisti understand, a very recognisable brand. It's a logo, a slogan. This is more than can be said for the parties on the left. The bucolic left-

wing coalition is called the Olive and is made up of the Sun-
flower (Greens and Socialists), the Daisy (Democrats, the
People's Party, the Union of Democrats of Europe, and the
former Prime Minister's "Dini list"), the Oak (the former
Communist Party, now called Democrats of the Left), and
one-half of the Communist Party proper (the Italian Communists). Then there are various fringe parties (the Refounded Communist Party, the "Di Pietro list," the Radicals).
Given this confusing plethora of parties, few ordinary voters
understood these coalitions, let alone what they stood for. Indeed, during the 2001 election it was hard even to know
what had happened in the last five years: during the thirteenth
Parliament of the Italian Republic (1996–2001), 158 politicians had changed political allegiance, and the country had
had three different prime ministers (Romano Prodi, Massimo
D'Alema, and Giuliano Amato) presiding over four different
governments. Political debate and front-page scoops had often simply been about who was building or breaking which
coalition, who was redesigning his party flag, or who was
reinventing himself as a politician of the right or of the left.
Amidst that sea of political alphabet soup, Berlusconi un-
doubtedly stands out. There's something, many of his supporters say to me, rather admirable in the way the leader is so
brash. "He's got balls," they say. He offends other people's
political correctness, punctures all their flowery words by
speaking *alla pancia*, "to the belly." When I phone the offices
of Forza Italia to check facts or quotations, they are so slick
that I sometimes forget I'm phoning an Italian political party.
They are polite, efficient, always helpful. That, Forza Italia
voters keep telling me, is all they want from the Italian Parliament: quick decisions, clarity, less red tape. Berlusconi, they
said, is good for business. "He's on our side."

He also benefits from the fact that the anti-establishment
vote in Italy is always influential. Politicians are held in such

low esteem that anyone who appears outside the old guard is immediately more appealing than the incumbent government. (One politician from the centre-left coalition admitted recently that any politician who denied taking bribes was a *bugiardo matricolato*, an "out-and-out liar.") So it's one of Berlusconi's strengths to be able to portray himself as the non-politician leading a party of entrepreneurs, not politicians. (About 90 per cent of the parliamentary intake of Forza Italia deputies in 1994 had never been in Parliament before.) Another advantage was that, as Machiavelli recognised, Italy seems ever to be "waiting to see who can be the one to heal her wounds . . . See how Italy beseeches God to send someone to save her from those barbarous cruelties and outrages; see how eager and willing the country is to follow a banner, if only someone will raise it."[4] There is in Italy a yearning for a redeemer, for a politician who will raise a new banner and "cleanse those sores" arising from years of misrule. That was the appeal of Mussolini in 1922 and of the Christian Democrats in 1948. Each new political regime is seen as a bright dawn before being furiously rejected when that dawn appears as false as the last (which, naturally, only increases the yearning for another "redeemer").

Beyond the symbolism of the non-politician healing wounds, Berlusconi's bedrock of support comes from the business community. As a man whose business acumen has never been doubted, Berlusconi appeals even to the traditionally "red" areas of Italy, in the richest parts of the centre and the north. Even the most left-wing commentator accepts that Italy's labour laws beggar belief. Contracts run on for "time immemorial," and it is virtually impossible for any company with more than fifteen employees to lay anybody off. Wages may be measly, but they are still guaranteed for life. Companies are then forced to pay hefty pension contributions for any "full-time" employee, a figure which, given that anyone can claim a state pension at fifty-six, is crippling to Italy's small businesses.

Berlusconi's other great vote winner was the immigration issue. Italy, for decades one of the world's largest exporters of human beings, had in the space of a few years become a net importer. The country has invariably been the first port of call for refugees from the Balkans, eastern Europe, and North Africa. For a society which is so homogeneous (socially, if not politically), and one with, significantly, the lowest birth rate in Europe, the sudden influx had been traumatic. The problem of immigration was compounded by the much more serious problem of "illegal immigration": the number of *clandestini* in the country was estimated to be nearing half a million, and every day more *extracomunitari* were arriving, thrown out onto the shores of the Adriatic from inflatables.

The preceding left-wing government had also added to its own downfall. When Romano Prodi won the 1996 election, it seemed that Italy's *bipartitismo imperfetto* (with the Christian Democrats, or the right, permanently in power, and the Communists, or the left, permanently excluded) had finally, after fifty years, come to an end. In power, however, those Communists (or, as they're now called, Democrats of the Left) and their allies proved to be strict monetarists, determined to prepare the country very painfully for entry into the euro. In their five years in government, net borrowing as a percentage of GDP had fallen from over 7 per cent to 0.3 per cent; the national debt had fallen, as had inflation. Only taxes were increased, or new ones introduced, like the "tax for Europe." Most suggest that Prodi's government, and those which followed, had been very successful financially and fiscally. The consequence, however, is that they were politically a disaster.

The left's greatest blunder, however, was simply tactical. Raising the spectre of Berlusconi's conflict of interest should have been the Olive coalition's winning game plan, but having ignored the issue for five years in government, they were unable suddenly to argue that it was a pressing problem. Massimo D'Alema, the man who replaced Romano Prodi as Prime Minister once the Refounded Communists withdrew from the coalition, had effectively been "made" by a handful of votes from Francesco Cossiga (a former Christian Democrat and former President of the Republic). In an attempt to strengthen his hand, D'Alema, an astute, intelligent, but old-school politician, had been locked in bipartisan, bicameral constitutional debates with Berlusconi. The intention was to give Italy once and for all a powerful executive and a presidential leader, no longer hostage to the small parties of Proportional Representation. As leaders of the country's two largest political movements, D'Alema and Berlusconi clearly had interests in common when it came to the constitutional talks. Meetings (480 hours of them) dragged on for years, during which time legislation against Berlusconi was unthinkable. D'Alema, apparently desperate to pass a new electoral law, had thus leant over backwards to accommodate his rival in order to reach an accord. Because D'Alema appeared so cosy with the leader of Forza Italia in the late 1990s, his subsequent suggestion—after the constitutional talks had collapsed and as an election loomed—that Berlusconi really was a Faustian figure after all lacked any credibility.

Finally, Berlusconi was able to portray himself, bizarrely, as a *garantista*, a standard-bearer of civil rights. Having suffered firsthand various legal "attacks," he promised a complete overhaul of the magistrature. Whatever his motives, the "civil rights" slogan was a winning line. Everyone knows that the legal system in Italy is excruciating. Forty per cent of those in prison are still awaiting trial—not just for a few days, but for years. The accused, according to one book by a Forza Italia deputy, are effectively being sentenced even before their trial.

Thus the country warmed to a politician who promised radically to reform the whole judiciary. "Against me," Berlusconi said with his normal flair for overstatement, "they use the same methods which Goebbels used against the Jews." To adapt the famous adage about the usefulness of Communism for the Christian Democrats ("if the Communist Party hadn't existed, we would have had to invent it"): if Berlusconi didn't have pending judicial prosecutions, he would have to invent them. It's an opposition which is, strangely, very useful to him. These accusations play into a key part of his strategy: *vittimismo*. It's a brilliant tactic. First, everyone in Italy can identify and empathise with a man who appears plagued and persecuted by sinister, unseen forces. It's a recognisable narrative. It's the one aspect of his life which makes him "one of us." Second, it allows Berlusconi to play the patriotic card. The more he is accused of improper conduct from abroad, the more he is admired at home. Third—and this is only a fleeting impression—the prosecutions create a sense that he is Everyman: he is being accused only of doing what everyone in Italy has always done. It's that classic defence not of innocence, but that everyone else is just as guilty.

By now the sense that the leader is a victim, subject to biblical suffering, has become a central part of the Forza Italia iconography. The cult needs the persecution complex. It makes the leader, and his followers, appear downtrodden, unfortunate underdogs, crusaders for a better world in a land which doesn't understand them. The diction of this image is fascinating. Forza Italia candidates are called "apostles"; the time in opposition was the *traversata nel deserto*. Berlusconi, indeed, often compares himself to Noah or Moses, even Jesus. That importation of religious imagery into the political arena creates, almost subliminally, the sense that these are good people, comparable to early Jewish and Christian nomads. They, living humbly among us, are spreading "the word," distributing the "good book," singing their communal hymns (which are played to you when, phoning Forza Italia's offices, you're put on hold).

None of this, however, was really mentioned in the run-up to the 2001 election. The political issues were only a subtext. In reality, Berlusconi, as the journalist Indro Montanelli realised, had become the "millstone that paralyses Italian politics."[5] Issues and ideas weren't even debated. The election had become, in the words of Umberto Eco, nothing more than a "moral referendum" on the leader of Forza Italia. It was simply a case of "for" or "against" one man. It was an experiment in saturation advertising: the brand was Berlusconi, and the simple slogans were "liberty" and "democracy." He won the 2001 election, of course, by a landslide. The interregnum was over, the restoration complete. The tactic of demonising Berlusconi had badly misfired. The more he was seen as under attack from pointy-heads on the left and financial journalists on the right (especially foreign ones), the stronger and more patriotic he appeared. In the "moral referendum" the majority had chosen the "immoral option." Forza Italia was voted for by almost 30 per cent of the electorate. The left was decimated (only Francesco Rutelli's Daisy coalition didn't wilt, claiming 15 per cent compared with 9 per cent five years earlier), and the few independent parties (Di Pietro's Italy of Values Party, the ambiguous Radicals) failed to make the 4-per-cent minimum required for a parliamentary seat from the allocation of Proportional Representation votes. Even so, the election might have been a close finish had the Refounded Communists, full of pomp and principle, been allied with the Olive. In the new, "two-coalition" politics, the Communists' 5 per cent of the vote would almost have guaranteed a hung Parliament. Outside the coalition, however, that 5 per cent simply translated into eleven inconsequential seats in the lower house.

...

It's part of the rewiring process of living in Italy that, as one experienced journalist described it to me, "it's entirely useless to think in terms of left and right. Politicians swap so often between the two that that will leave you utterly confused." To understand what goes on in the country, it was explained, the only possible definitions for slippery politicians are "pre-political" ones: not "right" or "left" wing, not historical dinosaurs like "Fascist" or "Communist," but old-fashioned judgements like "honest," "law-abiding," "tax-paying," or simply "moral." Given these definitions, Berlusconi's politics was thrown into sharp relief: the man who had so earnestly painted a picture of himself as a free-marketeer in the Thatcher mould was actually nothing of the sort. With his first legislative act Berlusconi decriminalised false accounting. He had, I felt, removed one of the foundation stones of capitalism: probity with the accounts.

That summer, a historic sentence was handed down by the courts. After almost eighteen months, on 30 June 2001, the judge and jury in the Piazza Fontana trial reached a decision on the bombing which had taken place thirty-two years previously. The announcement of three life sentences, for Delfo Zorzi, Carlo Maria Maggi, and Giancarlo Rognoni, was greeted in court by applause from the families of the bomb victims. The verdict barely raised a stir in the press. We were all suffering from scandal fatigue and overexposure to contrite *pentiti*. The revelations that the Italian state machine colluded with Fascist bombers decades ago were either unbelievable (given the farcical court case) or so obvious already that they weren't even news. What was news was the fact that Gaetano Pecorella, one of Berlusconi's judicial advisers, had also been the defence lawyer for Zorzi; Carlo Taormina, the under-secretary at the Ministry of the Interior, had previously acted as defence lawyer for Maggi. "The outcome of political show trials is already written at their inception," Pecorella wearily told the cameras outside the court before pouring more scorn on the judiciary of which he had become one of the political heads. "History is being rewritten with a red pen," said Taormina.

A month later, the tensions came out into the open. The month before the G8 summit in Genoa in July 2001, the Italian media spoke about nothing other than the threat of riots and terrorism. Five hundred and fifteen million dollars had been set aside to organise the summit, and fifteen thousand "forces of order" had evacuated the streets of the city at the height of the tourist season. The country was whipped into a frenzy as it was treated to back-to-back broadcasts showing police and rioter rehearsals for the confrontation (truncheons and tear-gas for the former, gas masks and cardboard shin-pads for the others). Manu Chao, a popular and politicised French-Spanish singer, went on-stage to lend his support to the Tute Bianche (the "white overalls" anti-globalist lobby). Members of Tute Bianche, looking like astronauts, joined him on-stage days before G8, raising their left fists in their anti-global salute.

For anyone with a sense of history, the Genoa venue was ominous. It was here, in 1960, that the neo-Fascist party Movimento Sociale Italiano attempted to organise a conference. It was to have been chaired by the former (Italian) prefect of the city when it was under Nazi occupation. On 30 June 1960 the city saw riots which were unprecedented and which were intended to prevent the inclusion of the Fascists in government. Within days the riots spread elsewhere, particularly to Reggio Emilia, the "red" town a short drive east of Parma. There, five protesters were killed by police, raising to ninety-four the number of strikers and "rioters" killed by the Italian police between 1945 and 1960. That memory of martyrs from forty-one years before, and the history of trigger-happy policing, meant that the G8 summit was becoming a cause for acute concern.

Shortly before the summit, bombs appeared across the country. As usual they were "minor." Many didn't go off, and others were paltry packages with simply a dusting of dynamite. Benetton, Fiat, an office for "temporary work" were all targeted. (Employment agencies are seen as an affront to the "time immemorial" job and are thus as much a target of Italian anti-globalists as is McDonald's.) Emilio Fede, Berlusconi's favourite newscaster, was sent a bomb which did explode, hospitalising his secretary. The hysteria about terrorism and the G8 reached new levels. What actually happened in Genoa is well known. There were the usual looters and car burners (the so-called black block) amongst the quarter of a million protesters who marched around the outskirts of the city. The "white overalls" protesters had been infiltrated, according to Berlusconi's Mediaset channels, by a sinister new terrorist outfit. All one could see were a few dozen people dressed in black, banging drums and throwing bricks into shop-windows: hooligans certainly, but hardly the "terrorists" the government said they were. (One was decked out in blacked-up cricket pads, which hardly seemed like the livery of a dangerous revolutionary.)

Much more serious was the behaviour of the police. The problem of Italian policing (as at the football stadia) is that it's a combination of the incompetent and the very heavy-handed. The one exacerbates the other: the greater the incompetence, of course, the greater the need for heavy hands. If those hands are carrying loaded weapons which are fired at point-blank range, it seems fairly obvious that there will be casualties. The $376,890,103 spent organising the summit weren't enough to prevent an armoured car being "attacked." Defending himself from a fire extinguisher being thrown towards his vehicle, one *carabiniere* opened fire and killed the twenty-year-old Carlo Giuliani.

But even that tragic and unnecessary death was surpassed a

day later. The *carabinieri* then conducted a night raid on the Diaz school, where many journalists and protesters from the Genoa Social Forum were staying. The *carabinieri*'s brutality overshadowed anything which had happened before. It was thuggery at its crudest. Pictures the next day showed teeth strewn across the floor of the school. There were blood stains at head height on many of the walls. Ninety-three people were arrested, and others were taken to the temporary barracks at Bolzaneto, outside Genoa. There, various protesters suffered beatings to the accompaniment of the Fascist hymn "Faccetta nera." One *carabiniere* later confessed to *La Repubblica* what his colleagues had done to the journalists and protesters: "They lined them up and banged their heads against the walls. They urinated on one person. They beat people if they didn't sing 'Faccetta nera.' One girl was vomiting blood, but the chief of the squad just looked on. They threatened to rape girls with their batons."[6] Bones were broken. The injuries of the British alone were obscene: broken ribs, punctured lungs, ruptured spleens, broken wrists, severe head injuries. Months later many people, both Italians and indignant foreigners, were still imprisoned and awaiting charges, let alone a trial from the government of "human rights." The Italian press compared the behaviour to that of militarists in Pinochet's Chile, and for once the rhetoric didn't appear overblown. "This," said my normally reticent flatmate, "is just the beginning. It's a calling card from the Fascists in government."

When, that autumn, the war on terrorism found a "financial front," Berlusconi's position became ever more unfathomable. As the international community began taking an ever-tougher line on the movements of unsourced money, Berlusconi's domestic legislation was going in exactly the opposite direction. With the eclipse of the Italian currency, the lira, just around the corner, his government passed legislation which was little more than a licence to launder money. In return for a fine of 2.5 per cent of the sum involved, illegally exported (or earned) capital would be allowed to return to Italy. It was called, simply, *rientro capitali* and was introduced as a sly amendment to a vote on the introduction of the euro. Apart from the international derision which the legislation incurred, the government won on both counts: financially the Treasury would benefit from the fines and the influx of funds, and politically the Prime Minister seemed to have honoured his side of the dark bargain struck before the election. Stashes of illegally exported cash could now, for a small fee, be put through the governmental washing machine. Such was the unease at the legislation that only months after coming to power, the government was forced to make the "re-entry of capital" legislation a vote of confidence in the government.

Meanwhile, a parallel piece of legislation seemed, in the face of international efforts, even more perverse. The government had added two amendments to a treaty agreed to between Switzerland and Italy in 1998, which was only now being ratified in Parliament. These amendments, in effect, deliberately impeded international investigations into financial fraud. They rendered useless any documents used in ongoing trials for banking irregularities unless they met rigid and improbable conditions (adherence, for example, to a raft of laws from February 1961, which ratified the Convention of Strasbourg). It seemed apparent that certain trials would have to be postponed, or begun again from scratch. By that time, the statute of limitations would have taken effect, and further prosecution would have been impossible. The director of public prosecutions in Geneva, Bernard Bertossa, spoke of his "impression that this disgraceful law has a clear objective: to do away with certain evidence to neutralise certain judicial processes in Italy. It's a fact that amongst the Italian trials most at risk [from the legislation] are those involving Mr

Berlusconi."[7] Even on the government benches there was outrage at the legislation. For the first time, twenty-seven *franchi tiratori* ("snipers" from Berlusconi's own Pole of Liberties coalition) took advantage of the secret ballot to vote against the government. As the legislation was passed, physical fights broke out on the floor of the Parliament. It was described as a *rissa*: not exactly a punch-up, but a lot of pushing and shoving between opposing politicians. Indeed, as the amendments were being passed, opposition parliamentarians held up posters with the name of Cesare Previti (Berlusconi's lawyer currently on trial in Milan) and the number of his Swiss bank account.

It became very obvious that the backlog of court cases against Silvio Berlusconi and his allies was the main reason for the autumn's rushed legislation. He intended, it seemed, to defend himself not *in* the various trials but *from* them. Even the Northern League, which at the beginning of the 1990s had appeared a minor party intent on rooting out the corruption of Rome, had become entirely co-opted in the cover-up. The Justice Minister, Roberto Castelli (of the Northern League), repeatedly inveighed against the "dirty togas"; Carlo Taormina, the Sicilian lawyer, went further, saying that any magistrates who continued to prosecute Berlusconi should themselves be prosecuted. Each time he went abroad Berlusconi desperately tried to explain himself to his allies: Italy had "Jacobin judges," he said in Spain. "For the last ten years," he said in an interview with one of his own magazines, "there has been a civil war in Italy." In a move which seemed intimidating, and whose full significance would only be understood months later, protective escorts for magistrates were drastically cut back. By the beginning of December, after weeks of relentless attacks, the entire committee of the National Association of Magistrates had resigned en masse, the first time it had done so since 1924.

Days later, the partners of the European Union met to discuss plans for a European arrest warrant for thirty-two of the
most serious crimes: terrorism, arms trafficking, paedophilia,
and so on. It was expected to be a straightforward meeting,
but Italy unexpectedly, and for the first time in its postwar
history, had suddenly cooled on the idea of the European
Community. The Italian delegation refused to sign the agreement. The motives for Italy's reluctance to introduce a European arrest warrant were baffling. Others, though, suggested
it was only natural: at a time when the Italian government was
intending to stitch up its domestic judiciary, it wouldn't then
go create an international noose for the presidential neck.
Roberto Castelli, the Justice Minister, returned from Brussels
wearing his green Northern League necktie and duly announced to a rally in Milan that a European arrest warrant
was a sure way to guarantee Communist justice; nobody, said
Umberto Bossi—the Minister of Reforms and leader of the
league—would have been safe from the left-wing "executioners" had the legislation been signed. An agreement was eventually reached, but only once many of the crimes under
discussion had become subject to "dual incrimination": the
arrest warrant would only be valid if the crime was legally a
crime in both the country requesting extradition and the ex-
traditing country. As Graham Watson, the chairman of the
European Union's Justice and Home Affairs Committee, later
told me: "The whole episode raised further questions in Brussels about the cleanliness of Berlusconi's government. That a
Prime Minister should go so far to guarantee what is effectively a veto against the arrest of criminals is very worrying."

Meanwhile, the court cases against Berlusconi and his entourage continued, as, of course, did the attacks on the magistrature. As ever, the only real clues to Berlusconi's innocence
or guilt were the coincidences: the rude haste with which his
government had invalidated trials in which he was involved,

the refusal to countenance international arrest warrants. In fact, the beautifully cynical question immediately asked of any action in Italy, especially governmental, is *"Chi giova?,"* which means basically "Who's set to benefit?" Pose that question to any of the legislation passed by the government, and there was only one conceivable reply: *Il Presidente*.

To complete the restoration of the *ancien régime*, immunity has now been reintroduced. Most equate immunity with impunity. It's not protection but evasion. It's a defiant declaration that certain people are above the law. Fed by TV imagery which portrays Berlusconi as a victim, immunity is accepted almost without question by millions of Forza Italia voters as if it represented normal, sane parliamentary behaviour. In Britain we have, obviously, dozens of crooked politicians. Every country has them. The difference is that if found guilty, they go to prison. By contrast, Berlusconi has been convicted and absolved so many times that no one can declare, in black and white, his innocence or guilt. Leonardo Sciascia once characterised Fascism as "a constant evasion of its own laws"[8]; one could adapt the line for Forzismo and say that it is "constant legislation of evasion." When a government issues laws that decriminalise the forgery of electoral signatures (guilt now brings a small fine instead of a maximum four years in prison), there's something very worrying afoot.

Throughout the spring of 2002, the stakes between the two halves of the country were exponentially raised. For the first time, commentators started talking about the "regime" and the "resistance." In January, at the opening ceremony for the new judicial year, the *procuratore generale* of Milan and former head of the Clean Hands pool, Francesco Saverio Borrelli, took the microphone. The reduction of protective escorts, the attacks on the magistrature, the new laws which interfered with ongoing court cases—all, said Borrelli, carried the stamp of an authoritarian regime. He urged his colleagues and the Italian public in general to "resist, resist, resist" Berlusconi's government. Having invoked the Resistance, he then also invoked Italians' brave First World War defiance on the Piave front. His rhetoric was warmly applauded, and magistrates removed their ermine and red robes to mourn in black ones instead. Gerardo D'Ambrosio, the Milanese *procuratore*, echoed the sentiments. About Berlusconi's government he said ominously: "This is the night of Italian democracy."

Television became the next theatre of the encounter between the "regime" and the "resistance." When the conflict-of-interest bill was finally introduced to Parliament, politicians once again screamed abuse at each other. "Shame" or "Pinocchio," chanted the left, standing and shouting like a group of football fans before abandoning the Parliament in a walk-out. The tone of the *Oggi* editor was more sober: "This law on the conflict of interest isn't honourable. It's laughable. In fact, it's disgusting." The main cause for complaint, days after Berlusconi had appointed a new "advisory commission" for RAI, was the bill's second article. It stated that "mere ownership" of a business wasn't sufficient to preclude taking up of governmental office. The conflict of interest existed, effectively, only for those concerned with the day-to-day running of the business. Berlusconi wasn't even subject to the legislation. Umberto Eco, days later, wrote about the only type of resistance left: "To a new form of government," he wrote in the pages of *La Repubblica*, "a new form of political reply. This really would be an opposition." It was the kind of proposal which, from the outside, seems surreal. Eco was proposing a boycott of all the products advertised on Mediaset channels:

One doesn't reply to a government-business with flags and ideas but by aiming at its weakest point: money. If the government-business then shows itself sensitive to this protest, even its electors will realise that it's nothing more than a government-business which survives only as long as its leader continues to make money.[9]

One of the biggest unions, CGIL, organised a protest—against the repeal of Article 18 (guaranteeing workers' rights) and against terrorism—in Rome. Two million turned out. Red flags made the Circo Massimo, site of the Roman chariot races, look like an ocean full of masts and sails. The flags bobbed up and down in the sun, billowing and then going slack. The city even sounded like a marina: that sound of cloth twisting and clapping in the wind. "We are here to join the fight against terrorism and to defend our rights," said Sergio Cofferati, leader of the union.

I spent the afternoon wandering across the capital. Every hilly street was crammed with flags and banners against Berlusconi. Small bands played music on street corners. Kids kicked footballs from pavement to pavement. People were passing round flasks of wine. Everyone had his own theory of what was going on. "Italy," one wizened old man told me, "has always been like this: one-third ruled by the Vatican, one-third by foreign powers, and one-third by our home-bred tyrants. But the reason we have tyrants is the reason we survive them: we're completely lawless."

One shop owner told me how he hated these protesters: "I'm from the National Alliance and I've got absolutely nothing in common with those idiots," he said. "I think Article 18 should be repealed. Of course it should. Here it's impossible to lay anyone off. It's like having marriage without divorce. A lot of what the government wants to change is for the better: it wants an elected President, chosen by the people, not by

Parliament. It wants to reform the judiciary and RAI. All that is fine. It's just that . . ." He began rocking his hands in the imploring praying position. "It's just if there were one man in the entire country you wouldn't trust to reform all those things, the one man you shouldn't let near the whole project, it's Berlusconi!"

Another scene: almost exactly a year later, May 2003. I had caught the dawn train from Parma to Milan. It was a Monday morning. I walked slowly from the station to the Palazzo di Giustizia. It was a beautiful spring morning. People were walking their dogs, taking their children to school. So many banks, I thought. I have never known a city with so many banks, and so many cars. The brutal square columns of the Palazzo di Giustizia, archetypal Fascist architecture, loomed into view.

This was to be a lengthy, direct appeal to the people. Berlusconi's lawyers had alerted the court authorities, and—of course—television stations, that their client would make a "spontaneous declaration" to the court. Outside the court-room I was crammed against the shut doors. There were about sixty or seventy journalists, many from abroad. Every-one was sweating and swearing. I got elbows and camera tripods stuck into my spine. People kept pushing and com-plaining and shouting at a *carabiniere* who looked adolescent. Eventually they called in the cameramen and the journalists. There were no security checks. No one asked to look inside our bags and books. I squeezed through the narrow door at exactly the same time as five other people. Inside, of course, it no longer looked like a courtroom; it was more like a televi-sion studio.

Camera crews and sound technicians crowded around the Prime Minister as he began his monologue. It was masterful: he started so humbly you could hardly hear him. He wiped his bronze brow with a crisp white handkerchief. He looked tired and dispirited. Then, before you know it, he picks up the pace. He explains big business deals from the 1980s in elegant, clipped Italian. The style is that of a competent manager reeling off figures from the top of his head, juggling them all at once, reaching sound, reasoned conclusions. He never needs to pause for breath, it's all unscripted. He's fighting back, and, listening to him, you're almost hypnotised. It's truly mesmeric. He reels off a list of famous politicians and alludes to bribes elsewhere in the system. The volume is getting louder, you can hear every word very clearly now. He never uses "I"; it's always in the third person: "the undersigned." When he finishes, there's applause in the courtroom.

Then, just as we all shuffle out of the courtroom, a heckler gets up: "Submit to justice like an ordinary citizen, you great Smurf! You'll end up like Ceausescu!" Berlusconi turns to the *carabinieri* and asks them to take the man's details. It was distasteful and undignified: the comparison with a murdered ex-dictator was inflammatory and stupid; Berlusconi's reaction was, well, inflammatory and stupid. It was another moment, like the Rome protest a year before, in which the entire debate was crystallised in a second: this time, frozen in the photographers' flash bulbs, there was all the aggression, the delegitimisation, the mutual loathing. The one seems to exacerbate the other, and objective opinions become hard, very hard, to come by.

On the train back to Parma from Milan I decided to read Shelley. Writing about the long history of Italian tyranny, he spoke about the "viper's paralysing venom" (the snake was the symbol of the Visconti family). "Lawless slaveries" and "savage lust," he wrote, trample "our columned cities into dust."[10] It's much the same language which the country's left wing are now using: apocalyptic and pessimistic, convinced that democracy is in peril. Is it hyperbole to say Berlusconi is a danger to Italian democracy? Is Forzismo really a twenty-first-century televisual version of Fascism? How could one possibly contextualise someone who is so unique, so *sui generis*? Walter Benjamin wrote that Fascism was the aestheticisation of politics and that Communism was, by response, the politicisation of art. Both were united, of course, by those personality cults which create and sustain dictatorships. Is Forzismo, then, the beautification of politics? Or is it the politicisation of the art of television? Is it simply a crude personality cult? Or are millions of Italians getting slightly hysterical about what is, simply, a democratic leader of a democratic party democratically elected to government?

For many foreign observers, Berlusconi is fascinating because he represents the incarnation of various literary figures, figures from a dystopian future in which democracy has been superseded: the obvious comparisons come from *Brave New World*, from *1984* or *Citizen Kane*. Foreigners see in Berlusconi a worrying media magnate who uses propaganda for political purposes; many on the Italian left would echo the accusation. Orwell, for example, described a "Party" which had introduced contradictory slogans to underline the creed of Big Brother: "War Is Peace," "Ignorance Is Strength," and so on. They were examples of *"doublethink,"* the neologism of the regime which, according to Orwell, "means the power of holding two contradictory beliefs in one's mind simultaneously, and accepting both of them."[11] When foreign political commentators observe Berlusconi's political movement, *doublethink* always comes to mind. His whole political cause is built upon contradiction, the most obvious being his choice of political allies: the Northern League (urging federalism, if not outright secession) and the National Alliance (the patriotic, statist post-Fascist party). Other Orwell phrases, like *"crimethink"* (the crime of thinking badly of the Party) and *"prolefeed"* ("the rubbishy entertainment and the spurious news which the Party handed out to the masses"), fit Berlusconi like a glove.

And yet Berlusconi is very adept at self-irony. The leader often jokes that he has a superiority complex. He laughs at the way he is represented. He teases both those who love and those who loathe him by occasionally dropping self-deprecatory remarks at press conferences. In fact, in those media scrums when he finds himself surrounded by microphones and bodyguards, the leader is chummy. Some of the jocular, laddish behaviour is surely deliberate: the joke that he would imprison footballers if they didn't win the 2002 World Cup is typical of the way the leader punctures the alarmist voices. It's not particularly funny, no one laughs. But it's effective. Indeed, his friends say he is a *gaffeur* of such epic proportions that he could never pose a threat to democracy, because he is, genuinely, a kind of clown. A happy-go-lucky chancer who rides his luck. He's amusing company: a bit vulgar, a great raconteur, someone who's larger than life. The idea that he could be dangerous is, according to his fans, unthinkable.

Millions, however, are very worried. They will say that, no, there's not a regime. It's absurd to say Italy isn't a democracy. But then they shrug pessimistically and say it's equally impossible to say that it is a democracy. It's "blocked," or "problematic," or "imbalanced." What's certain is that the iconography of the country is changing month by month. The best barometers of the change, as always, are the politicised plaques, memorials, and graffiti. Throughout 2001 and 2002 there was clearly a new symbolism emerging as an assiduous renaming of streets began (one for Benito Mussolini in Catania; two for Giorgio Almirante, the historic leader of Italy's postwar Fascism). In Friuli, in the north-east of the country, a plaque bearing the Fascist slogan outside a second-ary school was restored to its former glory: "Believe, Obey, Combat," it read. In Benevento, the name of the central square, Piazza Matteotti (Giacomo Matteotti was a Socialist parliamentarian killed by Fascists in 1924), was changed to Santa Sofia. All the mayors responsible for the new urban appearances were from the ranks of the National Alliance, as was the mayor of Latina (a town built from scratch by Mussolini) who decided to replace the marble plaque on the town's modern bell-tower (it had been removed after the Second World War): "Peasants and rural people should look at this tower which dominates the plain and which is a symbol of the power of Fascism."

Little by little the landscape of the country has altered. The changing of the political guard didn't imply only new policies; it implied the complete overhaul of every institution: the magistrature, the television, the street names, the syllabus. Even the dignified President of the Republic, Carlo Azeglio Ciampi (in what could only be interpreted as an attempt to maintain the fragile sense of national unity), said publicly that the *"ragazzi di Salò,"* those Fascists who fought the civil war to the bitter end in 1945, at least had the merit of fighting for a unified Italy. He was rounded on by the left, who accused the former Resistance fighter of offering yet another "customs clearance" for Fascism. Berlusconi's choice of political allies only adds to concern that Fascism is being rehabilitated. Under the right-wing Pole of Liberties coalition is the National Alliance, which is simply the new name of the Movimento Sociale Italiano, the postwar Fascist party. Its leader, Gianfranco Fini, is a chess player and always appears mea-sured, calm, and cerebral. In the ranks of his party, however, are many who have dark pasts, former Fascists who, according to the accusations, took a very active part in the country's *anni di piombo*. The granddaughter of Il Duce Alessandra Mussolini is another of the party's "big names." More extreme, and more maverick, is Umberto Bossi, the gravel-voiced leader of the Northern League. He's always decked out in the party's green livery and its symbol: a wagon wheel. He's the prime example of what is called *qualunquismo*—"Everymanism"—a term for crude, vote-grabbing populism. His electoral base is the rich industrialised north, which views Rome and the south as the epitome of all that's wrong with Italy. ("Garibaldi didn't unite Italy, he divided Africa," goes the rhetoric.) When a piece of land at Lodi, south-east of Milan, was recently set aside for a mosque, Bossi's *leghisti* protested, marching under banners proclaiming, "Our pigs have urinated there." Recently Bossi has suggested the use of cannon to dissuade immigrants from attempting to enter Italian territory.

Even cultured political commentators on the right, however, are dismayed. Italy, they say, has never produced a "normal" right-wing party. Mussolini's Fascism and the Christian Democrats' Christian Democracy were both, by anyone's reckoning, highly unorthodox political movements. Berlusconi's business-political party appears, if anything, even more idiosyncratic. Indro Montanelli was a right-wing nonagenarian writer whom many saw as the soul of Italian journalism (he was editor of Berlusconi's paper *Il Giornale* before resigning because of editorial interference). In the weeks before the election he called the Forza Italia leader a "systematic liar," someone whose methods are "of the truncheon . . . akin to those of Fascism."

In truth, however, Forzismo is very far from Fascism. Berlusconi is (in a complicated definition which could only make sense in Italy) an anti-anti-Fascist. The roots of the First Republic were nurtured on the nutrients of anti-Fascism; it was, perhaps, the defining, unifying theme for much of the divisive postwar years. Recently the breathtakingly quick rehabilitation of Il Duce has eulogised the spirituality, the esotericism, and the stately aspirations of Fascism. None of this implies that Forzismo is comparable; but it certainly makes anti-Fascism inimical to the Berlusconi project. Every year, when 25 April (the day of liberation in 1945) arrives, Forza Italia politicians refuse to take part. Or they do so grudgingly, saying that the real enemy was Communism from Russia, not home-grown Fascism. Berlusconi is more likely to be seen at a football match than at a 25 April anniversary. For the last two years he has pointedly stayed away.

But in a strange way, the leader is outside the old Fascist-Communist dichotomy. He is the perfect product of post-ideological politics in which the packaging is more important than the product. It has nothing to do with ideology, with Fascism or anti-Communism; it's simply about power and *Realpolitik*. One of Mussolini's political slogans was "ideas, not men." It expressed the notion that policies were more important than politicians. Contemporary Italian politics, though, is the inversion of the slogan. For all the talk about Fascists and Communists, it's really about "men, not ideas." The culture is one of *clientelismo*, the habit of mutual back-scratching. A politician sits at the top of his pyramid of clients, looking after their needs as he tries to outmanoeuvre opponents. It's an organic supply and demand of favours which, given the size of the public-sector workforce and the reach of political appointments, runs through all levels of society. A new government implies a clean sweep through the ranks of RAI; it implies new magistrates and new teachers, all chosen upon the basis of their personal allegiances. Meritocracy, always at a premium, is nowhere to be seen. Beyond the personality cult there are, it seems, dynastic aspirations.

So the strange thing is that despite the hysteria regarding the government of "Blackshirts" and "white-collar criminals," Forzismo isn't about the return of Fascism. It's about something much more subtle, much more amorphous. It's about a style of government based upon crude power, using as its motto the old Sicilian proverb *"potere è meglio di fottere"*: "Power is better than screwing." It's pure, exalted cynicism. That's why any notion that one might voluntarily remove a conflict of interest is anathema. It goes counter to every notion of *Realpolitik*. Days before the general election, Berlusconi had melodramatically signed his "contract with the Italian people." He promised that within one hundred days of entering office, he would resolve the anomaly of a politician whose telecommunications empire dominated domestic broadcasting. Years later nothing had been done. The conflict of interest had become blatant when an American offer of 800 billion lire for a 49-per-cent interest in the RAI infrastructure was bluntly turned down by the government's Minister of Communications. As soon as the lucrative deal fell through, Mediaset shares soared on the stock exchange.

Pure power politics is something at which the Italians excel. As one of Orwell's characters explains: "The Party seeks power entirely for its own sake. We are not interested in the good of others; we are interested solely in power . . . We are different from all the oligarchies of the past in that we know what we are doing."[12] In Italy, there's an understanding of power, of its deployment, which leaves most other nations looking painfully naive by comparison. That's why the words of a Catholic priest quoted at the top of this chapter appear eerily relevant, even though they were written in 1881. They describe a political system in which everything is dressed up in ideology but nothing is ideological, still less idealist. That is why foreigners feel so disorientated on analysing Italian politics: Socialists are in alliance with post-Fascists, Thatcherite economists in alliance with the post-Communists. The inverse of the power politics is the attitude of the powerless, and here many writers have mentioned a strange *cupidigia di abiezione*, a "cupidity of abjection," whereby the powerful are subject to adulation and admiration rather than criticism.

Taken as a movement in an ideological vacuum, Forzismo is thrown into sharp relief. It's about the conquest and main-tenance of power. There is no ideology behind it; without the leader the whole project would collapse. It's often argued that the leader is Italy's Thatcher, the iron chancellor who will introduce market economics into the Italian economy. It's the closest Forzismo comes to a clear-cut identity, and it's where the rhetoric is furthest from reality. Abroad Forzismo is fiercely criticised by right-wing economic publications precisely because the Thatcher comparison is absurd. Many of the government's most significant acts since coming to power—from the decriminalisation of false accounting to the legislation on the re-entry of (illegally exported) capital—seem contrary to transparent, free-market economics. Add to that the fact that there has been yet another pardon for tax evasion, and you begin to appreciate why the Thatcher com-parison is risible. One of Berlusconi's closest allies admitted in the witness stand in Milan that billions of lire in a Swiss bank account had been deposited there to avoid tax. He was vocif-erously defended as if this were normal behaviour.

All this leads to the best judge of character I know: people should be judged by the company they keep. By that yard-stick, Berlusconi is in an awkward position. One doesn't have to take the Vittorio Mangano story (the Mafioso-gardener on Berlusconi's estate) to its possibly sordid conclusion to realise that his presence shows an acute lack of judgement. Marcello Dell'Utri had been conclusively convicted of inflating invoices at Publitalia and is currently on trial in Palermo for proximity to the Mafia. Cesare Previti, in most countries, would be in prison. These, however, are the loyal outriders for the Forzismo project. Winning sixty-one out of the sixty-one available parliamentary seats in Sicily doesn't necessarily imply that Forzismo willingly cohabits with organised crime, but it certainly raises questions. In 2001, indeed, the powerful Minister of Infrastructure came out with a comment which sent a shiver down the spine of the body politic: "One needs to get along with the Mafia and the Camorra [the Neapolitan Mafia]," he said. "Everyone should resolve problems of criminality as he sees fit . . . the Mafia has always existed, always will." If anyone was still in any doubt, his words were a chilling indication of whom the government was prepared to accommodate. It was, wrote one newspaper, as if the martyred anti-Mafia judges had never existed, as if all the mourning at their deaths had suddenly been forgotten. One cartoon in the (left-wing) *Unità* newspaper spelt it out: "The government says we should get along with the Mafia," says one character. "Judging by the election results in Sicily," replies the other, "someone's getting along with them very nicely."[13]

The role of the media is equally worrying. The ability of one man, in front of the camera, to talk directly to us, in front of the TV set, is the ace up his sleeve. He only needs to courier a video cassette to television channels—which, mostly, duly broadcast it—and he has shifted the terms of the debate. The public, as anyone who works in the media knows, is amazingly malleable. Opinions can shift, especially when we are bombarded by various messages. TV isn't only direct propaganda; it also provides the iconography on which Forzismo is based: first, it idealises a fantasy world of rich men and beautiful women. The main problem isn't the lack of a free press or biased news reporting; it's that Italians seem hooked up to a lifestyle sell which has nothing to do with reality. Mediaset, more than any other channels, is desperate to sell a way of life in which, subliminally, the leader becomes *primus inter pares*. There is, thankfully, no architecture associated with Forzismo: there are none of the eagles, the Lictorian buildings, and the anabolic classicism of eighty years ago. But, in a strange way, the skyline has been physically changed by Forzismo: the television aerial and the satellite dish are sacred symbols, almost like flags we parade to demonstrate our allegiance.

To adapt Benjamin's phrase: Forzismo isn't the aestheticisation of politics but its subliminalisation. Berlusconi becomes the interface for millions of daily transactions which, on the surface, appear outside the sphere of politics. When one buys a book or a magazine, it's highly probable that the product is part of the Prime Minister's empire. Many of the films we watch have been distributed either by Medusa (his production company) or by Blockbuster. When we pay for the ticket to go see Milan at the San Siro stadium, when we watch the cup final of the Champions' League at Old Trafford transmitted by Mediaset channels, when we buy any of the fifteen hundred products advertised on Mediaset channels, we end up inextricably linked to Berlusconi. His presence hovers in the background, and to be financially free from his influence is impossible. The most simple choices assume political connotations. Even media gossip becomes part of the political process: we're told that Natalia Estrada (a young Spanish showgirl) is on the verge of becoming the Prime Minister's sister-in-law, and, before we know it, we're being nudged into a reassessment of our political position. The information has no political content, but it maintains the iconography of dynasty at the apex of high society.

"I'm incapable of saying no," Berlusconi once joked. "Fortunately, I'm a man and not a woman." There is, it's very obvious, something voracious and rapacious in his make-up. There's no end to his ambition, which is either infectious or infecting, depending upon your politics. Roberto Benigni, the comic actor, once sang an aggressive song on the subject, growling out the chorus, "It's all mine." That, in the end, is the enduring image: a spoilt child who wants all the toys in the nursery. It's greed of the first order. He seems rather like Cecil Rhodes, the nineteenth-century British colonialist who robbed large parts of Africa for the empire, and I suspect his motto is similar to Rhodes's famous, depressing adage: "Every man has his price."

The more you watch Berlusconi, the more you realise he is simply the political equivalent of a television salesman: he has the same slick presentation, the breathless narrative, the quick grin, the hand gestures. He squeezes each finger between the thumb and the index finger of his other hand, enunciating his points one by one. He has magnificent rhetorical flourishes. We enjoy the ride; we eagerly listen. When, as occasionally happens at press conferences, I am in the same room as him, I personally find it riveting. He talks and talks and talks. You never want him to stop. But by then, of course, you've been taken in. As happens when watching the man selling cheap jewellery on TV, if you listen for too long you're lost. You'll pick up the phone and order that new slimming pill or promise monthly instalments to pay for plastic jewellery. But if the leader were only a tarot-card reader, I would still be glued. It is his genius to identify his own self-promotion with the common weal, to conflate the two as if they were inseparable. And it is probably only when it becomes blindingly obvious that the good of one isn't closely related to the other that the whole theatre will close down.

Foreigners simply can't understand it. Foreign journalists, of course, love it when Berlusconi comes to town because a journalist's job—to print news—is always safe when the leader speaks. In Israel, confronted with one of the most sensitive issues in world politics, Berlusconi will be cynically prodded by journalists who want to know if he's going to buy David Beckham, the British footballer. He immediately falls into the trap: he smiles, glad that everyone remembers how important he is, and makes a few quick quips. He goes to Turkey, and his diplomacy—as with France—consists in telling the indigenous politicians that he likes Turkey because he's had a Turkish girl. He goes to Bulgaria and announces who should be sacked from the public RAI television channels.

Many foreigners just laugh. For Italians, though, it's much more poignant, much more painful. In July 2003, Berlusconi took over the rotating presidency of the European Union. In the opening debate within the European Parliament, he accused a German Socialist of being a Nazi. The entire Parliament fell silent, astonished at the insult. Berlusconi kept going, however, as his spokesman ran down the aisle to urge him to sit down. At a press conference later, he explained, with all seriousness, that his political ability was all down to "visionary madness." Within months Berlusconi declared in an interview that Mussolini had never killed anyone, he had simply sent undesirables to the Italian border for a holiday.

It is, of course, impossible to know where it will all lead. I suspect that Berlusconi will be in power for ten or fifteen years; he will almost certainly be tempted to run for head of state, thereby turning the ceremonial role of President of the Republic into a politicised one. Everything in his character suggests that he would find the position irresistible. Television, slowly but imperceptibly, will become ever more sycophantic to the government. Examination of policy and politics will become ever more scarce. Opposition will be increasingly and shrilly denounced and identified with indigenous terrorism. Every position of importance in the country will gradually come under control of Forzismo. And we will all continue much the same as before. Nothing, ultimately, will change much. The law will still be slow and unreliable. Employers and employees will still argue about wages and work conditions. The government, as always in Italy, will change little other than the personnel.

...

So, Berlusconi: *una bella persona*? Only now do I realise how wrong I have been. I used to think, when I first arrived here, that the Italian obsession with beauty was the negation of morality, that the beautification of everything and everyone was so obsessive that good and bad got left behind. Now, thinking about real *bellezza*, I finally understand that the notion of beauty in Italy is a conflation of aesthetics and ethics. I finally understand that Burckhardt quotation suggesting that Italians have "outgrown the limits of morality and religion." The beauty syndrome isn't the vanity and superficiality I thought it was; it's a means, much more nuanced than the moralising of northern Europe, to identify who someone is.

Saying someone is ugly isn't only a physical judgement; it's a moral one. Ugliness implies in Italian repulsion, which isn't only an analysis of visual presentation. It's also an analysis of someone's worth, his or her "goodness." A *bella persona* isn't only a good-looker (literally a "beautiful person") but also a "good person," someone who has an attractive personality. Because the words "good" and "bad" are so rarely used, beauty is the litmus paper by which everyone is judged. It's more sophisticated than morality because, in some strange way, it is more comprehensive. A description of beauty covers more ground than goodness; it includes more characteristics: not just righteousness, but civility, dignity, stature, and so on. *Bellissimo* is used not just for appearances but also for *il gesto*, "the gesture." Someone doesn't do a "good" deed; he does a "beautiful" one. It's like the old Greek idea of *kaloskagathos*: beauty and goodness are, rather than mutually excluding opposites, actually the same thing.

Talking about immorality is thus irrelevant in Italy, because it sounds preachy and prescriptive. Every time left-wing politicians, foreign journalists, and the public in general accuse Berlusconi of immorality, his popularity ratings with the other half of the country soar off the scale. He actually benefits from shrill attacks and immoderate language about immorality. The funny thing is, though, that no one has ever accused him of being a *bella persona*—even though, for his age, he is looking suspiciously good. That in itself gives the true measure of Italian beauty: it contains a moral message.

Late spring. I was in a bar watching a late-night football match. In one corner I recognised a blond guy I had taught almost two years before. Marco was one of those silent types who very rarely spoke in the lecture hall. When he did, it was normally a memorable put-down to one of his fellow students. He wasn't superior, just very studious, a little sarcastic, and aloof. I liked him a lot, though I didn't really know him.

"Zio Tobia!" He called me over to his table, and I sat down opposite him. "Are you still writing that book?" he asked.

"I'm afraid so," I replied.

"What are you writing about now?"

"The government."

He looked at me and went quiet. Then he began shaking his head, grimacing. *"Ma tu, non ti rendi conto?"* he hissed ("Don't you get it?"), as if he were accusing me of something. And he was accusing me of something, however indirectly. "You foreign journalists are so facetious and condescending. You only write about how terrible our country is."

"But I'm only repeating what you all tell me. And it's true, it is terrible."

"I know. But that's exactly why you foreign journalists fuck me off. You come here and laugh at the farce, not realising that for us it is a tragedy. You come here with your British patriotism and laugh at us before going back home. If you want to stay here, you mustn't laugh anymore," he said. "This is a terrible country, and Berlusconi is a tragedy for Italy. It's all an unbelievable tragedy. Italians are pricks who elect the first person they think will make them richer. Berlusconi only speaks to the belly. But you mustn't laugh about anything anymore. You must write that there's another side to Italy." He was exceptionally angry, tears rolling down his cheeks as he prodded his finger against my chest. "You must write that there's a completely different country which hates Berlusconi and all his corrupt henchmen. Life for us will be very difficult from now on. You don't understand, but you will."

We sat in silence for five minutes, ignoring each other and pretending to watch the game. He was right of course. By then, after years abroad, I had begun to long to go back home. I was sickened not just by what was going on but by the acceptance of it all. Saturated by Mediaset television, everyone seemed indifferent. I, by contrast, was feeling vitriolic and very foreign. I knew I was beginning to write bilious prose and probably, as a writer, becoming both irritated and irritating. Marco, though, somehow knew that I would be staying, and he knew that there was still "a different country," one outside the reach of Il Cavaliere, which I had entirely ignored in the book.

He caught me looking at him and began to apologise. "Excuse me, Tobia," he said finally. "Excuse me. It's just that Berlusconi brings so much shame upon our country, and you mustn't add to that. You must write about the other sides of the country."

"I will. I promise, Marco, that's what I'll write next. And I didn't mean it's all terrible here. I love it here, it's just that . . ."

"It's terrible." He nodded, smiling.

9

PENISOLA FELICE

The countryside around Parma is exquisitely beautiful, like a garden or better a wild cultivated expanse, where the grain and the grass of the lawn grow under large, tall trees, united one with the other by regular festoons of life.

—PERCY BYSSHE SHELLEY

A few months ago I was back watching football. It was an international match, and the tinny trumpets were rasping out the national anthem, "L'inno di Mameli." For some reason I found it intensely moving. The melodramatic words seemed to express the immense suffering and bravery in the country, and I sang along with the rest of the stadium. *"Siam pronti alla morte, pronti alla morte,"* "We're ready for death! We're ready for death! Italy has called!"

I realise I have become something I never thought possible: patriotic and proud about being an adopted Italian. In more honest moments, I realise that I might never quite be able to leave the country. That longing to leave, and the in-

ability to pull yourself away, have been written about for centuries. Using the usual obligatory metaphor, one of the country's most important patriots, Massimo d'Azeglio, wrote: "I
can't live outside Italy, which is strange because I continually
get angry with Italian ineptitude, envies, ignorance, and lazi-
ness. I'm like one of those people who falls in love with a
prostitute."[1] That, in fact, is precisely the feeling of living
here: it is infuriating and endlessly irritating, but in the end it
is almost impossible to leave. It's not just that everything is
troppo bello, "too beautiful," or that food and conversation
are so good. It's that life seems less exciting outside Italy, the
emotions seem muted. Stendhal wrote that the feeling one
gets from living in Italy is "akin to that of being in love," and
it's easy to understand what he meant. There's the same kind
of enchantment and serenity, occasionally insecurity and sadness. And writing about the country's sharp pangs of jealousy
and paranoia, Stendhal knew that they exist precisely because
the country's "joys are far more intense and more lasting."
You can't have the one without the other.[2]

Singing the words to that national anthem—"We're ready
for death!"—I noticed that there's one, admittedly morbid,
theme which is the reason I feel patriotic: *i morti*, "the dead."
The rituals of mourning and commemoration are incredible,
touching, communal, noble, even creative, in a way unthinkable elsewhere. If you spend long enough in the country, you
begin to notice that there's something very unique about
death in Italy. I noticed it during my first few days here. It
was during a question about birthdays in a bar (the conversation, as it often is, was about horoscopes). Someone asked
me when mine was, and I told him the date. In Britain, sharing a birthday with "All Souls" had never raised eyebrows.
Here, within seconds, everyone was frowning, backing off
whilst touching their testicles (warding off bad luck), or
laughing, slapping me on the back and telling me I was a

bit *sfigato*, "jinxed." My birthday, I was told, was the day of *i morti*.

I'm normally surprised by the collective amnesia, by the speed with which recent history in Italy is brushed under the carpet. But when it comes to *i morti*, the memory in Italy is very long. Every city or village feels like Shelley's "widowed" Genoa, where the "moonlight spells ancestral epitaphs."[3] From every direction the faces of the dead stare back at you, either in sculptured busts or in photographs. Each country, of course, has its memorials, but only in Italy is there such a sense that you're walking in someone else's footsteps. Perhaps it's because of the Catholic notion of purgatory, of companionship with and prayers for the dead; or maybe it's because, especially in the south, there's a kind of ancestor cult. Almost every alley-way seems to have its own plaque or memorial. I've often paused to look up at them, only for someone to stop and explain who the local dignitary was and the highs and lows of his or her life. It's that communal, public side of death which is different. In Sicily especially, but all over the country, you see handwritten notices up on the street corners of parishes: "The Gambino family thanks everyone who has been close to them in their time of mourning." Even football supporters, endlessly criticised in Italy for their violence and lawlessness, display—as they say—their "honour" as regards death. At every Roma home match, on the southern terrace of the stadium, there's a banner to supporters who have died that week, or even one to those who died on that day years ago. It's hard to imagine something so noble happening on the terraces at a British football ground.

If you open the back pages of Italy's oldest newspaper, the *Gazzetta di Parma*, dozens of faces stare back at you: these are *i morti*, "the dead." Some have passed away recently; others have had their photograph put there by relatives or friends on the anniversary of their death. In many other newspapers, national or local, the obituaries section runs on for as many pages as do the financial or sporting sections. When someone from the editorial team of a television channel or a newspaper dies, or even one of their relatives, there are often long thren-odies for the following days and weeks.

Funerals themselves are ostentatious. When there's a par-ticularly famous passing away, the funeral will always, without fail, be televised. Flags and fists are raised, huge crowds ap-plaud coffins. It doesn't matter if the deceased is an actor or an anonymous victim of a sadly spectacular murder, the fu-neral is more than just a send-off; it's a pageant. Millions of viewers watch the catwalk of politicians who come to pay their respects. The coffin is open, the cameras rolling; micro-phones are placed near sobbing mothers. In more remote parts of Italy there's even someone called the *prefica*, the hired female mourner who guarantees that the wailing will be at a respectable pitch.

But the dead aren't just seen; they are also "heard." The point about hearing the dead is that in Italy words are habit-ually put into the mouths of *i morti*, as if there really were voices from the grave. Just as the photographs are still seen, the voices are still heard. It's part of the uncanny continuum which happens between Italy's life and death. In one ceme-tery in Naples, after the first, extraordinary football champi-onship won with Diego Maradona in the 1980s, someone wrote graffiti in the local dialect: *"Guagliò, che ve site persi!"* "Kid, what you've missed!" Legend has it that a few weeks later the reply from the cemetery, scrawled on another wall, arrived: "I didn't miss a thing!" It might simply have been an idle piece of graffiti, but "voices from the grave" are Italians' favourite poetic genre. *Spoon River Anthology* is, by a very long way, the best-selling poetry book in Italy. With its voices from the other side, the dead seem to be heard as they re-count their simple, short lives. (When Pino Pinelli was finally laid to rest in 1980—after his body had been re-exhumed and again examined for evidence—he was buried in the anarchist section of the graveyard at Carrara, with an inscription from *Spoon River.*) Fabrizio De André, the plaintive Genovese singer, once issued an album of songs which were "liberal" translations from *Spoon River Anthology.* Apart from the fact that his choice of literary inspiration is indicative of the curious aesthetic surrounding death, I've always had a personal attachment to the album. The last song is called "Il suonatore Jones":

> *Libertà l'ho vista svegliarsi*
> *ogni volta che ho suonato,*
> *per un fruscio di ragazze*
> *a un ballo,*
> *per un compagno ubriaco.*[4]

(The English translation of the adaptation sounds, by comparison, rather dull: "I've seen liberty wake up / every time I have played / for a rustle of girls / at a dance / for a drunken friend.") His life finishes "in nettled fields . . . with a broken flute and a raucous laugh and so many memories."

The accommodation of *i morti* has always been a major architectural event. Tombs and sepulchres and catacombs have always been ostentatious. They even became the country's top tourist attractions. The beginning of Via Appia, the road which heads out of the capital towards Brindisi, used to be the chosen place of Romans for a Sunday stroll, there to enjoy and admire new mausolea which lined both sides of the road. A vital part of the Grand Tour was to search out the tombs of famous poets and emperors (even though many, including Virgil's and Nero's, were probably fakes). Dante's tomb at

Ravenna is still an important stopoff for modern travellers, and the catacombs in Palermo are probably more visited than any other site in Sicily.

The first of November, the day before *i morti*, is another national holiday, the day on which it's traditional to visit ancestors in their cemeteries. (Towards the end of October bones suddenly start appearing in the patisserie. The day of *i morti* is an opportunity not just to mourn, of course; it's also culinary tradition. The bones, pastry-coated with garish cream, represent the bones of the dead.) As every Italian schoolchild knows from reading one of the country's most famous poems, Ugo Foscolo's "Dei sepolcri," Napoleonic law was responsible for Italy's breathtaking cemeteries. Napoleon decreed that burials had to take place outside the city walls. The result across Europe was the phenomenon of vast out-of-town graveyards. Unlike in Britain, where burial was more usually within church grounds, huge suburbs for the dead grew up outside Italian cities. They are the country's most beautiful, serene sites. In Genoa, for example, the cemetery of Staglieno is built on a hill towards the north-east of the city.

On 1 November I went along as a tourist. Since thousands of Genovese were visiting the cemetery, the florist outside must have made half his annual salary within a few hours. There were four trucks selling bouquets to the queues of mourners. The cemetery's centrepiece is an arcaded square which leads you to the pantheon. The inscription in Latin above the entrance reads: "To the glory of God and to the memory of the illustrious Genovese." It's at Staglieno that Giuseppe Mazzini, the nineteenth-century revolutionary and nationalist, is buried, next to his mother, in a low, leafy temple. The inscriptions are political rather than religious. Today there are about two dozen fresh bouquets laid out. David Lloyd George, in 1922, left the inscription: "To the champion of the oppressed people and the prophet of European brotherhood." (The irony is that Mazzini, like Dante and many others now lauded as political or poetic heroes, died exiled from his city. He was, at the time of his death, living under the assumed name John Brown in Pisa.) In the English part of the cemetery there's the gratitude of the empire to Italians in the Great War: "The British Empire will always remember, together with those of her children who have fallen for her, those of Italy who gave their lives during the Great War of 1914–1918."

Genoa is a grandiose example. The following year I went to one of the smaller rural cemeteries outside Parma. Because it was for less illustrious souls, it looked like a complex of giant filing cabinets. *I morti* are slotted into place, and then rotated according to age and "rent" in deep walls, which are often three or four metres high. The funeral itself involves plasterers sealing off the end of the opening to the file, called the *loculo*, "niche." It might sound soulless, but it isn't: the dead can still be visited; you know where to find them. Almost all the headstones (in reality, the edge of the filing cabinet) carry photographs. On the day of *i morti* you go visit your ancestors, and can even look at your own slot, already booked in the family's allocated space. The point is that the dead are on display. Silvio Berlusconi has even built his own mausoleum on the grounds of his Arcore estate. It's designed along the lines of an Etruscan necropolis. Inside are thirty-six burial slots, reserved for members of his family and his business and political partners.

Before Italy became, for foreigners, a symbol of the vitality of life (the Edwardian stereotype), it was a symbol of the opposite: the land of the dead or the dying. Henry James had called Venice "the most beautiful of tombs." "Nowhere else," he wrote, "has the past been laid to rest with such tenderness, such a sadness of resignation and remembrance." The otherworldly quality of the floating ghost town of Venice meant that James saw it as a kind of Avalon to which bodies were carried in gondolas:

> [T]he little closed cabin of this perfect vehicle, the movement, the darkness and the plash, the indistinguishable swerves and twists, all the things you see and all the things you do feel— each dim recognition and obscure arrest is a possible throb of your sense of being floated to your doom.[5]

Italy's "old age" made it the natural place for mourning writers to visit during and after the First World War. For modernists it became imagined as a metaphorical mausoleum, a place where they could come to examine what it meant to be old and to die. James Joyce wrote "The Dead" in Trieste. Thomas Mann's *Death in Venice*, in which "the pale and lovely summoner" smiles and beckons Gustave von Aschenbach to his death, is just the most obvious example of the genre.

Given the country's civil strife, though, death in Italy is often more divisive than communal, and memorials and mourners are sometimes acutely politicised. On one of the walls in the main square in Bologna there's a collage of all the partisans from the city who died in the 1943–45 civil war. It's like looking at an auditorium of the fallen: a wall of hundreds of black-and-white faces watching you, almost defying you to challenge their political creed. Often little vases of flowers are left there, or candles are lit. This in itself is enough to tell you where the political loyalties of the city lie. In fact, the odium between right and left, which became militarist in the 1970s, now finds its most acute expression in the bickering over the wording of memorials. A mile away, outside the station in Bologna, the clock is permanently stopped at 10:25. There was recently a move by the railway authorities to get the clock working again, but the plan was shelved because of a local outcry. Ten-twenty-five was the time at which the bomb ripped through the waiting room of the station in 1980, killing eighty-five people. A little later, revisionists wanted to excise the word "Fascist" from the memorial to those who died; the move—either a worthy attempt to heal wounds or a rude attempt to whitewash history—was blocked by the city's (Forza Italia) mayor. It's like that monument in Pisa, "Anarchist killed by police at an anti-Fascist rally," provocative as much as it is conciliatory.

Connected to the politicisation of death is its aestheticisation. Death in Italy has frequently had its aesthetic edge, especially in the country's terrorism. Non-Italian writers had hinted at the mesmerising quality of violence and terror: Yeats wrote of the "terrible beauty"; Shelley about the "tempestuous loveliness of terror." But it was Umberto Eco who really analysed the politics of death, and thereby gave a political dimension to the ways in which Italian death and terrorism had become attractive and almost longed for. Not only did he discern that death had become aestheticised and adored; he identified the necrophilia as profoundly Fascist:

> [I]t's very elusive . . . but there is one component by which Fascism is recognisable in its purest form, wherever it shows itself, knowing with absolute certainty that such a premise will bring The Fascism: it is the cult of death.[6]

The taste for killings and martyrs was, for Eco, Fascism in its purest form. The beautification of terrorism in Italy, perceived by generations of writers, was for him more telling than any professed political dimension. Fascism meant adoring and serving death, be it as the slayer or as the slain:

> To love death necrophilically is to say that it's beautiful to receive it and risk it, and that the most beautiful and saintly love

is to distribute it . . . This stench of death, this putrid need of death, one feels today in Italy [1981]. If that's what terrorism (in its deep, ancestrally *squadrista* soul) wanted, it's got it.[7]

Fascism, for Eco, was political nihilism: a desire for martyrdom, a servitude to death.

Perhaps it's because of all that proximity to death that there's a discernible spirituality in Italy. It's impossible to write about because it's intangible, but the country really does appear, as so many foreigners write, prelapsarian, a fusion of natural beauty and human temptation. The "ancient cults" Fellini wrote about still exist. Compared with that in other countries, the modernist rupture has been minimal. There's an intimacy with the past, and those who have passed away; there's an umbilical cord to remote eras and ages. There is a proximity, mentally and physically, to preceding centuries. Perhaps it's because of that long history, that sense of a people with a unique and difficult destiny, a people with limitless creativity and suffering, that some writers have compared Italians to Jews. Limiting the comparison to Sicilians, Sciascia wrote that both speak "by allusion, in parables or in metaphors. It was as if the same circuits, the same logical processes operated in both their minds. A computer of distrust, of suspicion, of pessimism. Jews, Sicilians: an atavistic affinity in their own condition. Of energy. Of defence. Of suffering."[8]

The strange thing is that I'm no longer sure where my homeland is. Nathaniel Hawthorne once wrote about the melancholia of the expatriate, who becomes a global vagabond, rootless and outside reality:

The years, after all, have a kind of emptiness, when we spend too many of them on a foreign shore. We defer the reality of life, in such cases, until a future moment, when we shall again breathe our native air; but, by and by, there are no future moments; or, if we do return, we find that the native air has lost its invigorating quality, and that life has shifted its reality to the spot where we have deemed ourselves only temporary residents. Thus, between two countries, we have none at all, or only that little space of either in which we finally lay down our discontented bones.[9]

But there's more to it than that. If you live not only outside your own country but also outside your own language, it comes to affect your whole personality. We're different beings when we enter a foreign language; it changes our psyche somehow. Speaking Italian imperceptibly changes you. You get used to the tonality of the language and slowly realise that there are nuances and subtleties in Italian that don't exist in solid, stolid English. Even the family of little words which pepper Italian conversation—*ma, boh, mica, allora*—are able to proffer a judgement simply according to the tone in which they're uttered. They have a dozen different meanings; they can be comic or serious according to the tone you give them. A single word can open or slam shut a conversation. That is why foreigners always note the musicality of Italian: words are simply instruments on which the musician can express himself. And the sound of words is so important, words are so onomatopoeic, that one can usually guess the meaning without a dictionary. Given its tiptoe lightness and syncopation, a word like *solletico*, you know almost subconsciously, means "tickle." *Rigogliosità*, with its plump, portly vowels, clearly means "luxuriance."

Then there are words which remain entirely untranslatable so that, as you learn the other language, you become conscious of a very different mind-set. *Spregiudicato* is the adjective most frequently used to describe Silvio Berlusconi, but it remains completely inexplicable in English. It implies someone who is "without prejudice," someone who is daring, against the grain, cut from an original cloth. But it's twin meaning is very different: someone without scruples, someone who is untrammelled by the niceties of good and evil. With its Janus meanings, *spregiudicato* (and its noun, *spregiudicatezza*) contains a sense of admiration for the Machiavellian, a nod of acknowledgement to the slightly naughty, which is entirely absent from English.

Then there's something else about Italian as a language which I wouldn't call honesty, because it sounds too judgemental. It's more frankness, instinctive straight talking. In Britain, there's a politeness which means that conversation is often like driving with the handbrake on. As far back as Shakespeare, in *King Lear*, there's the plea for the British to speak straight: "The weight of this sad time we must obey, / Speak what we feel, not what we ought to say." Britain's studied politeness and formal observation of etiquette often veer off into hypocrisy: the inability to say openly what you think. There's a mental filter between what you think and what you say, and when you speak with someone, you have to understand precisely which filter she's using and where she is on the politeness-sincerity spectrum. Here, by contrast, there's a refreshing frankness. *"Non fare complimenti"* is one of the most common phrases I hear: meaning, please take what you want from our table. It combines generosity whilst prompting sincerity. So for a few days you eat as much as you've been kindly offered. And then someone else will roll up at the house and say: *"Porco cane*, Zio Tobia, you've got so fat! You look like a hot-air balloon!" There's something incredibly liberating about not having to walk on conversational eggshells, as you do in Britain, about not having to be on the lookout for everyone else's feelings instead of your own. Here the frankness is so habitual, so amusingly intimate, that it's never even hurtful.

On the subject of food, I'm finally beginning to understand the digestion thing. Most people outside Italy don't know what digestion is. I had never heard of the word before moving to Parma. On one of my first evenings at a restaurant in Parma, I found myself sitting next to a grown man who was tying a scarf around his belly. He explained he was worried about "a cold draught" on his stomach, and he then proceeded to tell me what he had eaten for the previous four days and the effect that it had all had on his intestines. I thought at the time that he was an incurable hypochondriac, but I now appreciate that the intestines are metaphysical here, the way one's lawn is to the British. Here, the intestines have the same slightly obsessional purpose. Talking about digestion is a metaphor for our happiness. And if the food is astonishingly good, it's not only because of the recipes: a good meal implies family, company, conversation, communal digestion, siesta, talking about what's for supper. All of this will be blindingly obvious to Italians but is strangely alien to English-speaking cultures in which, to the understandable astonishment of Italians, the words *buon appetito* don't exist.

Parma calls itself *l'isola felice*, "the happy island." It's the island that time forgot, a peaceful oasis of calm. There's a little trickle of tourism, but nothing like that in other, comparable cities. Perhaps because its charm is unquantifiable, no guidebook can adequately capture the blissful pace of life within the peaceful community; perhaps it's because it doesn't have one grandiose building which has become, like Pisa's tower or Brunelleschi's dome, a recognisable, global brand. And yet the city really is an *isola felice*. There are, doubtless, many others in Italy; so, although the circumstances might be different, I hope the specific—described here—illustrates what is surely general.

You're on your way home from the railway station. It's only May but the heat is oppressive. Everyone at the station is good-humoured. You step across the road and lean over a low wall. The river, ironically called the *torrente*, is dry. Trees are sprouting on the parched river bank where, only a month before, water had surged with huge trunks of driftwood washed down from the mountains to the south of the city. Hidden for much of the year by fog and clouds, the majestic mountains against a deep blue sky are visible now. The frogs are beginning their deafening chorus on the river banks, billowing their throats in search of a mate. There are boxes of petunias all across the bridge. It's the *passeggiata* hour, that blissful pre-dusk period in which the whole city goes for a walk. People are calmly strolling up and down the same streets: lovers on the paths above the Cittadella, the adolescents in Via Cavour, retired couples walking arm in arm along the wide pavement which lines the river. Children are walking with their grandparents, as they do every evening.

You walk into the Parco Ducale. It's got glistening white gravel. At this time, the statues are all in the shade, but you can still see where the sun kisses the plaster through the leaves of the trees. There's the old Palazzo Ducale with its fox-hunting prints. You went round it years ago, disturbing the kind *carabiniere* who was asleep at the reception desk of the station. As you walk towards home, you bump into the butcher. Big Vanni, hands like spades. All smiles. An old student is there pushing a pram, and you stop to chat, admiring the child and asking why she never did go to London the way she longed to. There will be that girl, the one you fancied with the freckly nose, walking across the grass with her shoes in her hands, and you wave at her.

The shop-windows on the way are unbelievable. It's worth stopping to admire not the products but simply their placement. The record store has loads of posters, but Luca has hung plastic ice-cube packets, the ones you put in the freezer for cocktails, from the ceiling. They're filled with blue foam. No idea why, and the shop's closed now so you can't go in and ask him. But the placement is kind of perfect. Visual brilliance: it just makes you want to go in, which is precisely the aim. Then the furniture shop. Then the carpenter's next door. The picture framer's, the cobbler's. All those artisan boutiques: an incredible crossover between high fashion and honest trade.

You go into a grocer's and there's a long queue. But everyone is talking to everyone else, happy to wait their turn. One woman starts describing to you how to illuminate your driveway by finding hollow snails' shells. You apparently have to fill them with oil and sand, and place them at metre intervals all the way to your front door. "You light them and they make the drive look like an incredibly elegant runway," she says with a laugh. When it's your turn, the shopkeeper notices what you're buying and offers you advice on the preparation of the meal. The advice lasts ten minutes, but no one is impatient. Others chip in with their own observations. You realise with embarrassment that you haven't got enough cash, but she laughs and tells you to drop by another time. "There's no hurry," she says.

You catch the bus. You stand by the driver and end up talking about football. Since the thing is empty of passengers, he doesn't follow the bus route but, squeezing the bus through narrow backstreets like a cork through a keyhole, drops you at your door. "Ci vediamo," he says cheerfully. "See you around."

There, just below your house, is the photographer standing outside his little studio. He complains to you about the heat, and you tease him, saying the *parmigiani* talk about the weather all the time. It's always either too hot, too cold, too humid. "You talk about the weather more than the English!"

And that phrase from Giovanni Guareschi about the *parmigiani* comes into your head:

> Political passion often reaches a disturbing intensity, and yet these people are highly attractive and hospitable and generous and have a highly developed sense of humour. It must be the sun, a terrible sun which beats on their brains during the summer, or perhaps it is the fog, a heavy fog which oppresses them during the winter.[10]

Humour, hospitality, and political passion: you can sense it all as you and the photographer sit down on the pavement in the shade of his shop awning. The barman next door brings out a couple of glasses of squeezed grapefruit. You talk for twenty minutes.

Back home there are messages. You don't even need to call back to know where they'll be tonight. You remember when you first came here you used to be amazed at the way people went out, always in groups, always with the same people week after week. In Britain, most people would be happy if they saw close friends more than once a month. The friendship wouldn't be any less close for that, but it's very different. People live so far apart. You pick them off one by one because they've all moved away or abroad, and you'll have a reunion, all together, only when someone gets married. In Parma, though, you would meet the same people in an almost ritualistic way: the same places and faces. You wouldn't even need to make a date, a time, and a place. It was as if you all met there by a happy combination of chance and habit. Pensioners still see, daily, the people they sat next to at school. The durability of an Italian friendship is breathtaking.

When you're at the usual dark grotto, a bottle of wine on the table, you realise, listening to the endless stories and laughter, that there's another Italian word which doesn't really have an adequate translation in English: *raccontare*. We say "recount," but that's formal and neutral. Or else "narrate," but that's a little literary. "Tell" is simply standard and dull. That word, *raccontare*, is why going out in Italy is so amusing. Perhaps the only, inadequate equivalent in English is "wit." "Witty" is the adjective I would use to describe most Italians I've met. It implies a humour which is highly intelligent but light and amusing: it combines the cheerful with the profound. It's a bit like the French *bon mot* but less fleeting. And another quality of these friends, another word without translation: *estrosità*. It means flair, *élan*, whimsy, fancy. It's the ability to be capricious and creative, to adapt to every situation.

Then, the following night, you go to the stadium. You're standing on the Curva Nord next to a woman who looks like she's in her nineties: her face is wrinkled like a raisin. But she's smiling broadly, and, minutes before kick-off, the PA is announcing the list of the opposition players. At each name, she does a very lively "umbrella gesture" (that movement of a straight right arm swiftly coming into contact at the inner elbow with the left hand, the right fist then bending upwards: the Italian version of the middle finger). The game kicks off and you find Pino. A few minutes later he starts shouting, "*Vedi,*" pointing at the attack: "Adriano's a lizard; he's untouchable." The Brazilian jinks inside onto his right foot and slots away another goal, and the entire Tardini enters into a "communal hug." The old lady is repeating her favourite gesture, grinning as she shows the opposition what she thinks.

All the fans are wearing sunglasses. They look like an army of pleasure seekers, all dressed in the same colours, shouting the same phrases in unison. It's something you've seen for years. There are such marked uniforms here, not just on the football terraces, but everywhere. Political positions are prismatic, expressed as much through the simplicity of colour as through the subtleties of argument: red, white, blue, and so on. What's important is adhesion to the flag, the belonging to a visual code. It's astonishing, you often think, that in Italy and especially in Parma you're expected to judge "a monk by his habit." Dress codes are exactly that: codes to be constructed and deconstructed. Sartorial eccentricity is incredibly rare. Even protests are visual, like the rainbow peace flags which still, months after the second Iraq war, flutter in the hot summer air from millions of Italian balconies. It's not only that everything is aestheticised; it's that there's a strict uniform for almost everything and it begins to look, to a foreigner, strangely close to uniformity.

The homogeneity, though, is only an appearance. You're on your way back from the stadium. It's a short walk. Outside your house, on the other side of the street, is the retirement home. In front of you are two twenty-something fans who are walking into the reception. You call them over and they turn round. You explain that you were just wondering what they were doing wandering into the old people's home. You're still wearing your yellow-and-blue scarf so they look at you, immediately trustful, and explain: it's Sunday night, their turn to be with some of the elderly patients. "You know," one of them says, "they can't do it on their own."

"Do what?"

"Eat. We have to feed them, spoon the food. Takes ages because they're like babies. Strangely fun, though. Afterwards we have a chat, talk about everything. Here, take this." And they pass you a leaflet from the local voluntary organisation which sends hundreds of youngsters into the retirement homes across the province. Not for the first time, you feel very humbled by the sheer humanity of this community.

By then it's dusk. Back in your flat the light is falling through the shutters. You pull them up and walk out onto the balcony. The neighbours are on theirs, opposite, and shout, *"Salve."* Children are everywhere. There's something in the light. It's the cusp between night and day, and swallows are beginning to give way to the bats. It's this light which is incredible. It bounces off the "Parma yellow," the city's favourite colour. Everything seems gentle, pastel, reposed. The reason those Thomas Jones paintings from the eighteenth century are so moving is because here was a Welshman who had found, in Italy, a completely new type of light. The colours might be the same, but they're infused with that placid, serene light which northern Europeans spend their whole lives yearning for.

There are other things which, cause of consternation years ago, now make you feel at home. It's your domestic duty once a week to go to the dry-cleaner. Each time you go and put a few clothes on the counter. The kind lady asks your name.

"Jones," you say, and she, exasperated by the impossibly foreign surname, passes you the Biro. But she knows you.

"Why don't you just say Calebich?" she asks, looking at you.

"Because that name belongs to my wife's grandfather," you say, laughing. "Do I really have to use that surname?"

"The Calebich family," she replies with admiration, "have been coming here for over fifty years."

Precisely what used to irritate you years ago you now find blissful. You used to get mildly annoyed at the gerontocratic nature of Italy, at the fact that old age and tradition are so dutifully deferred to. It all seemed, at the beginning, incredibly static, subconsciously conservative. Now, though, you would be sad if it weren't this way. Again, it's not that communities and traditions don't exist in England; it's just that they're very, very different there. It's more fractured there, perhaps more flexible. People move on, move away. You can't imagine that any of your friends takes his clothes to the same dry-cleaner that his grandparents went to. You suspect many don't even know what a dry-cleaner is.

It all means that life is more sophisticated here. Italy is infinitely more gentlemanly, more dignified. When you go to the
mountains, you can sit outside in the evening sun and hear,
from miles away, the sound of someone playing the guitar,
entertaining friends with old folk-songs. You normally go to
the mountains to play pool, or rather, the Italian version, *boc-
cette*. Normally you'll sit on the terrace of the old farmhouse,
overlooking the city in the distance, and just talk for hours.
Then, depending on the season, you go for a walk to pick
wild strawberries or blackberries or mushrooms in the woods.
Eventually you go to the upstairs room. Maurino, inevitably,
will put on some music. Then, and this is the crux, he asks if
the temperature is all right.

"Fine," you say, enjoying the sunshine.

"No, no." He'll come back, putting his palm on the felt.
"The temperature." It slowly sinks in what he is talking about.

"Unbelievable! You guys have actually heated the table
felt? In England only the oldest aristocratic houses do that."
And there you are in the middle of nowhere, in some country
villa which is as rustic as it is stunning—chickens were cluck-
ing around the garden—and you're about to play on heated
felt. And you play, not with pewter tankards of warm ale, as
one would in the thuggish pubs in Britain, but with tiny
thimble glasses of chilled Erba Luigia liqueur. And there are
no pockets. As Maurino teaches you the game, showing the
skittles and the possible angles, you realise—not for the first
time—how much you still have to learn. "They heat the felt!"
you keep whispering in admiration as you miss your shots. It's
that refinement, the delicacy with which friends enjoy the
simplest, most innocent pleasures together, which is incompa-
rable. And for all the complications, Italian life can sometimes
seem incredibly simple. A phrase of Cesare Pavese's comes
to mind. Asked by a student if he loved Italy, he paused,
thought, and then replied: "No, not Italy. The Italians."

NOTES

1. "PAROLE, PAROLE, PAROLE"

1. James T. Boulton, ed., *The Letters of D. H. Lawrence*, vol. 1 (Cambridge, UK: Cambridge University Press, 1979).
2. Fabrizio De André, *Come un'anomalia* (Turin: Einaudi, 1999).
3. Italo Calvino, *Una pietra sopra* (Turin: Einaudi, 1980).
4. Carlo Levi, *Christ Stopped at Eboli* (London: Penguin, 1982).
5. Marco Rogari, *Burocrazia fuorilegge* (Milan: Sperling & Kupfer, 2001).
6. Corrado Stajano, *L'italia nichilista* (Milan: Mondadori, 1982).
7. Jacob Burckhardt, *The Civilisation of the Renaissance in Italy* (London: Penguin, 1990).
8. Luigi Barzini, *The Italians* (London: Hamish Hamilton, 1964).
9. Ernesto Galli Della Loggia, *L'identità italiana* (Bologna: Il Mulino, 1998).
10. Dante, *The Divine Comedy*, trans. Peter Dale (London: Anvil, 1996).
11. Carlo Ginzburg, *The Judge and the Historian* (London: Verso, 1999).
12. Ibid.
13. Stendhal, *The Charterhouse of Parma* (London: Penguin, 1938).
14. Leonardo Sciascia, *L'affaire Moro* (Milan: Adelphia, 1994).
15. Luigi Pirandello, "So It Is (If You Think So)," in *Six Characters in Search of an Author and Other Plays*, trans. Mark Musa (London: Penguin, 1995).
16. Maurizio Dianese and Gianfranco Bettin, *La strage* (Milan: Feltrinelli, 1999).
17. Pier Paolo Pasolini, *Lettere luterane* (Turin: Einaudi, 1976).
18. Leonardo Sciascia, *L'affaire Moro* (Milan: Adelphi, 1994).
19. Umberto Eco, *Sette anni di desiderio* (Milan: Bompiani, 1983).

20. Donald Sassoon, *Contemporary Italy* (New York: Longman, 1997).
21. Carlo Levi, *Le mille patrie* (Rome: Donzelli, 2000).

2. "THE MOTHER OF ALL SLAUGHTERS"

1. Giovanni Fasanella, Corrado Sestieri, and Giovanni Pellegrino, *Segreto di stato* (Turin: Einaudi, 2000).
2. *Cuore*, 16 Dec. 1991.
3. Leonard Weinberg and William Lee Eubank, *The Rise and Fall of Italian Terrorism* (Boulder, Colo.: Westview, 1987).
4. Cesare Pavone, *Una guerra civile* (Turin: Bollati Boringhieri, 1992).
5. Weinberg and Eubank, *Rise and Fall*.
6. Franco Ferraresi, *Minacce alla democrazia* (Milan: Feltrinelli, 1995).
7. Robert Putnam, "Atteggiamenti politici dell'alta burocrazia nell'Europa occidentale," *Rivista Italiana di Scienza Politica* 3, no. 1 (1973).
8. Sergio Zavoli, *La notte della repubblica* (Milan: Mondadori, 1992).
9. Alessandro Silj, *Mai più senza fucile* (Florence: Vallechi, 1979).
10. Ibid.
11. Anonymous, *La Strage di stato* (Roma: Samona e Savelli, 1970).
12. Ibid.
13. Ibid.
14. *Corriere della Sera*, 13 Dec. 1969.
15. Camilla Cederna, *Pinelli: Una finestra sulla strage* (Milan: Feltrinelli, 1971).
16. Zavoli, *La notte della repubblica*.
17. Maurizio Dianese and Gianfranco Bettin, *La strage* (Milan: Feltrinelli, 1999).
18. Fabrizio Calvi and Frédéric Laurent, *Piazza Fontana: La verità su una strage* (Milan: Mondadori, 1997).
19. Dianese and Bettin, *La strage*.
20. Giorgio Bocca, *Il filo nero* (Milan: Mondadori, 1995).
21. Ernesto Galli Della Loggia, *L'identità italiana* (Bologna: Il Mulino, 1998).

3. PENALTIES AND IMPUNITY

1. Antonio Ghirelli, *Storia del calcio in Italia* (Turin: Einaudi, 1990).
2. Gianni Brera, *Storia critica del calcio italiano* (Milan: Baldini & Castoldi, 1998).
3. Antonio Papa and Guido Panico, *Storia sociale del calcio in Italia* (Bologna: Il Mulino, 2002).
4. Vittorio Malagutti, *I conti truccati del calcio* (Bologna: Il Mulino, 2002).
5. *La Repubblica*, 25 April 2001.

6. Various, *Una storia italiana* (Milan: Mondadori, 2001).
7. Ibid.
8. *La Stampa*, 19 Dec. 1993.
9. Quoted in Giovanni Ruggeri, *Berlusconi: Gli affari del Presidente* (Milan: Kaos, 1995).
10. *Gazzetta dello Sport*, 21 Feb. 2003.

4. THE SOFRI CASE

1. Quoted in Daniele Biacchessi, *Il caso Sofri* (Rome: Editori Riuniti, 1998).
2. *La Repubblica*, 7 Oct. 2000.
3. *Gazzetta di Parma*, 7 Oct. 2000.
4. Dario Fo, *Accidental Death of an Anarchist*, trans. Ed Emery (London: Methuen, 1992).
5. Quoted in Sergio Zavoli, *La notte della repubblica* (Milan: Mondadori, 1992).
6. Pietro Calderoni, *Servizi segreti* (Naples: Pironti, 1986).
7. Zavoli, *La notte della repubblica*.
8. Biacchessi, *Il caso Sofri*.
9. Ibid.
10. Adriano Sofri, *Memoria* (Palermo: Sellerio, 1990).
11. Biacchessi, *Il caso Sofri*.
12. *La Repubblica*, 7 Oct. 2000.
13. Sofri, *Memoria*.
14. Antonio Carlucci in *L'Espresso*, 4 Jan. 2001.
15. Alberto Arbasino, "In questo stato (1978–1998)," in *Paesaggi italiani con zombi* (Milan: Adelphi, 1998).
16. Giorgio Bocca in *La Repubblica*, 21 July 1982.
17. Leonardo Sciascia, *L'affaire Moro* (Milan: Adelphi, 1994).
18. Angelo Panebianco, "Democrazia sommersa," in *pM*, no. 10, June 1993.
19. Giulio Bollati, *L'Italiano* (Turin: Einaudi, 1996).
20. Giorgio Galli, *Storia del partito armato* (Milan: Rizzoli, 1986).
21. Arbasino, "In questo Stato (1978–98)."
22. *La Repubblica*, 18 Dec. 2000.
23. Thomas Sheehan in *New York Review of Books* 27:21, 22 Jan. 1981.
24. *Il Giornale*, 11 May 1978.
25. Maurizio Dianese and Gianfranco Bettin, *La strage* (Milan: Feltrinelli, 1999).
26. Ibid.
27. Giovanni Fasanella, Corrado Sestieri, and Giovanni Pellegrino, *Segreto di stato* (Turin: Einaudi, 2000).
28. Franco Ferraroti, *L'ipnosi della violenza* (Milan: Rizzoli, 1980).

5. The Means of Seduction

1. Charles Dickens, *Pictures from Italy* (London: Penguin, 1998).
2. Italo Calvino, *La speculazione edilizia* (Milan: Mondadori, 1994).
3. Quoted in Roberta Gisotti, *La favola dell'Auditel* (Rome: Editori Riuniti, 2002).
4. Quoted in Edward Murray, *Fellini the Artist* (New York: F. Ungar, 1976).
5. Pier Paolo Pasolini, *Lettere luterane* (Turin: Einaudi, 1976).
6. Calvino, *Speculazione edilizia*.
7. Quoted in Ernesto Galli Della Loggia, *L'identità italiana* (Bologna: Il Mulino, 1998).
8. Pasolini, *Lettere luterane*.
9. Aldous Huxley, *Brave New World* (London: Chatto & Windus, 1959).
10. *Diario*, 30 March 2001.
11. Huxley, *Brave New World*.

6. Pietra and Parola

1. Padre Pio da Pietrelcina to Padre Benedetto, 22 Oct. 1918.
2. I Millenari, *Via col vento in Vaticano* (Milan: Kaos, 1999).
3. Henry James, *Letters*, 4 vol., ed. Leon Edel (Cambridge, Mass.: Harvard University Press, 1984).
4. Charles Dickens, *Pictures from Italy*, ed. Kate Flint (London: Penguin, 1998).
5. *L'Espresso*, 4 Oct. 1981.
6. Paul Ginsborg, *L'Italia del tempo presente* (Turin: Einaudi, 1998).
7. Tina Anselmi, *Relazione della Commissione parlamentare d'inchiesta sulla loggia massonica P2* (Rome: Senate, 1984).
8. John Milton, *A Critical Edition of the Major Works*, ed. Stephen Orgel and Jonathan Goldberg (Oxford: Oxford University Press, 1991).
9. Quoted in Mario Infelise, *Libri proibiti* (Bari: Laterza, 1999).
10. Giorgio Tourn, *Italiani e protestantesimo: Un incontro impossibile?* (Turin: Claudiana, 1997).
11. Quoted in Alessandro Manzoni, *Osservazioni sulla morale cattolica* (Milan: Mondadori, 1997).

7. "Fewer Taxes for Everyone"

1. Eurostat, *Enterprises in Europe* (Brussels, 1996).
2. Quoted in *New York Review of Books*, 18 Oct. 2001.

3. Carlo Pirovano, ed., *Italia moderna: La difficile democrazia* (Milan: Electa, 1985).

4. Stendhal, *The Charterhouse of Parma* (London: Penguin, 1958).

5. Luigi Barzini, *Gli Italiani* (Milan: Bur, 1997).

6. Pirovano, *Italia moderna*.

7. Salvatore Bragantini, *Capitalismo all'italiana; come i furbi comandano con i soldi degli ingenui* (Milan: Baldini & Castoldi, 1996).

8. *Corriere della Sera*, 3 May 1992.

9. *L'Espresso*, 7 Feb. 2002.

10. *Corriere della Sera*, 29 May 1992.

11. *Il Giornale*, 27 Jan. 1994.

12. Laertius Diogenes, *Lives of Eminent Philosophers* (Cambridge: LOEB, 1989).

13. Italo Calvino, *La speculazione edilizia* (Milan: Mondadori, 1994).

14. Leonardo Sciascia, *Candido ovvero un sogno fatto in Sicilia* (Milan: Adelphi, 1990).

8. FORZISMO

1. *Corriere della Sera*, 19 Jan. 2002.

2. *The Economist*, 28 April 2001.

3. William Makepeace Thackeray, *Vanity Fair* (London: Penguin, 1994).

4. Niccolò Machiavelli, *Il principe*, ch. 26.

5. *Corriere della Sera*, 14 July 1998.

6. *La Repubblica*, 26 July 2001.

7. Francesco Tuccari, ed., *Il Governo Berlusconi* (Bari: Laterza, 2002).

8. Leonardo Sciascia, *The Knight and Death* (London: Granta, 2003).

9. *La Repubblica*, 20 April 2002.

10. Percy Bysshe Shelley, "Ode to Naples," in *The Complete Poems of Shelley* (New York: Random House, 1994).

11. George Orwell, *1984* (New York: New American Library, 1962), p. 176.

12. Ibid., p. 217.

13. *Corriere della Sera*, 27 Aug. 2001.

9. PENISOLA FELICE

1. Quoted in Giorgio Bocca, *Il Secolo sbagliato* (Milan: Mondadori, 1999).

2. Stendhal, *The Charterhouse of Parma* (London: Penguin, 1958).

3. Percy Bysshe Shelley, "Ode to Naples," in *The Complete Poems of Shelley* (New York: Random House, 1994).

4. Fabrizio De André, *Parole e canzoni* (Turin: Einaudi, 1999).

5. Henry James, *Italian Hours* (London: Penguin, 1995).
6. Umberto Eco, *Sette anni di desiderio* (Milan: Bompiani, 1983).
7. Ibid.
8. Leonardo Sciascia, *Il cavaliere e la morte* (Milan: Adelphi, 1988).
9. Nathaniel Hawthorne, *The Marble Faun* (Oxford: Oxford University Press, 2002).
10. Giovanni Guareschi, *Lo spumarino pallido* (Milan: Rizzoli, 1981).

INDEX

abusivismo ("illegal building"), 227–35
Accattone, 155
Accidental Death of an Anarchist (Fo), 111–12
accounting laws, 102–103, 255, 273
advertising on television, 144–46, 149–50, 156, 157–58
aesthetics, 23, 24–25, 135–41, 228, 278, 289, 298
Agca, Mehmet Ali, 184
Agnelli, Gianni, 83
Agricola, Riccardo, 97
Agrigento, Italy, 228–33, 235
Agusta, Francesca Vacca, 134
Alessandrini, Emilio, 185
Alighieri, Dante, *see* Dante
Amato, Giuliano, 127, 221, 249
Ambrosini, Vittorio, 65
Ambrosoli, Giorgio, 185
Amnesty International, 50
anarchism, 43, 55, 112, 119, 126
Andreotti, Giulio, 66, 132, 181
anni di piombo, viii, 46, 62, 107, 119, 128, 133, 269
anti-globalization, 256, 257
Antonioni, Michelangelo, 153
Arab-Israeli conflict, 132–33
Arbasino, Alberto, 127, 130, 131
Arnone, Giuseppe, 230, 231, 232
artisan class, 199
Auditel, 145–46

Avventura, L', 153
Azione Cattolica, 181

Badoglio, Marshal Pietro, 41, 42
Baggio, Dino, 74, 91
Baldelli, Pio, 56
Banca Rasini, 244
Banco Ambrosiano, 187–88
Bank of America, 216–17
Bank of Italy, 185, 188
banks, 198, 204–205, 207, 265
Barbacetto, Gianni, 218
Baresi, Franco, 99
Barzini, Luigi, 213
Basile, Carlo Emanuele, 44
Batistuta, Gabriel, 76
Beckham, David, 74, 276
Beckwith, General Charles, 193
Bellissima, 152–53
Benedetto, Padre, 168–69
Beneduce, Alberto, 211
Benetton, 257
Benigni, Roberto, 275
Benjamin, Walter, 267
Berlinguer, Enrico, 119
Berlusconi, Paolo, 224
Berlusconi, Silvio, ix–xi, xii, 61, 143, 149, 162, 188, 208, 223, 227, 232, 240–80, 287, 291
    business empire, 211, 240–41, 247–48
    defense of, 225–27, 252–53, 260

Berlusconi, Silvio (*cont.*)
  "false accounting" legislation,
    102–103, 255, 273
  football team ownership, 83, 85,
    99, 100–102, 243, 247
  Forza Italia, *see* Forza Italia
  investigations and legal prosecution
    of, 100–101, 159, 224–25, 241,
    247, 253, 260–61, 265–66
  Mafia links, allegations of, 240,
    243–44, 245, 273–74
  media businesses, 68, 121,
    157–63, 225, 240–41, 257,
    263, 272, 274–75
  polarization over, 241, 244,
    262–63
  re-entry of illegally exported cash,
    legislation on, 259, 273
Bertolotti, Francesco, 98
Bertolucci, Bernardo, 154–55
Bertossa, Bernard, 259–60
Biagi, Enzo, 162
Biagi, Marco, 127–28
Big Pantomime with Flags and Puppets
  (Fo), 155–56
Biscardi's Trial, 79
Blob, 148, 151
Bocca, Giorgio, 63–64
Boccaccio, 17, 194
Bompressi, Ovidio, 119
Borghese, Prince Junio Valerio, 43,
  115–16
Borrelli, Francesco Saverio, 262–63
Borsellino, Paolo, 220, 243
Bossi, Umberto, 261, 269–70
Bragantini, Salvatore, 198, 217
Brave New World (Huxley), 162,
  163–64, 267
Brera, Gianni, 71, 79
Brigate GAP (Gruppi di Azione
  Partigiana), 112–13
Burckhardt, Jacob, 22
bureaucracy, 18–21, 201–203,
  205–206, 210, 212–13, 218
Bush, George H. W., 55

Calabresi, Luigi, 56, 57, 109, 111,
  112, 118, 119, 124
Calabresi, My Husband (Capri), 120
Calvi, Roberto, 184–89
Calvino, Italo, 9, 10, 140–41, 156,
  233–34

Calzolari, Armando, 65
Camilleri, Andrea, 137, 163, 231,
  232
Cannavaro, Fabio, 76, 88
Canzonissima, 149
Capello, Fabio, 93, 94, 100
Capitini, Aldo, 110
Capri, Gemma, 120
Carraro, Franco, 83, 85
Carret, David, 54, 58
Castelli, Roberto, 260, 261
Castro, Fidel, 113
Catenacci, Elvio, 54–55
Catholic Church and Roman
  Catholics, 131, 155, 174–97,
  220, 283
  anticlericalism, 177–78, 194, 197
  moral attitudes and, 23–24
  Padre Pio, 165–74
  see also Vatican; *individual popes*
cattocomunismo, 131
Cecchi Gori, Vittorio, 83
Cederna, Camilla, 56
cemeteries, tombs, and catacombs,
  285–88
Central Intelligence Agency, 54, 55,
  62, 69
Chao, Manu, 256
Charles, John, 78
Charterhouse of Parma, The
  (Stendhal), 213
Chaucer, Geoffrey, 194
Che Guevara, Ernesto, 113, 118
Chiesa, Enrico, 74, 78
Children of the Sun, 54
Christian Democrats, ix–x, 45, 62,
  113, 129, 131, 159, 181, 211,
  219, 222, 234, 250, 251, 253,
  270
Churchill, Winston, 75
Ciampi, Carlo Azeglio, 185, 188,
  221, 269
Ciampi, Franca, 150
Cimminelli, Franco, 85
city-states, 14–15, 198
Civilisation of the Renaissance in Italy
  (Burckhardt), 22–23
civil war, World War II and Italian,
  27, 41–43, 61, 223
Clean Hands initiative, ix, 101,
  218–26, 223, 224, 262
Cofferati, Sergio, 264

Comare secca, La, 155
Commissione Giustizia alla Camera, 58
Commissione Stragi, *see* Slaughter
    Commission
Communism and Communists, 26,
    27, 43, 63, 109, 113, 119,
    131–32, 181, 219, 222, 241,
    251, 253, 254, 267, 271
conflicts of interest, 83–84, 85, 263,
    272
Conformist, The, 154–55
Congregation for the Doctrine of the
    Faith, 176
conspiracy theories, *see dietrologia*
    (culture of suspicion)
Correggio, 137
Corriere della Sera, 145–46, 162,
    187, 218, 241
Corriere dello Sport, 89
Corrocher, Graziella, 187
Cosmi, Serse, 91
Cossiga, Francesco, 252
Craxi, Bettino, 109, 142, 159, 188,
    221, 225–26
credit crisis, 215
Crespo, Hernán, 74, 91
Cuccarini, Lorella, 170
Cuccia, Enrico, 210–11
Curci, Father, 240, 272
Curcio, Renato, 45

D'Alema, Massimo, 84, 249, 252
D'Ambrosio, Gerardo, 130–31, 263
D'Annunzio, Gabriele, 170
Dante, 17, 27, 285–86, 287
D'Antona, Massimo, 128
Davids, Edgar, 95, 96, 97
"Dead, The," 288
De André, Fabrizio, 8, 134, 149, 285
death, 282–90
Death in Venice (Mann), 288
De Beneditti, Carlo, 225
de Boer, Frank, 96
Decima Mas, 115
De Gasperi, Alcide, 181
De Gregori, Francesco, 149
"Dei sepolcri," 286
Dell'Utri, Marcello, 224, 245–46,
    273
Del Piero, Alessandro, 90
de Michelis, Gianni, 221
Democrats of the Left, 222

"Democrazia sommersa" (Submerged
    democracy), 129
Di Canio, Paolo, 73
Dickens, Charles, 137, 178
dietrologia (culture of suspicion),
    29–31, 123, 164, 189
    football and, 80–82, 84–85,
    89–93
Digilio, Carlo (Zio Otto), 54, 57,
    58–59, 69
Di Pietro, Antonio, 223, 224, 226,
    254
Doctor Zhivago (Pasternak), 113
Dolce vita, La, 153–54, 173

Eco, Umberto, xiv, 31, 136, 254,
    263–64, 289–90
Economist, The, 246–47
economy, Italian, 198–227
    Clean Hands initiative against
    corruption, ix, 101, 218–26,
    223, 224
    "illegal building," 227–33
Elementi di un'esperienza religiosa
    (Capitini), 110
employment, 18–21, 201–206, 210,
    212–13, 218
Ertl, Monica, 118
Espresso, L', magazine, 63, 112, 225
Estrada, Natalia, 275
European Court of Human Rights,
    50
European Union, 277
Evola, Julius, 53
exports, 211–12

Falcone, Giovanni, 220
Fascism and Fascists, 26, 27, 43–46,
    52–55, 58–60, 64, 98–99, 114,
    126, 154, 155, 181, 267, 269,
    270–71, 289–90
Fashanu, John, 77
fashion, 138–39
Fátima Madonna, 183, 188
Fede, Emilio, 161, 246, 257
Fellini, Federico, 149–50, 153–54,
    166, 174–75, 290
Feltrinelli, Giangiacomo, 113, 118,
    119
feminism, 148–49
Ferguson, Duncan, 73, 77
Ferlaino, Carrado, 98

Ferrigno, Massimo, 98
Fiat, 211, 257
films, Italian, 16–17, 64–65, 112,
    133, 152–56, 234
Fini, Gianfranco, 222
Finivest, 243, 244–45
Flamigni, Sergio, 129
flirtation, 141–42
Fo, Dario, 110, 111, 155–56
football, Italian, 25–26, 71–105,
    124, 163, 279
  banned substances, 94–97
  Berlusconi's interest in, *see*
    Berlusconi, Silvio, football team
    ownership
  betting system, 87–88, 91
  buying and selling of players, 87
  coaches, 73, 77, 99–100
  the fans, 77–78, 97–98
  journalists and media, 78–79,
    86–87, 99
  the *moviola*, 80
  penalties in, 80–81, 88–92
  politics, business, and, 82–88,
    98–103
  the referees, 80–82, 84–85,
    88–93
Forza Italia, x, 37, 51, 60, 101, 109,
    163, 247–50, 252, 253, 254,
    261, 271–73
  formation of, 222–23, 244–45
  see also Berlusconi, Silvio
Foscolo, Ugo, 286
Foxe, John, 193–94
Franceschini, Alberto, 45
Francis of Assisi, Saint, 174
Franco, Ciccio, 114, 115
Freda, Franco, 55, 65
Fronte Nazionale, 115
Frossi, Annibale, 100
funerals, 284, 287

G8 summit of July 2001, 256–58
Gaddafi, Muammar, 132
Galli, Giorgio, 107, 130
Galliani, Adriano, 85
Garibaldi, Giuseppe, 191, 270
Gaucci, Luciano, 85
Gazzetta dello Sport, La, 89, 103
Gelli, Licio, 185–86, 187, 188
Gente, 170
Geronzi family, 85

Ghirelli, Antonio, 79
Giannettini, Guido, 55
Giraudo, Antonio, 97
Gladio, 132
Greece, 46, 60
Guareschi, Giovanni, 296
Guariniello, Raffaele, 97
Guida, Marcello, 48
Gullit, Ruud, 99

Haring, Keith, 110
Hateley, Mark, 77
Hawthorne, Nathaniel, 290–91
Hobbes, Thomas, 130
Holocaust, 181
housing, 208–209
  "illegal building," 227–35
Huxley, Aldous, 162, 163–64

I cento passi, 133
illiteracy, 137, 156
Illustrious Corpses, 64–65
immigration, illegal, 251
Indice, 195
inflation, 212, 217
Insabato, Andrea, 126–27
Institute for Industrial Reconstruction
    (IRI), 210, 211, 224–25
*Investigation of a Citizen above
    Suspicion*, 112
investigations:
  of Berlusconi, 100–101, 159,
    224–25, 241, 247, 253,
    260–61, 265–66
  Clean Hands, *see* Clean Hands
    initiative
  Piazza Fontana, *see* Piazza Fontana
    bombing
  Slaughter Commission, *see*
    Slaughter Commission
I promessi sposi (Manzoni), 67
Istituto per le Opere de Religione
    (IOR), 184–85, 188
Islam, 192
Italian, The (Radcliffe), 194
Italia Nostra, 227

James, Henry, 177–78, 287–88
Jews, 191–92
John Paul II, Pope, 167, 169,
    182–84, 188–89
Jones, Inigo, 195

Joyce, James, 288
judiciary, Italian, ix, 50–51, 58, 69, 124
   Berlusconi's charges against, 226, 227, 252–53, 260
   Clean Hands and, *see* Clean Hands initiative
Juliano, Pasquale, 65

language, 3–31, 4, 6–18, 20–25, 70, 140, 278, 291–93
Lario, Veronica, 143
Lateran Pacts of 1929, 181
Law 222, or Mammí law, 159
legalism and lawlessness, 66–68, 93–94, 95–96, 102–104, 196, 225–26, 234
   "official pardons," 232–33
Legambiente, 227, 230
Lentini, Gianluigi, 100, 103
Leopard, The (Tomasi di Lampedusa), 30, 113
Levi, Carlo, 15
Lippi, Marcello, 85
Lloyd George, David, 286–87
Loren, Sofia, 148
Lotta Continua (Continuing Struggle), 56, 108, 109, 111, 118, 119, 120, 121, 124
Luther, Martin, 190

Maastricht Treaty, 217
Maceratini, Giulio, 37
Machiavelli, Niccolò, 17, 22–23, 250
Madonna, the, 179, 181
Mafia, the, 220, 231–32, 246
Maggi, Carlo Maria, 53–54, 255
Maldini, Paolo, 99
Malloppo, Il (The Swag) (Pansa), 218–19
Mangano, Vittorio, 245, 273
Manifesto, Il, 59, 126–27
Mani sulla città, Le (Hands over the City), 234
Mann, Thomas, 288
Manzoni, Alessandro, 67, 197
Marcinkus, Bishop Paul, 184, 188
Maria Luigia, Duchess, 138
Marino, Leonardo, 109–10, 119, 121
Marino libero! Marino è innocente!, 110

Maroni, Roberto, 128
Marsala, Italy, 236–37
Mattei, Enrico, 133
Mazzini, Giuseppe, 286–87
Mediaset, 145, 149, 157, 159, 160, 161, 163, 246, 257, 263, 272, 274, 280
Mediobanca, 210–11, 213
Mereu, Antonio, 103
Miceli, General Vito, 116–17
Mihajlovic, Sinisa, 97
Milan, Italy, 38–39
Milano degli scandali (Veltri and Barbacetto), 218
Milo, Sandra, 143
Milton, John, 191, 194
Mina, 149
Ministry of Interior, 54–55, 255
Miss Italia, 148
Moggi, Alessandro, 85, 96
Moggi, Luciano, 82
Mondadori, 225, 241
Montale, Eugenio, 32
Montanelli, Indro, 131, 254, 270
Monte Sant' Angelo, 167, 173–74
Montesi, Wilma, 133
Moratti, Massimo, 83
Moravia, Alberto, 154
Moro, Aldo, 31, 33, 181
Movimento Sociale Italiano (MSI), 37, 44, 59, 115, 116, 117, 222, 256, 269
Mussolini, Benito, 41, 42, 43, 61, 98, 110, 161, 181, 250, 269, 270, 271, 277

Nakata, Hidetoshi, 94
National Alliance, 108, 118
Newman, Cardinal John Henry, 175
New Resistance, 45
noise, 4–5
National Alliance, 267, 269
Northern League, 222, 224, 267, 270
Notte, La, 153
Nuclei Armati Rivoluzionari, 127

Observer, The, 46
Odore dei soldi, L', 243, 244, 245
Oggi, 263
oligarchies, 82–86
Olivetti, 214

312 INDEX

Ordine Nuovo, 52, 53–54, 55, 58, 59–60, 64, 114
Orwell, George, 267–68, 272
Osservatore Romano, L', 153
Otto III, Holy Roman Emperor, 167–68, 174

Panebianco, Angelo, 129, 241
Panormama, 68
Pansa, Giampalo, 218–19
paranoia, *see dietrologia* (culture of suspicion)
Parenti, Tiziana, 223
Parmalat empire and scandal, 84, 215–17
Partisan Action Group, 45
partisans, 42–43, 44, 45
Pasolini, Pier Paolo, 30, 114, 154, 155, 156
Pasternak, Boris, 113
patriotism, 16, 180, 281–82
Paul VI, Pope, 195
Pavese, Cesare, 299
Pecorelli, Mino, 66
Pecorella, Gaetano, 58, 102, 255–56
Pellice, Torre, 193
Pellegrino, Giovanni, 36, 65
pentitismo, 51–52, 54, 68–69, 109, 118, 255
People's Party, 222, 249
Petri, Elio, 112
Piano, Renzo, 166
Piazza Fontana bombing, 38–70, 105, 111, 123, 185
  background information, 41–47
  facts of, 47–48
  Pinelli's suicide, 48, 56–57
  trials, 40, 48–69, 255
Pietrostefani, Giorgio, 119
Pinelli, Pino, 48, 56–57, 107, 111, 118, 119, 284–85
Pio, Padre, 165–74
Pirandello, Luigi, 29, 228–29, 237
Pisa, Italy, 110
Pius XII, Pope, 181
Poggiolini, Duilio, 219–20
politics and politicians, 43, 45, 63, 142–43
  Clean Hands and, 218–26
  football, business, and, 82–88, 98–103
  trasformismo, 64, 86, 129–30

see also names of individuals and political parties
Pontano, Giovanni, 153
Previti, Cesare, 162, 225, 260, 273
Prodi, Romano, 102, 128, 224, 249, 251
Propaganda Due (P2), 186–88
Protestantism, 176, 182, 190–91, 192–95

Quelli che il calcio, 162
Quintanilla, Roberto, 118

Radcliffe, Ann, 194
Raggio verde, Il, 245
RAI, 146, 148, 158, 159, 160, 162, 207, 243, 245, 246, 263, 272
Ranieri, Claudio, 73
Ratzinger, Cardinal Joseph, 176
Rauti, Pino, 43, 52, 53, 59–63, 222
Ravanelli, Fabrizio, 75
real estate, *see* housing
Red Brigades, 37, 45, 109, 112, 119, 128, 131
Red Brigades–Combatant Communist Party, 128
Reder, Major Walter, 42
Reformation, 190, 195
Reggio Calabria, 114, 115
Reggio Emilia, 256
Repubblica, La, 108, 225, 258, 263
Repubblica Sociale Italiana (Republic of Salò), 42, 43, 44
Rhodes, Cecil, 276
Rijkaard, Frank, 99
Rispoli, Luciano, 170
Rivista Storica Italiana, 129
Rizzoli family, 187
Rognoni, Giorgio, 97, 255
Roman Catholics, *see* Catholic Church and Roman Catholics
Ronaldo (Brazilian football star), 77–78
Rooney, Wayne, 73, 74
Rosa dei Venti, 117
Rosi, Francesco, 64, 234
Rumor, Mariano, 113
Russo, Marta, 133, 134
Rutelli, Francesco, 254

Sacchi, Arrigo, 99–100
Sacco and Vanzetti, 112

Saccucci, Sandro, 116
Salò, 154
Salsedo, Andrea, 112
Salvini, Guido, 52, 60, 65, 69
San Giovanni Rotondo, 166–73
Santa Maria delle Grazie, 170–71
Sant'Anna di Staazema, 42
Santoro, Michele, 245
Santuario di San Michele, 167, 173–74
Santuzza, the day of La, 238–39
Sartori, Giovanni, 145
Scalfaro, Oscar Luigi, 220
Sciascia, Leonardo, 29, 31, 52, 64,
    106, 129, 237, 261, 290
Scoppola, Pietro, 219, 226
Scuola dell'uomo, La, 110
Second Vatican Council, 179–80
secret services, 34, 45, 55, 65–66, 117
Selva, Gustavo, 37
Sensi, Franco, 85
Serantini, Franco, 110, 119
Sgarbi, Vittorio, 143
Shelley, Percy Bysshe, 266, 281, 283,
    289
Siciliano, Martino, 54, 68–69
Sicily, 227–38, 273–74
Signorini, Gianluca, 97
Sindona, Michele, 184, 185, 187
Sismondi, Jean-Charles-Léonard
    Simonde de, 197
Skorzeny, Otto, 41
Slaughter Commission, viii, 34–38,
    41, 51, 55, 66, 133
small enterprises, 198–99
Socialist Party, 109
Sofri, Adriano, viii, 105–25, 134, 144
Sole 24 Ore, Il, 87
Solidarietà Internazionale, 126
Sonnino, Baron Giorgio Sidney, 191
Sordi, Alberto, 17
Speculazione edilizia, La (Calvino),
    233–34
Spencer, Bud (Carlo Pedersoli), 13
Spider's Stratagem, The, 155
spoils system, 212
Spoon River Anthology, 284, 285
sports journalism, 78–79
Stajano, Corrado, 38
Stam, Japp, 96
state, attitude toward the, 16, 21–22,
    197, 207–208
Stendhal, 213, 282

Storia italiana, Una (Berlusconi),
    100, 241–43, 244
strikes, 46, 49, 114

Taine, Hippolyte, 175
Tanzi, Calisto, 215–16, 217
Tanzi family, 84
Taormina, Carlo, 255–56, 260
taxes, 204, 206–208, 218, 221, 251,
    273
television, Italian, 144–52, 156–64,
    274–75, 277
    advertising on, 144–46, 149–50,
        156, 157–58
    Berlusconi's media businesses, 68,
        121, 157–63
    female body on, 147–48, 163
    imported programming, 151
    karaoke and cabaret on, 149–50
    local channels, 151
    news programs, 146–47
    see also Mediaset; RAI
terrorism, viii, 27, 198, 258–59, 264,
    289
    justifications for, 21
    political, 43, 126, 128–33
    Slaughter Commission, see
        Slaughter Commission
Terza Posizione, 127
Titian, 137
Tomasi di Lampedusa, Giuseppe, 30,
    113, 237
Torniamo allo Statuto (Sonnino), 191
Tortora, Enzo, 52
Tosatti, Giorgio, 75
Totti, Francesco, 78
Tourn, Giorgio, 3, 196
Transparency International, 217
trasformismo, 64, 86, 129–30
Tronchetti Provera, Marco, 83, 214
Turone, Ramon, 84

Unità, L', 274
United Nations Relief and
    Rehabilitation Administration
    (UNRRA), 172

Valpreda, Pietro, 52
Vatican, 153, 177, 179–80, 188
    finances of, 184–89
    Italian state and, 180–82
    Padre Pio and, 170

Veltri, Elio, 218
Ventura, Giovanni, 55
venture capital, 215
Verga, Giovanni, 237
Veron, Juan Sebastian, 74, 93, 94
Vialli, Gianluca, 73
Vieira, Patrick, 97
Vincenzi, Guido, 97
Visconti, Luchino, 152–53
Vittorio Emanuele III, King, 41, 42
Vogliamo i colonnelli, 46

Waldensians, 190–91, 192
war on terrorism, 258–59

Watson, Graham, 261
Wenger, Arsene, 73
Whitaker, Joseph, 238
"Window on the Slaughter, A,"
　56
World War II:
　civil war in Italy and, 27, 41–43,
　　61, 223
　postwar reconstruction, 210–12
Wren, Christopher, 195

Zola, Gianfranco, 73
Zorzi, Delfo, 53, 55, 57, 58, 59, 68,
　255